D1191424

BERDYAEV'S PHILOSOPHY OF HISTORY

BERDYAEV'S PHILOSOPHY OF HISTORY

AN EXISTENTIALIST THEORY OF SOCIAL CREATIVITY AND ESCHATOLOGY

by

DAVID BONNER RICHARDSON

Utah State University

Preface by

CHARLES HARTSHORNE

MARTINUS NIJHOFF / THE HAGUE / 1968

PRINTED IN THE NETHERLANDS

TABLE OF CONTENTS

PREFACE

How shall a non-Russian, above all a North American, assimilate the extraordinary assemblage of ideas which is Berdyaev's philosophy? Dr. Richardson does not exaggerate the difficulties. And he introduces us with great care (and what a formidable task it must have been) precisely to what is most strange in this writer, his fusion of historical-eschatological-metaphysical-mystical-Christian conceptions. By some standards Berdyaev is a theologian rather than a philosopher; for he takes the truth of the Christian revelation for granted and his work can readily be viewed as an elaborate apologetic for one religion against all others and against irreligion. Yet I incline to sympathize with him in his claim to be a philosopher. What an eccentric one, however! There are indeed some partial analogies in the general European tradition. Certainly this Russian is a disciple of Kant, and strong traces of Kantianism survive in him. He also moved away from Kant somewhat as did Fichte, Hegel, and, above all, Schelling in his last period. His sympathetic response to Heracleitos and Boehme recalls Hegel. The interest in Boehme and Schelling is found also in Tillich. Like the late German-American, Berdyaev rejects conceptual in favor of symbolic speech about God. Like Bergson, he stresses intuition and makes a radical distinction between scientific logical analytic thought and the mode of apprehension by which, he believes, metaphysical truth is to be appropriated. Here one thinks also of Heidegger.

Since Berdyaev is an extremely bold imaginative thinker, almost the opposite of the fashionable types of positivistic, agnostic, merely linguistic, or commonsensical philosophers of today, it seems fair to compare him with his counterpart in speculative boldness outside of the Russian tradition, the Anglo-American mathematician and metaphysician, A. N. Whitehead. The following ideas or concerns are common to the two.

    1. A universal principle of "creative advance" (Whitehead) or

creativity (that most positive idea of our century) by which reality perpetually transcends all rational or causal necessities and enriches itself, not merely, as in Platonism, by realizing eternal or preexistent patterns or images, but by producing new patterns, "new images" (Berdyaev). Berdyaev uses both "creativity" and "freedom" for this idea; Whitehead uses chiefly the first of these terms. In both writers there is a rejection or limitation of the deterministic conception of causality. The difference is that for Whitehead this does not mean a rejection of scientific causal explanation, or its limitation to a secondary role, but rather a revision of the concept of causality itself, a revision readily related, though Whitehead was not in a position to relate it, to what has happened in physics and biology in recent decades. Whitehead's "eternal objects" might be too Platonic for Berdyaev; but on the other hand it is Whitehead who most radically universalizes freedom so that it applies even to atoms or particles.

2. The explanation of evils in the world, not by some mysterious divine justice, but by the universal presence of creative freedom in reality. Creatures are not free to make decisions of their own because God decided they should be so, but because freedom is an ultimate aspect of reality as such, any reality, divine or otherwise. "God does not create freedom" (Berdyaev); creativity is the "ultimate category," of which all other universals are special aspects (Whitehead).

3. The most concrete or complete value is beauty, not moral goodness or mere truth.

4. Tragedy is not basically the conflict of good with evil but of good with good. Indeed evil itself is (in a large part at least) this very conflict; it is "good in the wrong place" (Whitehead) or out of proper relation to other things or to God. There are incompatibles and not even God can realize all possible good. There is in some real sense tragedy even for God. See (6).

5. God has ideal power, but no power could simply suppress creative freedom in the creatures or monopolize decision-making, leaving no genuine option for other creatures. To be is to be in some degree free. Hence the conventional notion of "omnipotence" is not an ideal that God falls short of, but a pseudoconception, a rationalistic myth. God is not and could not be "author of the play" (Whitehead), since the players help to write it. We are co-creators with God.

6. God, though primordial and everlasting and in this sense eternal, is not the unmoved mover, but is in some real sense in process of creation, is both eternal and in some sense temporal, in some way creature

as well as creator, and we participate in the creation of God himself, contribute real value to his life. Indeed we contribute *ourselves*, as creatively selfdetermined, to that life; for "pantheism though rationalistically false is mystically true" (Berdyaev), or as Whitehead puts it, "all things are together in the consequent nature of God," though he suggests we can hardly hope to have clear understanding of this togetherness. The "self-created creature" (Whitehead) is thus in God, hence in that way creates God. We "enrich the divine life itself" (Berdyaev). God is not immune to suffering but is "the fellow sufferer who understands" (Whitehead).

7. The ethical imperative is to create beauty, harmonious experience, in oneself, in and for others, ultimately in and for God.

8. There is no eternal damnation; the doctrine of hell is a "piece of sadism" (Berdyaev). The only immortality is God's imperishable possession of us "transmuted" (Whitehead), "transfigured" (Berdyaev) into his own. For Whitehead this is meant in a fashion farther from conventional views of personal immortality than for Berdyaev, who says that all will achieve beatitude. Whitehead's "transmutation" is meant in a more modest sense; God makes the best use in his own life of a bad human life on earth. He does not turn it into a good one in another sphere. Berdyaev's "spiritual determinism," which he characteristically leaves in some apparent conflict with his rejection of causal determinism, may represent a more complete or more anthropomorphic optimism than Whitehead would accept.

These are some at least of the striking analogies between two thinkers whose backgrounds are widely diverse and whose styles are no less contrasting. Among the ideas which one finds in Berdyaev but *not* in Whitehead are: the radical centrality of man in the cosmos (there is no such anthropomorphism in Whitehead); the centrality of Jesus, the Godman, in both man and the cosmos (for Whitehead Jesus is only a supreme teacher and symbol of the basic place of love in reality); the notion of a "Fall" affecting the entire cosmos; something like the traditional idea of personal immortality; the notion of the substantial ego as a preexistent or eternal entity (remarkably like ideas one finds in some Hindu thinkers); the eventual radical community of all souls (*Sobornost'*); and finally and pervasively the radical distrust of rational or univocal concepts and radical trust in mystic experience of the Christian type.

Whitehead, like the Buddhists, is a sharp critic of soul-substance and, like them, holds that this doctrine is an ally of egoism or self-interest

theories of motivation. (If Berdyaev escapes this unfortunate conse-
quence, it is only, Whitehead might have argued, by taking *Sobornost'*
in so extreme a sense that it is dangerously close to the Hindu denial of
individuality). Here I go with Whitehead and the Buddhists. We are
indeed only relatively distinguished from our fellows, truly "members
one of another," but this is possible just because we are only relatively
self-identical with ourselves through time. Neither self-identity nor
nonidentity with others is absolute.

Berdyaev has affinities not only to Whitehead but also to a broader
tradition. Basically there have been two ideas of deity in the theistic
religions: (1) the divine nature is the eminent form of independence,
immutability, impassibility, infinity, simplicity or absence of parts or
composition – in short, the negative theology taken without qualifi-
cation; (2) the divine nature is *both* the eminent form of independence,
changelessness, simplicity, etc. *and* the eminent form of dependence,
changeability, complexity, etc. God is both supreme creator and supreme creature, supreme cause and supreme effect. He has alike supreme permanence and supreme capacity for novelty. He is thus the
synthesis of eternity and time, absoluteness and relativity. The following thinkers, among others, more or less explicitly and clearly affirm
this view:

Socinus and his followers, Schelling (late period), Fechner (the
German psychologist), Heinrich Scholz (the German theologian and
logician), J. Lequier (the brilliant though tragic French philosopher),
Bergson, Varisco (the Italian metaphysician), James Ward (the English
psychologist and philosopher), W. P. Montague (the American moralist
and metaphysician), W. E. Hocking (my first and in a sense only teacher
in metaphysics), N. Berdyaev, A. N. Whitehead, Charles Hartshorne.
I list these people because this tradition is often omitted from the histories of philosophy and other works of reference. They are a small but
increasing number. From their standpoint the identification of God
with "the absolute," or "the unconditioned," i.e., with the object of the
negative theology, is a blunder of the first magnitude and indeed a
typical piece of philosophical idolatry. Eternity, absoluteness, infinity,
by themselves are the merest abstractions; they cannot apply without
radical supplementation to the living God. Of those who have seen this,
Berdyaev is surely not the least. He is sharp and clear on the main
issues: God is not simply unmoved, eternal, or independent. He is not
immune to all suffering. He is not identical with being in contrast to
becoming.

If, as these authors hold, God is the eminent being-becoming, cause-effect, creator-creature, then ordinary individuals are simply nonemment forms of the same duality. They, too, in their humble way both create and are created. But then it is no longer cogent to refute belief in God by taking the evils of the world to be divinely chosen. Certain outlines of reality are divinely chosen ("spiritually determined"); but the details result from partly self-determined creaturely choices. And what an individual creatively decides no one else, not even God, can have decided. Thus at long last the old problem of Job has a reasonable solution. Odd that Berdyaev, the professed irrationalist, should give the most rational of all theories concerning perhaps the nost perplexing of human puzzles. How far other matters are reasonably dealt with by the Berdyaev method I leave to the reader.

CHARLES HARTSHORNE
The University of Texas

INTRODUCTION

I

Nicolas Alexandrovich Berdyaev (1874–1948) was born in the city of Kiev, into an aristocratic and landed Russian family.[1] He was interested in philosophy from the time of his childhood and read Schopenhauer, Kant and Hegel in his father's library when he was fourteen. From his earliest days he never complied with any philosophical tradition but always had a sense of radical freedom and repudiation of authority.[2] When he became a Marxist it was as a Fichtean idealist and as a rebel against the society into which he was born.[3] His true master in philosophy was Kant, though he may not be called a Kantian.[4] He became very widely read in philosophy and found thinkers in the German mystical tradition and in 19th century Russia congenial to his thought.[5] Indeed, the authors he mentions that he read would make a very long list and would include names from all periods of Russian and Western thought. In 1900, as a Marxian idealist, he began a literary activity, writing books and articles, which was to continue until interrupted by his death in 1948. At the same time he entered upon a life-long participation in and leadership of various philosophical societies and meeting-groups,[6] and a career of speaking on the platform.[7] I would say that he was whole-heartedly a professional philosopher all his life. As his autobiography and other books show, he was enormously erudite in philosophy, especially in 19th- and 20th-century European thought. He kept up with contemporary European movements, especially Existential-

---

[1] N. Berdyaev, *Dream and Reality* (Bles, London, 1950), 3–4.
[2] *Ibid.*, 48–50.
[3] *Ibid.*, 50, 55, 92.
[4] *Ibid.*, 93.
[5] *Ibid.*, 83.
[6] *Ibid.*, Chapter V.
[7] *Ibid.*, 135.

ism.[1] And he maintained constant association with other philosophers all his life.

About 1905 he was attracted to the Orthodox Church and became a friend of some of the great Orthodox theologians.[2] As he says, he became conscious of himself as a Christian (conscious of his faith),[3] and he turned from Marxism to a Christian philosophy. Very active in various intellectual circles at this time, he became president of a religious-philosophical society in St. Petersburg [4] and in 1907 participated in a similar society in Moscow. He was then in constant association with the greatest intellectuals in Russia. The magnitude, catholicity and ferquency of his various associations with Russian thinkers from that time until he was expelled from Russia in 1922 are very impressive. He was professor of philosophy at the University of Moscow for two years just previous to being exiled by the Communist government (he had been teaching a Christian philosophy).

His activity in lecturing, writing and meeting with intellectuals continued in his exile, first in Berlin for two years and then in Paris for the rest of his life.[5] Both in Berlin and in Paris Berdyaev had various associations with a large group of exiled Russian intellectuals; and in both cities he wrote numerous articles and books which were printed and published in Russian.[6]

In Paris "he took the initiative in arranging interconfessional gatherings between Orthodox, Catholics and Protestants." [7] He had a frequent and long association with Catholic theologians and philosophers. As in Russia, so, too, in Paris he associated variously with leading intellectuals and maintained in different ways a close contact with the thought of contemporary European philosophers. Berdyaev died suddenly, while working at his writing table, on March 24, 1948.

Nicolas Alexandrovich Berdyaev writes so vividly, goes so quickly from one subject to another and refers so frequently to historical traditions that his books appear very easy to read. He is so popular a philosopher that most of his works have been translated from the Russian or French into the English tongue, and about ten translated books are now in print. We soon find that what Berdyaev says looks easy to understand when we glance through the majority of his works (though

[1] *Ibid.*, Index.
[2] *Ibid.*, Chapters VI and VII.
[3] *Ibid.*, 180.
[4] *Ibid.*, 162.
[5] *Ibid.*, Chapter X.
[5] *Ibid.*, Chapter X.
[7] *Ibid.*, 258.

there are one or two exceptions). And we cannot but be struck by his predominent interest in the meaning of history and by the clarity of his insights into the course of world history.

Why, then, should one attempt to penetrate Berdyaev's philosophy of history when he sets it forth so brilliantly himself? Why re-examine lucid texts when Berdyaev repeatedly returns to the various themes of his philosophy of history in his numerous books? Further, why attempt to simplify what seems already simple? A reader unfamiliar with Berdyaev may take away the first impression of an always brilliant and sometimes profound author, but a superficial philosopher who seems unable to follow out a line of thought in close argumentation.

Berdyaev's style is deceptive. Despite appearance, he is a very deep philosopher. In his own way he has elaborated a philosophy which constitutes a very full and complete doctrine. At the very time he is moving so nimbly from one subject to another in his books – for that is his method – he has a great and complex philosophy in mind.

When one reads his books he sees the outlines of this doctrine only sporadically and vaguely. At one and the same time that one finds Berdyaev's comments on the course of world history so clear, brilliant and meaningful, his complete philosophy lies obscurely at a deeper level. I may almost say that there are two levels in Berdyaev's writings, and one could, in fact, understand Berdyaev's comments on world history without understanding the philosophic principles which inspire them. The various historical and political traditions and cultures to which Berdyaev so often refers, serve not only to exemplify his deepest principles but also exist in their own right as the materials of his philosophy of history.

Yet, because the historical materials are presented by Berdyaev in the light of his first principles, one cannot rest content to understand him superficially. What those first principles are and how they function in the whole structure of Berdyaev's philosophy need still to be determined. For only when one understands his first principles can it be decided how far one may assent to his comments on the course of world history.

Berdyaev's first philosophy is so deep, complex and strange, and so closely related to his philosophy of history, that it takes considerable efforts to understand it. That is why this book is an analysis, not a criticism. We must understand the philosopher before we can truthfully say anything about him. It was not possible to understand his definitive position until recently because his most important books – several of them – were published in the fifties. *Truth and Revelation* and *The Realm of Spirit and the Realm of Caesar*, his last writings, were first published in 1952 and 1953, and *The Meaning of the Creative Act* (originally published in 1916) became available to English speaking readers in 1955.

Further, his outlook itself is unfamiliar to the Western mind because he is a Russian philosopher. The Russian mind has received a peculiar world-outlook from the Orthodox Church. There are striking differences between the outlooks of Western and Eastern Christianity and between the civilizations which they have formed. What is more, there exists no tradition of scholarship about his doctrine and writings. There is no tradition of learning about the "school" to which Berdyaev belongs, as for example we find for the German Idealists or the Greeks. These, then, are some of my reasons for undertaking this study.

I have not investigated the Russian aspects of this doctrine by means of a philological study of the language. English texts of Berdyaev have been exclusively used, and a half dozen important words in his vocabulary have been investigated. I rely partly on Berdyaev's own stated interpretation of the Russian quality of his philosophy and partly on my own. These philological limitations are not so serious as they might seem. Most of the key philosophical terms have Western origins and are used in the light of Western thought as well as that of the Russians. However, the technical terms of Berdyaev must be defined, in the last analysis, through a study of his own peculiar doctrine. The terms, *will* and *existence*, for example, have to be defined finally in the light of no other theory except that of Berdyaev. It is a commonplace in the history of philosophy that the primary principles of a philosopher are expressed by terms common to a multitude of differing systems of thought, but defined finally by reference to his own doctrine.

II

I would like to raise a question about a recent problem, to be found, not only in Berdyaev, but in many recent Christian philosophers. It is the problem of *adjusting* a Christian philosophy to the historical fact of a world in which other higher religions exist; and prominent among them are the Jewish, Mohammedan, Buddhist and Hindu religions. It is an anachronism to be unconconcerned with this problem. During the interval between the early centuries of Christianity and the seventeenth century theologians took it for granted that Christianity might be forcibly imposed on a people, and eventually, by law or fiat, on the entire world. During those centuries Christianity, or a particular form of Christianity, had usually been imposed on a people because their ruler or their conqueror had decided what their religion would be.

The presupposition of Christianizing by coercion, in my opinion, or by exterminating rival religions, is the only presupposition whereby a Christian philosopher can actually think of the destiny of mankind in solely Christian terms. This all-embracing sort of thinking really requires the premiss that a Christian nation shall conquer the world, and then, through a ruthless dictatorship, extirpate or isolate all the other religions of mankind. Such a presupposition is, of course, far from Berdyaev's mind; he is pre-eminently a philosopher of freedom, for whom totalitarian coercion is a loathsome solution of human problems. So far as I can see, this question never did attract the attention of Berdyaev. He thought of the salvation of mankind with ideas shared with Dionysius the Pseudo-Areopagite, Scotus Erigena and a large number of subsequent theologians and mystical writers. A universal Christianization of mankind was a thoroughly feasible possibility to those earlier Christians, however, but not for Berdyaev.

Despite his brilliant solution of the problem of developing a philosophy of humanity, he was caught in the dilemma of the nineteenth and twentieth century Christian eschatologists whose eschaton had not come to grips with the fact that a huge mass of religious humanity will never in the foreseeable future be converted to Christianity, except by force. To be sure, one may claim rightly that Berdyaev's eschatological emphasis leads finally [1] to a state of apokatastasis (the resurrection of all), and perhaps Berdyaev personally did slip between the horns of the dilemma by anticipating the end of the world (and, thereby, the salvation of *all* mankind) in a not very distant future. Nevertheless, could not the idea of Godmanhood, one of his key concepts, a notion in which the second Person of the Divine Trinity figures very importantly, be brought into a fertile relationship with the theories and doctrines of the non-Christian world-religions? Indeed, he wrote, in an early essay at the time of his conversion to Christianity (1905):

We are living in an epoch ... of the beginning of a new religious renaissance, a dawning *new religious consciousness*, which fascinates by its universal significance.

The man of the new religious consciousness cannot renounce either paganism or Christianity: in both he sees divine revelation ... There can be no return to

[1] C. S. Calian, *The Significance of Eschatology in the Thoughts of Nicolas Berdyaev* (Brill, Leiden, 1965), 211 212.

paganism as thesis and Christianity as anti-thesis ... If religion in general is possible and useful, then we must consider the whole world-historical process as divine revelation, as the intimate mutual action and reaction between humanity and Divinity.[1]

Berdyaev's writings contain a proposal which, I think, points the way to the answer to the problem: "Perhaps an *anthropodicy* is the only way to a theodicy..." [2] One of the most far-reaching revolutions of the past hundred and fifty years has been a massive movement of Western Civilization, and, more lately, of all mankind, toward a humanism, not like that of the Renaissance, but a metaphysical humanism, based on an "anthropodicy," rather than on a theodicy. We encounter numerous cults of Humanity, among which are that of Comte, that of Marx and of his contemporary, Feuerbach, whom he admired and Frank Lloyd Wright's religion of Humanity. Subsequent to the Western development of various religions of humanity, twentieth century scholars have been discovering the presence of humanisms in the venerable civilizations of India and China. Chinese Confucianism was a strikingly successful cult [3] of humanity, as evidenced by its longevity. India, in its metaphysical fashion, has long possessed a humanism whose influence has sometimes been contrary to divine (non-human) worship. I refer, for example, to the "cosmic MAN of the Jainas." [4]

The most striking feature of Oriental philosophy, it seems to me, is its concern with the status of man in this world (China) and with man's ultimate goal (Indian). It is my impression that this interest in man clearly predominates over any interest in Nature or in God.[5]

Berdyaev's philosophy, in its extraordinary social awareness, and its mystical anarchism, is reminiscent, respectively, of the Confucianist and the Taoist currents of Chinese thought; and, in its peculiar emphasis upon religious gnosis – the fulfillment of human and divine history by means of *knowledge* – it is deeply evocative of ancient Indian wisdom.

[1] "Life's Questions," No. 9, 1905, selected and translated by D. A. Lowrie in *Christian Existentialism. A Berdyaev Anthology* (Allen and Unwin, London, 1965), 226.

[2] N. Berdyaev, *The Meaning of the Creative Act*, tr. D. A. Lowrie (Harper, New York, 1955), 19.

[3] See J. K. Shryock, *The Origin and Development of the State Cult of Confucius* (Paragon Book Reprint Corp., New York, 1966), including ch. VI, "The Worship Paid to the Spirits of Men in Ancient China," 79–92.

[4] "The Christian notion of God as a giant human form is rendered by the Swedenborgians in a figure that somewhat suggests the cosmic MAN of the Jainas. Emmanuel Swedenborg (1688–1772) experienced in his visions the whole of heaven in this anthropomorphic way." H. Zimmer, *Philosophies of India*, ed. J. Campbell (Pantheon, New York, 1953), 244.

[5] W. H. Werkmeister, "Scientism and the Problem of Man," in C. A. Moore, ed., *Philosophy and Culture. East and West* (Univ. Hawaii, Honolulu, 1962), 136.

A contemporary of Berdyaev, Whitehead, synthesized the philosophy of an almost human-like divine intelligence, together with a theory of almost human-like psyches in all material particles, in a new "social" description of the cosmos,[1] and more recently Hartshorne wrote: "Electrons and protons are, for all that anyone knows, simply the lowest actual levels of social existence." [2] Contemporary Judaism contains a trend which intensifies a keen Jewish sense of humanity, which this religion has always had. "(Buber's) rejection of mysticism for responsibility to his fellowman strikes a very Jewish note ... a mysticism operating within the law ..." [3] Berdyaev's own Boehmian theory is admittedly indebted to a "Semitic ingrafting of the Kabbala, with the exclusive position it accords to man, with its concrete spirit. In the nineteenth century Franz Baader and Vladimir Soloviev were permeated with the anthropological and concrete spirit of the Kabbala and of Jakob Boehme ..." [4]

Berdyaev is aware, moreover, of a profound East Asian influence which is affecting the religious and metaphysical thought of the West: "... Christianity is becoming more foreign and less acceptable to the modern mind than Buddhism," [5] and he finds that the "German spirit is ... somehow akin to the spirit of India: there is the same idealism, the same spirituality, the same vast distance from the concrete flesh of being ..." [6]

The massive religious and metaphysical revolution (and I include Marxism), which seems to be going on in the present century, recalls to mind one that occurred over two thousand years ago. E. V. Arnold, in his monumental work on Roman Stoicism, discerned a vast cultural revolution in the Mediterranean world in the time-interval extending from the Graeco-Persian Wars to the early Christian centuries. "The

---

[1] A. N. Whitehead, *Process and Reality. An Essay in Cosmology* (Macmillan, New York, 1927; Harper Torchbook, New York, 1960), 331, ff.

[2] C. Hartshorne, *The Divine Relativity: A Social Conception of God.* The Terry Lectures, 1947 (Yale Univ., New Haven, 1948), 28.

[3] (Rabbi) E. B. Borowitz, *A Layman's Introduction to Religious Existentialism* (Dell, New York, 1966), 165.

[4] *The Meaning of the Creative Act*, 307.

[5] *Ibid.*, 310.

[6] *Ibid.*, 329. Concerning the influence of East Asia on the West see, in particular, L. A. Maverick, *China A Model for Europe* (Paul Anderson, San Antonio, 1946); J. Needham, *Science and Civilization in China* (Cambridge Univ., Cambridge, 1954; seven vols. projected, vol. 6 to be published in 1967); A. Reichwein, *China and Europe; Intellectual and Artistic Contacts in the Eighteenth Century* (Kegan Paul, London, 1925); G. F. Hudson, *Europe and China. A Survey of Their Relations From the Earliest Times to 1800* (E. Arnold, London, 1931); R. Schwab, *La Renaissance Orientale* (Payot, Paris, 1951). This last-named book is devoted to the Indianization of European culture in the nineteenth century.

meaning of Persism and its immense influence on the Graeco-Roman world are still so little realized ..." [1] Persia's attack on fifth-century Greece was a war of religion, of a theodicy which was destined to establish itself victoriously over the Roman world, whether in Stoicism, Cynicism, Judaism or the other Near-Eastern religions. "... its warlike zeal is directed towards establishing throughout the world the worship of the 'god of heaven,' and the destruction of all images, whether in the shape of man or of beasts, as dishonoring to the divine nature." [2]

Something of comparable magnitude and metaphysical depth has been revolutionizing recent world thought, and, like the "Persian" revolution, the force and momentum of the movement has carried it beyond the simple removal of a religious status quo. The "destruction of all images" of ancient times, in its excess, is comparable to the "religion of Humanity"; and the essential purpose of "Persism," to establish an ideology of a perfect God, corresponds to the aim of the nineteenth and twentieth century movement, to modify the traditional ideology about God in order to include characteristics of the divine being which are limitations: the eminent forms, as Dr. Hartshorne states above, of dependence, changeability, complexity, etc.

It is not surprising that the recent revolution has taken various forms of "anthropodicy," in view of the extraordinary development of humanism since 1800; a development in which the ancient Chinese cult of Humanity seems to have communicated itself to the Western World.

Berdyaev, in his philosophy of history, his ideal of creativity, his eschatology, his Christian anthropodicy of Godmanhood and his existentialism, is one of the great moving personalities of this revolution. After his death in 1948, among his papers was found the outline of a new work on creativity, in which one of the main ideas is that man's co-creativity with God is even more important than man's personal salvation.[3] This movement progresses toward a *rapprochment* of all the higher religions, and the philosophy of history of Berdyaev might play a significant role.

---

[1] E. V. Arnold, *Roman Stoicism. Being Lectures on the History of the Stoic Philosophy With Special Reference to its Development within the Roman Empire* (Cambridge Univ., Cambridge, 1911; reissued 1958 by The Humanities Press, New York), 7.

[2] *Ibid.*, 8–9.

[3] D. A. Lowrie, *Rebellious Prophet. A Life of Nicolai Berdyaev* (Harper, New York, 1960), 248.

III

I would like to express my gratitude to the many whom I consulted for their friendly suggestions, to those who have underwritten the expense of writing the book, particularly in freeing me from other duties during two summers in order to study Berdyaev and interpret him and to those who prepared the final typescript. My particular thanks to G.E.A., M.S.A., C.S.B., C.S.C., E.F., L.E.L., A.M., B.M., A.P. and H.A.R. I am grateful, too, to Professor Charles Hartshorne who kindly consented to write a Preface in the light of his own valuable interpretation of Berdyaev's philosophy.

DAVID BONNER RICHARDSON
Utah State University
January 17, 1967

BERDYAEV'S PHILOSOPHY OF HISTORY

A. INTRODUCTION

We begin this study by considering Berdyaev's philosophy of history as a complete doctrine. But his philosophy [1] partakes of the great complexity of early 19th-century German philosophy. Numerous questions must occur to the reader of this chapter. Indeed, the most nagging questions must concern the deepest principles of Berdyaev. The chapters following, therefore, explain doctrines mentioned in Chapter I.

In the present chapter the subject matter of philosophy of history is studied first. Then, its definition is investigated. Next, the purposiveness, the eschatology, will be examined. Next, Berdyaev's doctrine of time and eternity will be seen. Finally, the main principle, the doctrine of Godmanhood, will be considered briefly.

B. THE "HISTORICAL" AND THE PHILOSOPHY OF HISTORY

(1) The "Historical"

Berdyaev, in a definitive work, *The Meaning of History*, gives a comprehensive view of his philosophy of history. This book, therefore, is given the most attention in the present chapter; nevertheless, many

---

[1] *Philosophy of history*, for Berdyaev means both *philosophy of history* and *theology of history* at once. When he speaks of his *philosophy*, he means philosophy that is both philosophy and theology at once. When he speaks of his metaphysics, he means, also, both a metaphysics and a theology at once. We must note this well because Berdyaev terms himself a philosopher rather than a theologian; and he constantly refers to his *philosophy* or his *metaphysics*. He never uses *theology* to name his work.

His terminology (and his rejection of the use of the term, *theology*) will be used in this study. When I speak of Berdyaev's *philosophy of history*, I use the term in the sense that Berdyaev uses it – with all its theological import, as well as philosophical. When I speak of his *philosophy* or his *metaphysics* I refer, like Berdyaev, more or less to the theological, as well as philosophical, subject-matter.

other books of Berdyaev, written later, enable us to clarify what is written in *The Meaning of History*.

Berdyaev begins his consideration of the "historical" early in *The Meaning of History*:

Historical knowledge has as its goal an absolutely specific and original object which cannot be sub-divided into other objects either material or spiritual. It is, of course, impossible to regard the 'historical' as a reality of a material, physiological or geographical order. It is likewise unthinkable to consider historical reality in terms of any psychic reality. The "historical" has its peculiar and specific nature; it is a reality of a particular kind, a particular stage of existence. The acceptance of historical tradition and of communion with history is indispensable for the knowledge of what constitutes the specifically "historical." Historical speculation is impossible outside the category of historical tradition. The acceptance of this latter forms a certain *a priori*, a certain absolute category for all historical knowledge.[1]

The philosophy of history – of historical knowledge – is one of the ways to the knowledge of spiritual reality. It is a science of the spirit bringing us into communion with the mysteries of spiritual life.[2]

In the first quotation, above, Berdyaev discusses both the historical reality and the knowledge whereby it is known. He distinguishes reality known and the knowledge of it.

He is not talking about historical science at all as he understands it. Historical science, for Berdyaev, tells us of the superficial causes which lead to events; but philosophy of history is concerned with the spiritual meaning of history.[3]

The historical reality is a "particular stage of existence." The knowledge of it is closely associated with the "category of historical tradition." The distinction between knowledge and reality is unmistakably stated. Why, then, does Berdyaev consider the "historical" and the knowledge of it in the same paragraph, in the same breath, as it were? The answer to this question is indicated in the second quotation, where he says: "the philosophy of history – of historical knowledge – is one of the ways to the knowledge of spiritual reality." Berdyaev

---

[1] N. Berdyaev, *The Meaning of History* (Bles, London, 1949), 12–13.

[2] *Ibid.*, 14.

[3] N. Berdyaev, *The End of Our Time* (Sheed and Ward, London, 1935), 148. Berdyaev says, in a last work, *Truth and Revelation* (Bles, London, 1953), 97:

"What historical science sees is not the primary break-through of the noumenal world into this phenomenal world, but what is already a derivative objectivization. That is why historical science, for all its knowledge, and for all its devotion to the discovery of truth, can say nothing in reality about the revelation of God in history."

We will see that "derivative objectivization" which historical science studies is only a superficial aspect of the true world and of true history. Indeed, for Berdyaev, objective and scientific disciplines, such as historical science, are incapable of getting at the truth of what they study. See Chapter IV, Section B.

means to identify history and historical knowledge. Yet, for him, history is a reality distinct from knowledge. Therefore, according to Berdyaev, the "historical" is a reality, a stage of existence; yet, according to philosophy of history, the historical is also knowledge. Historical reality is both distinct from knowledge and is knowledge. We will have to study both in Chapter III, which concerns existential reality, and in Chapter IV, which investigates Berdyaev's theory of knowledge, how the knowledge of the existential reality is at the same time reality.

Berdyaev says that historical knowledge has as its goal an object which cannot be sub-divided into other objects. *Object*, in this early work, here refers to historical reality. (In later works, Berdyaev, rejects the use of *object* to indicate a reality existing outside of knowledge.) [1]

This historical "object" (reality) is not physical or physiological; that is, it is not material. It is not psychological, either. When Berdyaev says it should not be considered in terms of any psychic reality, he means that the knowledge proper to the soul of man, alone, does not attain the "historical." [2] The philosophy of history (which attains knowledge of the "historical"), he says, is a science of the spirit.[3] That is, the philosophy of history is a spiritual knowledge, which is known by the spirit of man, rather than by the isolated soul.[4]

The "historical," then, is spiritual, and philosophy of history "brings us into communion with the mysteries of spiritual life." This means that the historical reality, which exists distinct from the knower, is spiritual and the knowledge of it is also spiritual. The identity which Berdyaev indicates to exist between the historical reality and the knowledge of it is a spiritual one.

The seeming contradiction of identifying historical existence with the knowledge of it can now be partly explained. The knowledge is not the knowledge by the soul but by the spirit; the identity is spiritual. Berdyaev associates this knowledge with the human spirit and also the historial existence with the human spirit. The "historical" (which is not material, physiological, geographical or psychic) pertains, somehow, in its existence to the human spirit.

---

[1] See Chapter IV, Section B.

[2] Concerning the knowledge by the soul, alone, see Chapter IV, Section B.

[3] Again, as in the case of *object*, Berdyaev uses a term, *science* (for true knowledge), which he will not use in later works. In the works written after he wrote *The Meaning of History*, Berdyaev does not use the term, *science*, to describe the true knowledge of philosophy or history. He rejects *science*, along with *object* from the terminology of the true knowledge which is philosophy of history. He does so because he rejects the scientific, rational and discursive method of philosophy. See Chapter IV, Section B.

[4] See Chapter IV, Section G, Part 3.

Berdyaev says, in the passage quoted above, that the historical must be known through the category of historical tradition. That is, historical tradition is a category, a mode of knowledge of the "historical." Berdyaev indicates that historical tradition is a part or aspect of the spiritual reality which *is*, on the one hand, the "historical," and, on the other hand, *knowledge* of the "historical." By "acceptance of historical tradition as a reality," Berdyaev means the recognition of historical traditions (such as, for example, the historical tradition of modern technocracy).[1] And he must accept these traditions as realities which have truly existed in their own right. Berdyaev associates knowledge of historical traditions with a "communion with history." And he says that philosophy of history "brings us into communion with the mysteries of spiritual life."

He says on the following page:

(Historical reality) is above all a concrete and not an abstract reality; and no concrete reality other than the historical does or can exist. The "historical" is essentially a coherent form of existence. For the concrete in its literal sense signifies something that grows together and coheres, as opposed to the abstract, detached, dissociated and divided. Everything abstract is by its nature opposed to the historical ... it is both concrete and particular ...[2]

After saying (we saw) that an important aspect of the "historical" is the historical tradition, Berdyaev says, in the above-quoted passage, that the "historical" is particular and concrete. The historical tradition, then, is particular and concrete according to his philosophy.

According to the above quotation, the historical is concrete. But how the *"historical,"* a *spiritual* entity, can be concrete and yet not material will have to be investigated in Chapters III and IV. Further, not everything (e.g. the material or the physiological), is *"historical."* We must study, in Chapters III and IV, how Berdyaev distinguishes things which truly exist (*"historical"*) from those that do not.

The "historical" is not an abstraction imposed upon our knowledge of history, but, to sum up Berdyaev's remarks, it is organic ("something that grows together and coheres"). This follows from Berdyaev's previous definition of the "historical" as something which is an existent and a being. It is "essentially a coherent form of existence." To explain why we must use the word, *organic*, to characterize Berdyaev's "historical," it will be necessary in the following chapters to consider the cosmology

---

[1] See Chapter IV, Section G, Part 2. Cf. N. Berdyaev, *The Realm of Spirit and the Realm of Caesar* (Gollancz, London, 1952), 47.

[2] *The Meaning of History*, 13.

of Berdyaev and the unifying principles of his doctrine. We must also consider, in a later chapter, how the preference for the concrete and the distaste for the abstract affects the theory of knowledge; that is, the *method* of philosophy of history.

Berdyaev continues and presents an example taken from history which is as singular and particular as anything can be, so as to illustrate the concreteness and particularity of the "historical":

> The "historical" . . . is both concrete and particular. . . . Everything genuinely historical has both a particular and a concrete character. Carlyle, the most concrete and particular of historians, says that John Lackland came upon this earth on such and such a day. This indeed is the very substance of history.[1]

Berdyaev does not mean here that the historical is restricted to momentary events (for we have already seen mention of the relevance of historical tradition). Rather, he is indicating two things: First, the historical refers not only to historical tradition but also to particular events. Second, the historical, when it refers to a tradition, is just as particular, concrete and existential as the fact that "John Lackland came upon this earth on such and such a day." That is to say:

> . . . there are cases in which the general may itself be the particular. As an illustration of this let us take the term "historical nation." This latter is a general concept; but a concrete historical nation is at the same time an absolutely historical concept. The age-long dispute between the Nominalists and the Realists reveals an insufficient grasp of the mystery of the particular. . . . The apprehension of being as a gradation of particularities does not necessarily imply Nominalism, for the general can also be the particular.[2]

The "historical nation," taken in itself, is an example of the historical. That is, when a philosopher of history considers the historical, one of the entities he knows is the "historical nation." In using this example, Berdyaev shows that the historical, though it is always concrete and particular, may be general so that it can be grasped in a general concept. Berdyaev indicates, above, that this existent reality – the historical – has an intelligibility which is not nominal but inheres in it, and which is not abstract or separate, but exists concretely. This existentialism of an intelligible existent will have to be considered later in detail. It is very important to our study because Berdyaev is much concerned with the metaphysics of the historical.

The remainder of the above paragraph throws more light on the complex notion of the historical. Berdyaev speaks of the "apprehension

---

[1] *Ibid.*, 13.
[2] *Ibid.*, 14.

of being as a gradation of particularities," and he means that the historical itself refers to a gradation of particularities. *Being*, in this text refers to existential reality. The term, *being*, like *object* and *science* (see p. 3, preceding), will be criticized in later books of Berdyaev.[1] Recalling the illustrations given above, we may note than the fact that John Lackland was born on such and such a date occupies a lower place in the hierarchy of particularities than does the entity of a historical nation.[2]

My book is concerned ... with the problems ... of the philosophy and the knowledge of historical destinies. The philosophy of history – of historical knowledge – is one of the ways to the knowledge of spiritual reality. It is a science of the spirit bringing us into communion with the mysteries of spiritual life. It deals with that concrete spiritual reality man ... The philosophy of history studies man in the concrete fulness of his spiritual being; psychology, physiology and the other sphere of human knowledge study him incompletely in one or other of his aspects. The philosophy of history examines man in relation to the world forces which act upon him, that is, in his greatest fulness and concreteness. By comparison all other ways of approaching man are abstract.[3]

The purpose of the philosophy of history is to help us to know spiritual reality. It is a "science of the spirit" because it deals with the concrete spiritual reality, man. We find, here, the emphasis on man explicit. We say that the study of the "historical" comprises such things as the birth of John Lackland and the historical nation. But these historical entities are in turn understood in respect to man. The philosophy of history studies man in the concrete fulness of his spiritual being and, hence, examines man in relation to the world forces which act upon him; that is, in his greatest fulness and concreteness. The particular historical, the historical nation, is ultimately understood in respect to man as one of "the world forces which act upon him." To sum it up, philosophy of history studies the historical in all its diverse complexity in order to understand man "in the concrete fulness of his spiritual being."

Berdyaev says, "by comparison all other ways of approaching man are abstract." We will see that he opposes the abstract approach to reality.[4] Philosophy of history is the least abstract way of approaching man. The implication is that this philosophy is the best approach to reality. We will see what sort of a metaphysics this implies in Section C of this Chapter; for Berdyaev considers himself to be a metaphysician.

---

[1] See Chapter III, Section D.

[2] This is not to say that the *existence* of John Lackland is inferior to the historical nation in the hierarchy of particularities. John Lackland, according to Berdyaev's psychology, which is based on his doctrine of Godmanhood, is absolutely eternal and is transcendentally superior to the "historical" as historical. See Chapter III, Section E.

[3] *The Meaning of History*, 14–15.

[4] Chapter III, Section D; Chapter IV, Section B.

Berdyaev says, a little further on:

It is as impossible to detach man from history and to consider him abstractly as it is to detach history from man and to examine it from without, that is form a non-human point of view. . . . The historical in the real sense of the word brings with it the revelation of essential being, of the inner spiritual nature of the world and of the inner essence of man, and not merely of the external phenomena. The "historical" is by its nature not phenomenal but deeply ontological. It has its roots in some deep primal foundation of being which it makes available for our communion and understanding. The "historical" is a sort of revelation of the deepest essence of universal reliaty of the destiny of the world focused in that of man.[1]

The philosophy of history cannot detach man from history or history from man because the two are understood in terms of each other. The "historical" reveals "essential being," that is, the deepest reality,[2] though the "historical" being itself is not essential being. It is not mere phenomena, but it is ontological because it is rooted in "some deep primal foundation of being." Berdyaev concludes the passage saying, "the 'historical' is a sort of revelation of the deepest essence of universal reality, of the destiny of the world focused on that of man." The historical is rooted in the spiritual. And the "historical" is a *revelation* of Divine truths. It reveals the deepest intelligibility of reality.

Berdyaev's notion of the "historical" becomes refined in this text. Note the use of quotation marks in *"historical."* With quotation marks *"historical"* refers to something not phenomenal but deeply ontological. Note the lack of quotation marks in *historical.* Without quotation marks, *the historical* is that which merely "brings with it the revelation of essential being." *Historical,* without quotation marks, refers not to the spiritual meaning of history, but to the material, geographical and natural conditions in which the meaning of history is imbedded.[3] The *"historical,"* with quotation marks, names the spiritual meaning of history, the true existential reality.

Thus, Berdyaev refers, in *Solitude and Society* to the "historical" as it characterizes the human personality and existence:

The personality is a biography one and unique, an "history." . . . Existence is invariably "historical." [4]

[1] *The Meaning of History*, 15–16.

[2] See Chapter III, Section D, which shows that the deepest reality is the concrete existent. This is what *"essential being"* refers to. Berdyaev uses the term, *"essential being,"* but in his later books, he develops an existentialism and a vocabulary according to which the "essential being" is a concrete existent. Cf. *ibid.*, notes.

[3] See the treatment of the mere historical by Berdyaev, discussed in Section C of this chapter.

[4] N. Berdyaev, *Solitude and Society* (Bles, London, 1947), 124.

When Berdyaev writes of the spiritual meaning of history, he is discussing something that is not historical in the common sense of the term,
historical. This is why he terms it *"historical,"* written with quotation
marks. It does not partake of the material conditions of historical traditions, although, the acceptance of historical tradition is indispensable
for knowing the "historical." (See p. 3).

The "historical," therefore, is different from the mere historical. The
true subject of philosophy of history (the "historical") is not the mere
historical. In later books Berdyaev is very critical of history as such.
Thus, in *Slavery and Freedom* [1] he says that "the greatest of all forms
of the seduction and slavery of man is connected with history ... he is
crushed by history."

We have said that the philosophy of history "studies man in the
concrete fulness of his spiritual being"; it is a philosophy of the spirit
and it primarily is concerned about man. This means, for Berdyaev, the
"historical," a spiritual meaningfulness, is also man, insofar as man
is a spirit.

Berdyaev does not speak precisely of the "historical," because it is
mysterious; there is, in his discussion, a great respect for the mystery
of it. He says that "the 'historical' is a sort of revelation of the deepest
essence of universal reality ..." The "historical," then, is not the
ultimate spiritual reality. It is not exactly historical, on the one hand,
nor is it precisely ultimate metaphysical [2] reality, on the other hand.
The "historical," however, is far more spiritual than the mere historical.
Berdyaev intends the term to express the ultimate reality insofar as the
reality has a historical quality or aspect. We will see in Section F of this
chapter how it is the ultimate metaphysical and religious Reality has
a historical quality or aspect.

We must recall, too, that Berdyaev has a strong sense of the organic
unity of the world. Further, his discussion of the "historical," which
has been in terms of both spiritual reality and plain history, shows a
strong sense of the unity of plain history with the spiritual. There is no
assertion of a sharp division between history and the "historical," or,
moreover, between the "historical" and the ultimate reality. Berdyaev
says, on the following page of the text: "history ... is synonymous
with the greatest spiritual reality." [3] We see in this assertion the
strongest sense of the unity of history with the ultimate (yet Berdyaev,

---

[1] N. Berdyaev, *Slavery and Freedom* (Bles, London, 1943), 255.
[2] For *metaphysical,* see Section C of this chapter.
[3] *The Meaning of History,* 17.

we saw, is very aware of the difference between them). Berdyaev is im-
plying that, history, in its inner existential meaning, is the "historical,"
and that the "historical," in its truest and most real aspect, is the
greatest spiritual reality.

Thus, Berdyaev does not employ the term *"historical"* in a strict and
rigid sense; he intends that the *"historical,"* in the truest sense of the
term, refers to the historical aspect of the ultimate reality. We will see,
in Chapter IV,[1] that Berdyaev characteristically uses philosophical
terms in this way. We will see how and why Berdyaev's terms have a
truest sense and a less true sense.

We should note, at this time, that the *"historical,"* in the truest sense
of the term, refers to man "in the concrete fulness of his spiritual being"
and at the same time to the ultimate reality.[2] In the truest sense of the
term, the *"historical,"* indicates something which is not historical in the
plain sense of the word, but which, nevertheless, has a certain historical
aspect.

In order to understand the "historical," we must investigate more
closely how Berdyaev relates his theory of it to his theory of man and
man's knowledge of it. Indeed, insofar as the "historical" is a revelation
of something beyond history, it can "be approached only through the
most intimate concrete tie between man and history ..." [3]

Berdyaev says: "the 'historical' is a revelation of noumenal reality." [4]
Revelation, according to Berdyaev, is properly not knowledge, it is,
rather, the ultimate reality in which knowledge is indistinguishable
from the metaphysical reality.[5]

When Berdyaev says, "the historical in the real sense of the word

---

[1] Chapter IV, Section G, Part 2.

[2] *The "historical"* refers both to the ultimate Reality, so far as it is the meaning of history,
and to man through whom the diffusion of meaning into history occurs. This is a Christian
spiritual doctrine which asserts the divine Logos, the Godman. See Chapter II, Section B.
Berdyaev says, in *Slavery and Freedom*, 29: "The triumph of the spiritual principle means,
not the subordination of man to the universe, but the revelation of the universe in personality." "The revelation of the universe in personality" refers to the "historical"; that is
the "historical" is a "sort of revelation" (*The Meaning of History*, 16). The "historical" is,
in part, the *true* universe, as it is in the ultimate reality; and it is revealed in the
human personality.

[3] *The Meaning of History*, 16.

[4] *Ibid.*, 16.

[5] Berdyaev asserts that the ultimate reality is ineffable and can properly be known only
negatively, or apophatically. See N. Berdyaev, *The Beginning and the End* (Bles, London,
1952), 102–103. This is so, though a positively asserted philosophy can be developed. For
Berdyaev, what can be asserted about the ultimate reality is only symbolic of it. See
Chapter IV, Section G, Part 2.

As for the distinction Berdyaev makes between revelation and knowledge, see Chapter IV,
Section G, Part 2.

brings with it the revelation of ... the inner spiritual nature of the
world and of the inner spiritual essence of man," he means that it
brings with it the "historical." [1] The "historical," the true reality, is
revealed in the historical.

Since the "historical" refers to the inner spirituality of man as well
as that of the world, we may penetrate the mystery of the true "historical" if we consider the relationship of man to it. Berdyaev's approach
to the problem is to consider historical knowledge.

(2) The "Historical" and the Human Memory

Berdyaev continues, in the passage quoted on p. 8,

In order to grasp the mystery of the "historical," I must have a sense of it and
history as something that is deeply *mine*, that is deeply *my* history, that is deeply
my destiny. I must situate myself within historical destiny and it within my own
human destiny. The presence of the historical destiny then becomes revealed in
the very depths of the human spirit. All historical epochs, from the very earliest
to that at the topmost peak of modern history, represent my historical destiny;
they are all mine. [2]

We have seen that the notion of the "historical" refers transcendentally
to all of history in its various levels of gradations of being and at the
same time to the human spirit. It follows that, if one is to attain the
mystery of the "historical," he must identify his own historical destiny
– in knowing – with all historical epochs: "a profound integration of
my historical destiny with that of mankind". [3]

We have, here, the expression of a personalism and an existentialism:
Berdyaev strongly advises the philosopher of history to identify himself, in the depths of his personality, with the historical destiny of the
world. We will see, in Chapter III, the way in which this doctrine
expresses a personalism and existentialism. We can observe the existentialism at this time. When Berdyaev speaks of the mystery of the
"historical" and the sense of history that is "deeply *my* history, that is
deeply *my* destiny," he is personalist and existential. That is, he refers
not merely to the person's knowledge of history and of the "historical,"
but also to an existential identity of the person with them, achieved by
"situating himself within historical destiny."

As always, we must note the subtlety of Berdyaev's discourse. This
Existential communion and identity with history, achieved by the
person is directed toward the "historical," rather than merely history.

[1] *The Meaning of History*, 16.
[2] *Ibid.*, 16.
[3] *Ibid.*, 17.

He qualifies "deeply *my* history" to say, "that is, deeply *my* destiny. I must situate myself within historical destiny and it within my own human destiny." That is, the activity is directed toward the "historical" the meaning of history to be achieved, the destiny of history.

Berdyaev speaks early in *The Meaning of History*, of a primitive wisdom that lingers in mankind.

Reason ought to be attuned to the primal wisdom of man, to those first apprehensions of being and of life which are born with the dawn of human history or even prehistory. ... This wisdom which is shared by the very earliest epochs persists in the inner mysterious depths of life throughout the history of the human spirit, the birth of Christianity and the Middle Ages, down to our times.[1]

Berdyaev means that the primal metaphysical apprehensions of primitive man (which are contained in their myths) should never be lost, sight of. In the context from which the passage is taken he criticizes the mind of the 18th century enlightenment which "was a self-assertive and limited reason." [2] He posits a continuity of human wisdom, which, if a mind loses it, it loses "all inner contact with the mysteries of the historical life." [3]

History, since it is synonymous with the greatest spiritual reality, is not a given empirical fact or a naked factual material. As such it neither exists nor can be apprehended. It can, however, be approached through the historical memory, that is, through a certain spiritual activity, a certain given spiritual relation to the "historical" within the sphere of historical knowledge which, as a result, becomes inwardly transfigured and transformed. The inner soul of history emerges in all its clarity only in the process of transformation and transfiguration which takes place in historical memory. This is as true for the apprehension of the soul of history as it is for that of man; for the human personality when not bound by memory into an integral whole, lacks the faculty of apprehending the human soul as a certain reality.[4]

History is synonymous with the greatest spiritual reality because (we saw) in its truest sense history is the "historical" (p. 9). History, for Berdyaev, cannot be known empirically because empirical knowing is a phenomenal knowing, which knows according to the ways of empirical and necessitarian nature. The historical memory, through which history is truly known, is a spiritual activity, "a certain given spiritual relation to the 'historical' within the sphere of historical knowledge." We will have to consider the natures of spirit and spiritual knowing in later chapters. But it is clear from our foregoing section that spirit is

---

[1] *Ibid.*, 7.
[2] *Ibid.*, 6.
[3] *Ibid.*, 7.
[4] *Ibid.*, 17–18.

able to penetrate beyond the natural world, seen by empirical sciences, to a mysterious realm where the spiritual instead of a natural necessity prevails.

Historical knowledge becomes inwardly transfigured and transformed in this spiritual activity upon condition that the knowing spirit sees beyond the natural and categorical intelligibility in which historycal actions, events and entities are encrusted: the transfiguration of the knowledge occurs because the historical memory achieves a spiritual relation "to the historical within the sphere of historical knowledge." This spiritual relation brings about the transfiguration of historical knowledge.

"The inner soul of history emerges in all its clarity only in the process of transformation ... which takes place in historical memory." When he next compares the soul of history to the human soul he exemplifies the organic, complex and unified character of universal history. And he implies that the soul of history is as superior and preeminent over the particular historical facts and institutions as the soul is over the body it vivifies.

We will see in Chapter II [1] that Berdyaev refers to a soul of the cosmos, as well. He refers, with the notions of a soul of history and soul of the cosmos, to the organic unity of history and of the cosmos. *Soul of history* should not be considered apart from the human soul or apart from Berdyaev's cosmological doctrine. [2]

This is how (obscure as the notion is) Berdyaev understands history "to be synonymous with the greatest spiritual reality." Note especially the *unity* of history this notion presupposes. We can see that Berdyaev's universal history presupposes a living unifying agent that vivifies all of history with the same life and the same intelligibility. The process of history is the process of this vivifying agent as it is participated in by history. We will see in Chapter III how this unifying agent unites history through the human soul and spirit.

This shows that the "historical" is truly interior, both in the human spirit of the philosopher of history, and in history. Historical tradition is both a metaphysical reality (in its meaningful depths) and the epistemological means of knowing that reality. This is, at present, somewhat mysterious and must be cleared up in chapters III and IV. Berdyaev continues:

---

[1] See Chapter II, Section D, Part 2.
[2] *Ibid.*

But the historical memory as a means of knowing the "historical" is inalienably part of the historical tradition outside of which it has no existence. The abstract use of documents never leads to the knowledge of the "historical." It does not bring us into communion with the latter. . . . historical tradition . . . only, undoes the knot that binds man's spiritual destiny to that of history, no great cultural epoch . . . is comprehensible unless we approach it through the historical memory whose data constitute our spiritual past, our spiritual culture and our ultimate source. To grasp these great epochs we must inform them with our own spiritual destiny, for, considered superficially, they are all inwardly dead to us. But the historical memory, which obliges us to commune inwardly with the "historical," is an inalienable part of the historical tradition.

The historical tradition is precisely this inner historical memory which is transposed into historical destiny.[1]

We learn in this passage that the abstract use of documents will not give knowledge of the "historical" for the simple reason that historical tradition (which reveals "historical") is none else than "this inner historical memory," so far as it is transposed into historical destiny. In this way the historical memory becomes an inalienable part of historical tradition. So that when Berdyaev says a great historical epoch is comprehensible only if we approach it through the historical memory, he means that it is comprehensible through historical tradition and ultimately through the "historical." Since tradition is historical memory, the epoch is comprehensible through historical memory. It will be obvious that historical memory can be considered external to the man who knows, since in knowing traditions he is knowing the memory in which the traditions are preserved. Nevertheless, Berdyaev says, "to grasp these great epochs, we must inform them with our own historical destiny"; that is, to see the "historical" through the expressed memory of somebody else is not enough. But we must inform it with our own spiritual destiny; we must understand the "historical" in the light of our knowledge of our own spiritual destiny. Historical traditions, then, are not spiritually dead, but live in the dynamic intelligibility of a known and sought-after historical destiny. (We have yet to see Berdyaev's explanation of what historical destiny is.) Indeed, in a later book, *Slavery and Freedom*, Berdyaev, says:

Memory of the past is spiritual; it conquers historical time. This however is not a conserving but a creatively transfiguring memory. It wishes to carry forward into eternal life not that which is dead in the past but what is alive, not that which is static in the past but what is dynamic.[2]

The manifestations of the "historical" (the traditions, cultures), there-

---

[1] *The Meaning of History*, 18.
[2] *Slavery and Freedom*, 111.

fore are not merely re-created in the knowing subject, but actively created in his historical memory. And this means, in knowing historical traditions, we create something new and better – this is the significance of Berdyaev's assertion that the historical memory carries into eternal life what is dynamic in the past. We must study the creativity of knowing in Chapter IV.

Berdyaev continues, in *The Meaning of History*, as follows:

The philosophy of history represents a certain spiritualization and transfiguration of the historical process. In a certain sense, historical memory implies a merciless war between eternity and time; and the philosophy of history is always the witness of the triumph of eternity over time and corruption. ... The goal of historical knowledge and philosophy is not natural but supernatural. For just as there exists an after-life in relation to individual life, so the great historical paths likewise lead us to such a world. And that explains why the historical memory, when directed to contemplating the past, evokes an absolutely peculiar feeling of communion with a world other than the empirical whose nightmare oppression we must overcome before we can attain to that historical reality which is the authentic revelation of other worlds.

The philosophy of history is therefore that of an after-world rather than that of empirical realities.[1]

The historical process is spiritualized and transfigured in philosophy of history and in the historical memory; that is to say, it is informed with the spiritual destiny which is known and asserted in philosophy of history. There is war between eternity and time in historical memory because the spiritualization of temporal entities, in a direction toward a supernatural goal, is the conquest of the temporal by the eternal. Indeed the spiritual is also supernatural, the goal is supernatural in Berdyaev's Christian philosophy.[2]

History is not annihilated in being spiritualized or subjectivized in the individual knowing man. There is not only an other-world for the individual knower but also an other-world for history in its true spiritual reality. Indeed, Berdyaev mentions a feeling of a "communion" with a world other than the empirical, which is experienced in the activity of the historical memory.

This communion with an other-world recalls our investigations a few pages back, of the organic unity of history (and of the cosmos, too), effected through the human soul. The historical memory, which is spiritual, in knowing history and the cosmos, spiritualizes them; thus, it communes with an other world. See chapters III and IV.

---

[1] *The Meaning of History*, 18–19. The Spiritual is supernatural.
[2] See Sections C, D and F.

The other-world is an after-world (which has been referred to in the term *historical destiny*). The after-world (the goal and final end of history) is communed with as an other-world in the historical memory. This is mysterious and will be clarified when we study the mystical principle of Godmanhood in Chapter II.[1]

The human memory is of the utmost importance in the doctrine. "Historical science ought to adopt to its needs, with certain modifications, it is true, the Platonic doctrine of knowledge as an act of remembranche." This theory is one of the distinguishing marks of Berdyaev's philosophy of history and doctrine of man, and we will need to study it later when we consider his metaphysics and epistemology.[2] So important is memory, that Berdyaev says, later, in *The Meaning of History:*

The historical memory is the greatest manifestation of the eternal spirit in our temporal reality. It upholds the historical connection of the times. It is the very foundation of history. ... Memory is therefore the eternal ontological basis of all history.[3]

For, Berdyaev says, "purely objective history would be incomprehensible."[4]

Each man represents by virtue of his inner nature a sort of microcosm in which the whole world of reality and all the great historical epochs combine and coexist. He ... is a world in his own right, a world revealed or hidden according as consciousness is more or less penetrating and extensive. In this development of self-consciousness the whole history of the world is apprehended.... assuming an external stimulus for every profound act of remembrance, it should be possible for man to apprehend history within himself; he should be able, for example, to discover within himself the profoundest strata of the Hellenic world and thus grasp the essentials of Greek history.[5]

Man is a microcosm because, as we saw, the "historical" is created and preserved in its integrity in the human spirit. We saw, too, that the living, organic unity of history (and the cosmos) unites history through the human soul and spirit. The "historical" is truly interior, in the human spirit. Berdyaev then says that the whole history of the world is apprehended in the development of self-consciousness. He means

---

[1] Chapter II, Section B.

[2] Let us note at this time, concerning the memory, that Berdyaev says in a later book, *Solitude and Society*, 107, "memory is the primary constituent of the personality." See Chapter III, Section F; Chapter IV, Section G, Part 2.

[3] *The Meaning of History*, 73.

[4] *Ibid.*, 22.

[5] *Ibid.*, 22–23.

that history and the cosmos are progressively spiritualized during universal history in man.[1]

"Assuming an external stimulus for every profound act of remembrance, it should be possible for man to apprehend history within himself." This indicates that the act of historical remembrance, in its essence, is unworldly with respect to the external world of the past and the present, and completely subjective. Berdyaev posits a Platonic doctrine of knowledge of remembrance, and it implies that our knowledge of the meaning of universal history, throughout its various epochs, comes from an *internal* principle. It is brought to consciousness in the historical memory.[2] We have here a philosophy of history in which man is a microcosm, containing, obscurely or consciously, universal history.[3]

"The profoundest stratum of the Hellenic world" is discovered by an

---

[1] See Chapter III, Section F.

[2] Is Berdyaev's adaptation of the Platonic doctrine of remembrance antihistorical? Not in Berdyaev's view, for the following reasons. One aspect of the divine Universal History posited by Christianity is a movement within the Godhead of the Blessed Trinity, and involving the Incarnation of the divine Logos. It is a Celestial History. Another aspect is the terrestrial history which occurs in the fallen cosmos and in fallen man. (See Sections C and E of this chapter). Berdyaev is unhistorical to the extent that he denies terrestrial history is a completely true reality. But he asserts the truth and reality of celestial history and that man, as well as God, participates in it. The meaning of universal history is spiritual (mystical) rather than rational or natural; it does not partake of the rationality of Platonic ideas. (Berdyaev opposes Plato on this point. See N. Berdyaev, *The Russian Idea* (Bles, London. 1947), 240–241.

[3] See preceding note. Berdyaev's doctrine of man is truly reminiscent of Leibniz' doctrine of the monad and properly so because Berdyaev in his early career was strongly influenced by a Russian movement of Leibnizians.

At that early period, Berdyaev asserted a hierarchical unity of spiritual monads bound together into a cosmic whole by the Primary Divine monad. See Chapter III, notes.

However, the definitive doctrine of Berdyaev is more historical than that of Leibniz. In Leibniz, the notion of law is extremely important. The laws of God unite and harmonize the monads. In political terms, we may say that the world of monads unites a maximum of individualism with a maximum of socialism. They are all together and they are all alone. See "The Monadology," translated by G. R. Montgomery in *Leibniz's Discourse on Metaphysics, etc.* (Opencourt, La Salle, Illinois, 1945).

Indeed, Leibniz says (No. 88, p. 271): "This harmony brings it about that things progress of themselves towards grace along natural lines, and that this earth, for example, must be destroyed and restored by natural means ... for chastisement ..."

In a universe dominated by rational laws, without Grace, and ordered by a pre-established harmony (*Ibid.*, 268–269), there is no real universal history. We may contrast Berdyaev's doctrine of a radical freedom of God and of man. The Divine Universal History which Berdyaev asserts is a historical movement. The meaning, the essential intelligibility of Universal History does not destroy its freedom or render meaningless its movement. See E. Gilson, *Les Métamorphoses de la Cité de Dieu* (Nauwelaerts, Louvain, 1952), Chapter VIII, "La Cité des Philosophes," which treats of Leibniz.

Berdyaev accepts Leibniz' ideas only so far as Leibniz has shown the necessitarianism and alienation which men have experienced as a result of the Fall of man from God. He says, in *The Beginning and the End*, 130: "Leibniz' monad loses its character of a microcosm as a result of alienation, the projection into the external of that which ought to be within, and is subjected to the forcible action of nature and society in their capacity of forces established as external things. The sun no longer shines from within man."

act of Platonic remembrance, provoked by an external stimulation. It is, then, "a penetration that is really into the depths of (man's) own nature. Only deep down in his own self can man really discover the secrets of time." [1]

The result of the external stimulations to historical remembrance is the historical myth:

Historical myths have a profound significance for the act of remembrance. A myth contains the story that is preserved in popular memory and that helps to bring to life some deep stratum buried in the depths of the human spirit. . . . This leads us to reconsider the significance of the part played by tradition in the inner comprehension of history. For historical tradition . . . makes possible a great and occult act of remembrance. It represents, indeed, no éxternal impulse or externally imposed fact alien to man, but one that is a manifestation of the inner mysterious life, in which he can attain to the knowledge of himself and feel himself to be an inalienable participant.

. . . The tradition of a people is valuable in so far as it symbolizes the historical destiny of that people. *This symbolism* is of primary importance for the elaboration of a philosophy of history and for the apprehension of its inner significance. . . .

. . . This inner tradition, this inner myth of history . . . [2] (my italics)

The historical myth is important for the philosopher of history because it reveals, not the superficial intelligibility of history, but "some deep stratum buried deep in the depths of the human spirit." Berdyaev does not identify the myth with historical tradition; for, as we shall see when we study his epistemology, the myth, that is, the symbol, is one of the most important forms of knowledge, while a tradition is only a particular kind of historical myth. The historical myth, created in the memory, is a way of truly and occultly knowing the "historical," which is to say, of knowing the mysterious depths of history, and of man. Berdyaev then says that the historical tradition symbolizes the historical destiny of a people. The destiny of a people is not merely historical but metaphysical. We are thus dealing with a philosophy of history which seeks reality in knowing symbolically.

Berdyaev speaks of a "manifestation of the inner mysterious life, in which (man) can attain to the knowledge of himself"; namely, the historical tradition or symbol [3] or myth. And he mentions, too, that this symbolism affords the philosopher the "apprehension of the inner significance" of the philosophy of history. An "*inner* tradition," he says.

---

[1] *The Meaning of History*, 23.
[2] *Ibid.*, 23–25.
[3] We will see, in Chapter IV that historical symbol and myth are synonymous.

Note the stress on the interiority of historical tradition, both in history and in the metaphysical depths of the philosopher. This knowledge has such a mystery because it is in the order of metaphorical or poetic knowledge. And, since tradition is a reality existing in history, outside the knower as well as within, history itself is a metaphorical and symbolic reality. In such an outlook, the organic unity of history (achieved through man) is provided for. But we will have to investigate how historical knowing and terrestrial history itself must be symbolic and metaphysical.

(3) The "Historical" and Universal History

Now we must consider Berdyaev's doctrine of the destiny of history. He says:

> In the destiny of mankind, I must recognize my own destiny, and in the latter, that of history. This is the only way we can commune with the mystery of the historical and discover in it the great spiritual destinies of mankind. And, inversely, this is the only way we can ... unite our own individual destiny with that of universal history instead of merely discovering the void of our isolation in opposition to all the riches of universal historical life. Thus the real goal of the philosophy of history is to establish a bond between man and history, between man's destiny and the metaphysics of history.[1]

In order to commune with the mystery of the "historical," Berdyaev exhorts the reader to realize that his own destiny is bound up with the destiny of mankind. Indeed, he points out the emptiness and solitude that occurs in a human life if the person will not recognize his own destiny in the destiny of mankind. He means that if one would achieve his proper goal ("commune with the mystery of the 'historical'"), he must establish a bond between his own individual destiny and that of mankind.[2]

When he speaks of the "goal of the philosophy of history" he means it in an axiological sense. The goal is not only to achieve the true knowledge of history, to commune intellectually with the "historical" but to establish a bond between the entire being of man and the "historical." This is the bond with the metaphysics of history, of which he speaks. (Concerning metaphysics of history see section E of this chapter.)

Thus, when Berdyaev shows the reader something of what he means by historical destiny (both of history and of man) he introduces the religious doctrine of Universal History.[1] His essay takes on the moral

---

[1] *The Meaning of History*, 17.
[2] *Ibid.*, 17.
[3] See Section B, Part 4 of the present chapter.

quality of a religious doctrine. Thus, his philosophy of history is moral. It is a religious and normative philosophy which seeks to bring about the destiny of man. He is saying, as it were, "en route!" See *The Destiny of Man*, an ethical work.[1]

Thus we see that the word, *philosophy*, pertains to Christian theology as well as to a religious philosophy expressed in philosophical terms.

> The goal of historical knowledge and philosophy is not natural but supernatural. For just as there exists an after-life in relation to individual life, so the great historical paths likewise lead us to such a world. . . .
>
> The philosophy of history is therefore that of an after-world rather than that of empirical realities.[2]

We may then add, concerning *metaphysics* (of history), that it is understood in a more spiritual sense than philosophy (of history); it also has the concrete meaning. The meaning of history, on any level, is concrete, according to Berdyaev's philosophy (see p. 8).[3] However, metaphysics of history is so spiritual, that it does not, like philosophy of history, refer to the material and historical conditions in which the "historical" is involved. I am describing (as we will find) the way in which Berdyaev's use of "metaphysics of history" tends to differ from his use of "philosophy of history." However, philosophy of history, in its truest aspect, is entirely metaphysical, about "an after-world rather than that of empirical realities." Metaphysics of history refers to that part of philosophy of history which considers the transcendental or religious intelligibles and norms, insofar as they are spiritual. (See Section C of this chapter.)

We saw that the philosophy of history "studies man in the concrete fullness of his spiritual being."

> But spiritual life is concrete and demands concrete study, since it is manifested in the knowledge of a concrete spiritual culture, and not in that of the abstract elements of the soul-life. The knowledge of spiritual life is a historical science which deals with culture and not a natural science . . . The materials of a spiritual life are contributed by the spiritual life of humanity itself as it has developed in history.[4]

Note how consistently Berdyaev refers to the historical aspect of the "knowledge of spiritual life." By "historical science," Berdyaev refers to philosophy of history insofar as it is a "science of the spirit." [5] Note,

---

[1] N. Berdyaev, *The Destiny of Man* (Bles, London, 1948).
[2] *The Meaning of History*, 19.
[3] See Chapter III, Sections D and F; Chapter IV, Section G.
[4] N. Berdyaev, *Freedom and the Spirit* (Bles, London, 1935), 19.
[5] *The Meaning of History*, 14.

too, that Berdyaev is treating philosophy as the "knowledge of spiritual life." Observe, also, though the materials of this knowledge are found in historical cultures (which are in historical and material conditions), they are seen from a spiritual point of view. Indeed, Berdyaev says: "the materials of a spiritual life (that is, of a life lived according to the 'historical,' the meaning of history) are contributed by the spiritual life of humanity itself as it has developed in history."

We are then dealing with a religious philosophy [1] in which the intelligibility of man and of history is sought through studying the relationship between historical entities and man and spirit. And this, Berdyaev says, is the way to the spiritual life. This life is one lived according to the "historical."

Berdyaev states in a later work:

Spirit is historically incarnated ... historical bodies ...[2]

Spirit is incarnated in man and, through man, in history and in historical entities. Spirit is manifested in a culture, and the knowledge of spiritual life must therefore be attained through historical knowledge. Philosophy of history then must refer to the merely historical as well as to the metaphysical. (This is not to say philosophy is historical.)

The historical entities with which philosophy of history is especially concerned are historical traditions and also cultures. We may say that though Berdyaev's doctrine deals with a whole order of gradations of historical facts and entities, it is especially interested in historical cultures. The meaning of history, aside from religious doctrine, is especially revealed, not in a study of man, nor in a scrutiny of visible historical events, but in a study of cultures. Indeed, for Berdyaev, our knowledge of man comes (in part) from a study of historical cultures.

This is Berdyaev's doctrine [3] and his practice. We saw (p. 2) that historical tradition is the indispensable category of knowledge in philosophy of history. Berdyaev studies cultures in order to learn the historical tradition embodied in them. The historical tradition, for Berdyaev, is a mode of knowing the "historical." [4]

On the one hand, he views culture as a sort of "living organism" [5] and "no great culture has been immune from decadence." [6] The his-

---

[1] See note I. We will see that Berdyaev unites philosophy and Christian doctrine.
[2] N. Berdyaev, *Spirit and Reality* (Bles, London, 1946), 64.
[3] See Chapter IV, Section G, Part 2.
[4] See p.4 above.
[5] *The Meaning of History*, 194.
[6] *Ibid.*, 194

torical tradition, on the other hand, is a symbol "of primary importance for the elaboration of a philosophy of history and for the apprehension of its inner significance. Tradition is synonymous with the knowledge of historical life ..." [1] Historical tradition, for Berdyaev, therefore, is more spiritual than historical culture, though "every culture ... is spiritual and the product of the creative work of the spirit as applied to the natural elements. ... Culture is the living process and destiny of peoples." [2] And cultures, in a deeper (spiritual) sense, continue to live in men after particular cultures have disappeared. [3]

He is, like Oswald Spengler, [4] contemptuous of *civilization* as he understands it.

Spengler proclaimed civilization to be the doom of every culture. ... The theme is not new. It has long been part of Russian thought, philosophy and history. [5]

Every culture (even the material one) is spiritual and the product of the creative work of the spirit as applied to the natural elements. But culture develops a tendency to disintegrate in its religious and spiritual foundations and to repudiate its own symbolism in passing to civilization. [6]

Culture, for Berdyaev, is an organic embodiment of the spiritual meaning of history. The loss of culture's religious and spiritual foundations, mentioned above, occurs in the passage to civilization. Civilization, he says, brings with it barbarism, the vulgarization or loss of the perfect forms contributed by culture. [7] It is not in civilization (as he understands it) that Berdyaev seeks the meaning of history. [8] He seeks a unity of history, realized in the material conditions of terrestrial existence, and it is to culture that he turns.

The most important culture in view of the unity and finite temporality of history is the total culture of all history:

The fall of Rome ... teaches us not only that culture has its stages of birth, flower and decay, but that it is also based upon an eternal principle ... (it is) a sort of historical catastrophe; an upheaval on the surface of the earth during which some new elements is added to the foundations of history, and the basic principle of ancient culture is left intact. Thus Roman law is still alive; and so are Greek art and philosophy and all the other ancient principles that constitute

---

[1] *Ibid.*, 24.
[2] *Ibid.*, 213.
[3] *Ibid.*, 221.
[4] See O. Spengler, *The Decline of the West* (Knopf, New York, 1939), Index: "culture."
[8] *The Meaning of History*, 207.
[6] *Ibid.*, 213.
[7] *Ibid.*, 221.
[5] Cf. *ibid.*, 207–224.

the foundations of our culture, which is one and eternal, though passing through various stages of existence.[1]

The most important culture that philosophy of history studies is the eternal culture of man, which preserves the deathless principles of peoples from cultures that have passed away. As we shall presently see, the cultures that have grown and declined will provide Berdyaev with a means of considering distinct moments in the development of the whole culture of mankind. "Culture," Berdyaev says, "is the living process and destiny of peoples." [2]

When Berdyaev speaks of one eternal culture what he has in mind is the Augustinian [3] doctrine of universal history:

Christianity ... supplied the postulate of universal history without which a philosophy of history is altogether impossible. Thus, while establishing itself upon the ground of a united East and West, Christianity offered the postulate of a united mankind and a Providence manifesting itself in historical destinies.[4]

That the postulate of a universal history is necessary to a philosophy of history is one of the implications of Berdyaev's doctrine of the "historical," as we have described it.

Though he admits to the growths and deaths of a succession of cultures, his Christian doctrine of the one culture of universal history excludes the possibility of accepting the Greek notion of ever-recurring cycles of cultures.

The dynamism introduced by Christianity derived from its idea of the immediacy and uniqueness of events which was foreign to the pagan world. ... The Christian consciousness ... held that events were immediate, non-recurrent and unique, and it imposed this conception on historical reality.[5]

While the Greek consciousness had conceived the time process as a cycle, Christianity passed beyond the cyclic idea, asserted the progression of history in time and discovered a historical purpose.[6]

The reason why Christianity went beyond the Greek consciousness and asserted the progression of history in time and a historical purpose is that:

It was convinced that an event of central importance in history had taken place; an event that had been completed once and for all; a non-recurring, indivisible,

---

[1] *Ibid.*, 121.
[2] *Ibid.*, 213.
[3] See *ibid.*, 33.
[4] *Ibid.*, 123. In his reference to the East and the West, Berdyaev is speaking of Christianity as it has been "the meeting ground of the Eastern and Western spiritual and historical forces."
[5] *Ibid.*, 33.
[6] *Ibid.*, 35.

incomparable and unique event that was both historical and metaphysical, ...
in a word, Christ's revelation.

History ... both ends and begins with the fact of Christ's revelation.[1]

Now we see why Berdyaev speaks of the one culture that is history.
There are really two reasons to be found in these passages why Christianity had to posit the uniqueness and unrepeatability of history: First,
the fact of Christ's Revelation is absolutely unique and unrepeatable,
yet, it is historical; consequently, it indicates that historical events –
not eternally recurring – are unique, not determined in the fact of their
existence nor the circumstances by the necessity of their intelligibility.
Second, to say that "history both ends and begins with the fact of
Christ's Revelation" is to mean that universal history is explainable
according to the doctrine of Sacred Scriptures. And that is to say,
history, from the beginning of history, has contained a revelation of
Christ (or a preparation for it); and with the Second Coming of Christ,
history will end. Hence, universal history itself is a unique fact.

Christianity introduced a *freedom* and a dynamism into the notion
of history through its insistence upon the unique character of historical
and metaphysical facts.

Consequently a great and distinct Christian world evolved – a world that was
dynamic by contrast with the static world of antiquity.[2]

This dynamic and historical character is peculiar to Christianity which alone
attributed a general and ultimate goal to mankind.[3]

That is, the coming to awareness, in Christianity, of the freedom of man
made it possible for Christians to choose freely the means of progressing
towards an ultimate goal. (The Greeks thought themselves bound and
determined in endless historical cycles.) [4] Hence:

... Christianity laid the foundations of philosophy of history.[5]

Hence:

... historical reality implies the existence of an irrational principle which makes
dynamism possible. Neither history not true dynamism is possible without this
principle, which is turbulent, mobile and pliant, and which kindles the conflict
between the opposing forces of light and darkness. ... the *sine qua non* of
freedom and dynamism.[6]

[1] *Ibid.*, 33–34.
[2] *Ibid.*, 35.
[3] *Ibid.*, 36.
[4] See *Ibid.*, 34–35.
[5] *Ibid.*, 36.
[6] *Ibid.*, 36.

In this passage Berdyaev sets forth the notion of an ultimate dynamic principle. We will find, in the following chapter, that the dynamic principle is an irrational Freedom or Will which is the deepest and most ultimate principle in God and in man. The uniqueness of the "historical," and the consequent meaningfulness of history, which Berdyaev asserts, is possible only upon the conditions of the radical freedom that Christianity finds in man. [1]

Universal History, for Berdyaev, has two main aspects (see Sections C and E of this Chapter); namely, a terrestrial history and a celestial history. The Greek doctrine of the eternal recurrence, or cyclical returns, is denied on two grounds: First, terrestrial history, according to Christian Universal History, has a beginning and an end, it is unique and unrepeatable. Second, there is a divine movement a celestial "history" involving, for example, the Incarnation of the divine Logos and a spiritualization of mankind. We will see how it happens that, for Berdyaev, terrestrial history is not a fully true reality and celestial history is a true reality. There is no doubt that Berdyaev means to assert a real and true history in his doctrine of Universal History. In contrast to the Greeks, Berdyaev asserts an intelligible principle (the revealed divine Logos) Who gives meaning to the unique history. He also posits an irrational principle, a radical freedom which makes the dynamism and movement of history possible.

(4) Universal History: An Interaction Between Man and Nature

Our encounter with the primacy of freedom in Berdyaev's philosophy reintroduces us to a "main theme of universal history":

What is the main theme of universal history? In my opinion it is that of man's destiny seen in the light of the interaction between the human spirit and nature, which constitutes the foundation and motivating principle of the "historical." We can observe in the history of mankind various stages of interaction between the human spirit and nature which falls into historical epochs.[2]

Universal history concerns man's destiny. And, here, man's destiny is seen in the light of the interaction of man and nature. But what is the "interaction of the human spirit and nature?" In order to retain the comprehensive viewpoint of Berdyaev, as we follow him in this passage, it is necessary to understand his notion of nature. "The interaction of

---

[1] Meaningfulness flows from radical freedom, from the irrational. Indeed, we will see, in Chapter II that the Holy Trinity, of which the divine Logos is the Meaning, is born out of a primal Will. Cf. Chapter II, Section C.
[2] *Ibid.*, 112.

the human spirit and nature" must be understood to refer not only to the relation of the human spirit and the cosmos, but also to the relation of the human spirit and historical entities.

We will see, in Chapter IV,[1] that he has taken his notion of nature from Kant and consequently defines "nature" in respect to phenomenal causality and necessity. Hence, the "natural" refers to the Newtonian external cosmos and to the Kantian phenomenal epistemology, presented in the *Critique of Pure Reason*. Berdyaev accepts the Newtonian universe of Kant as existing in fact,[2] but he calls such a cosmos an objectified world.[3] He dose not understand the knowing which is correlated with the natural world as merely phenomenal, however.[4] "Objectified" indicates the debased situation of the world and of man's knowledge, which occurred because of the Fall of man. He believes that it is possible to know in a truer manner (that is, subjectively) which overcomes the obstruction between reality and true knowledge. We must study this in Chapter IV when we investigate his theory of knowledge.

Guided by his religious doctrine he believes that, in the interaction between the human spirit and nature, nature and the fallen cosmos will not be transformed until the end of the world, but nature in man is gradually transcended and transformed into free spirit during history.[5]

Thus Christianity had affected man's deliverance from the terror and slavery of nature; but, in order to achieve this, it had been obliged to declare an uncompromising, passionate and heroic war on the natural elements both within and outside man, an ascetic war illustrated by the astounding lives of the Saints.[6]

Berdyaev says that this interaction between the human spirit and nature "constitutes the foundation and motivating principle of the 'historical.'" [7] Man's destiny, seen in the light of the interaction between the human spirit and nature, which constitutes the motivating principle of the "historical," is to transcend the natural, as such, completely. This is known in its simplicity through basic religious doctrine and known in its difficult complexity in the philosophy of history where a theory of freedom is developed.

Berdyaev associates the natural with necessity and the spiritual with

---

[1] Chapter IV, Section B, notes.
[2] *Ibid.*
[3] See Chapter III, Section B; Chapter IV, Section B.
[4] *Ibid.*
[5] *The Meaning of History*, 112, ff.
[6] *Ibid.*, 116.
[7] *Ibid.*, 112.

freedom;[1] therefore, the interaction of man and nature, with which philosophy of history is concerned, may be expressed in the following way:

The philosophy of history is concerned with the fundamental antinomy between freedom and necessity, between the freedom of man and his lot in history. The massive scale of history impresses man and imposes itself upon him to the extent of overwhelming him.[2]

"Antinomy" is here understood in the sense of "contradiction."[3] There is an antinomy which arises from the conflict of the freedom of man with the necessity that is imposed upon him by being immersed in history. By nature, alone, man is enslaved. The historical has the element of necessity, the natural element, because the fallen cosmos, visible nature, in its necessity is involved in history, along with the necessitarian outlooks of man which he has borrowed from the fallen cosmos.

He says, however, in a later book:

The word, *nature* can be interpreted in two ways: there is a preconscious existential nature, and there is a post conscious and objectified nature. The first admits of spiritual communion, the latter only of scientific or technical relations.[5]

That is, the struggle during universal history between man and nature (objectified world) will not culminate in the destruction of nature. For Berdyaev asserts there is an "existential nature," attainable in spiritual communion.

(5) *The Ages of the World*

Berdyaev's theory of the epochs or ages of the world, like the doctrine of time with which it is connected, was not set forth in its clarity until some years after *The Meaning of History* was written.[6] Earlier, in *The Meaning of History* (1921) and in *Freedom and the Spirit* (1926), he proposed three epochs of the world, but later, in a posthumous work, *The Realm of the Spirit and the Realm of Caesar* (1953) four epochs:

We may fix four periods in man's relationship to the cosmos. 1. Man's submersion in cosmic life, his dependence on the objective world. ... 2. Man is freed from

[1] Though the natural is necessitarian and the spiritual is fact, the two are not necessarily opposed. Nature will be completely spiritualized at the end of history. Nature, taken by itself (fallen) is opposed to the spiritual. See *Spirit and Reality*, 175.

[2] N. Berdyaev, *Truth and Revelation*, 84.

[3] See Chapter IV, Sections B and C.

[4] See Chapter III, Section F.

[5] *Spirit and Reality*, 175.

[6] Though the doctrine of time is not well-developed in *The Meaning of History*, yet Berdyaev composed Chapter VI, "Christianity and History," with the idea of the epochs of the world in mind; cf. *The Meaning of History*, 112, 116.

the power of cosmic forces, from the spirits and demons of nature – man struggles by means of ascesis . . . 3. the mechanization of nature, its scientific and technical control . . . 4. the disruption of cosmic order in the discovery of the infinitely great and the infinitely small . . . the terribly augmented power of man over nature, and his slavery to his own discoveries. These phases are typological and not chronological. . . .[1]

The cosmic epoch is exemplified by early societies where man is submerged in the visible natural world. But, as Berdyaev defines it, it could conceivably refer to an epoch in modern times which was dominated by a cosmic outlook. The second, ascetic epoch is exemplified by the Middle Ages. The third, mechanical epoch is exemplified by that which has arisen since the Renaissance. The fourth is exemplified by the present technical age, where man has become partly enslaved by his technical fabrications.

This outline is applicable to a chapter (VI) in *The Meaning of History*, entitled, "Christianity and History," where Berdyaev writes a short universal history which treats historical progress in terms of eras.[2] The main theme of universal history is that of man's destiny, seen in the light of the interaction between the human spirit and nature.

We can observe in the history of mankind various stages of interaction between the human spirit and nature which fall into historical epochs. . . .

The theme of man's worldly destiny is the liberation of the creative human spirit from the depths of natural necessity and its enslavement by the lowest elements.[3]

This elaborates how the epochs of history (itself an epoch) are essentially contained in the divine history as a necessary condition of its fulfilment.[4] That is, "the liberation of the human spirit" (a divine-human action) occurs through various stages of history, and consequently, through a historical progress which is described by the doctrine of the epochs of the world. Christianity enabled man to escape the rule of the cosmic and finally has mechanized nature, exalting man above nature.[5]

The four epochs correspond to cosmic time (the cosmic epoch) and to historical time (the other three epochs), and therefore mostly concern

---

[1] N. Berdyaev, *The Realm of Spirit and the Realm of Caesar*, 47.

[2] I refer this outline of the epochs of the world, taken from *The Realm of Spirit and the Realm of Caesar*, back to *The Meaning of History* because the short chapter where the outline is found, entitled "Man and the Cosmos – Technics," is concerned merely with the technical age.

[3] *The Meaning of History*, 112.

[4] See Chapter II, Section C; also the present chapter, Section E.

[5] *The Meaning of History*, 113–117.

the historical. Above all, they attest to the power of the "historical," a power which is grounded in the dynamism of the meta-historical.

Berdyaev prophesies in *The Realm of Spirit and the Realm of Caesar* a future epoch:

We may conceive of a fifth period in the relationship between man and nature. In this period will come man's still greater control of the forces of nature, the real emancipation of labor and the workers, technics made subject to spirit.[1]

This age will be the New Middle Ages, an epoch to follow the present age and which will be a preparation for the end of the world. It will be more spiritual than the present epoch and will be culminated by the appearance of Antichrist.[2] That is, the tragedy of history will culminate in the coning of Antichrist, though man will have attained the greatest spirituality in history. Men will culminate his progress in history towards meta-history with the final preparation in the last age, though the solution of the problem of evil will lie beyond its ability. As we shall see, Berdyaev develops a doctrine of the age of the Spirit where man and the world are reintegrated in God after the end of the world.[3] And just as this Christian doctrine controls his philosophy of history, so it controls his description of the final age of the world, the preparatory age, the New Middle Ages.[4]

C. PHILOSOPHY OF HISTORY AND METAPHYSICS OF HISTORY

(1) *The Relationship of Philosophy of History to the Metaphysical*

We saw that Berdyaev introduces philosophy of history in the light of both metaphysical and historical considerations and that he considers philosophy of history to include a metaphysics of history. But the question as to whether philosophy of history is or is not metaphysical in its essence has not yet been investigated. With this in mind, let us read the following passage from *The Meaning of History:*

The history of the world and that of mankind are fulfilled not only in the object, and, objectively, in the macrocosm, but also in the microcosm. The connection between these two fulfilments in essential to the metaphysics of history and implies a special relation between the historical and the metaphysical. The opposition between these latter had long been the dominant conception in science and philosophy ... It is based on the assumption that the metaphysical cannot

---

[1] *The Realm of Spirit and the Realm of Caesar*, 48.
[2] See conclusion of Section D of this chapter.
[3] See Chapter II, Section D, Part 3.
[4] *Ibid.*

manifest itself in the historical; and it did not consider the possibility of the historical being other than a merely external and empirical fact which, methodically, must always be antithetical to everything metaphysical.

Another] point of view holds that the metaphysical may be transposed and made manifest in terms of the historical. This standpoint is particularly favorable to the elaboration of a philosophy of history, postulating as it does a sort of historical center where the metaphysical and the historical meet.[1]

We may note, first of all, that Berdyaev says that there are two fulfilments: that of the history of the world (and of mankind) which occurs in the *macrocosm* (the reality external to the individual subject), and that which occurs in the *microcosm*. When he says, "the connection between these fulfilments ... implies a special relation between the historical and the metaphysical," he implies, exactly, that the historical is particularly concerned with the macrocosm, and the metaphysical is particularly concerned with the microcosm.[2]

Berdyaev adds that the historical has been predominantly understood to be only an "external and empirical fact which, methodically, must always be antithetical to everything metaphysical." Berdyaev allows the traditional meaning of *historical* to define his own notion of the historical; that is, he agrees it essentially refers to the macrocosm, rather than to the metaphysics of the microcosm. Only, he adds, "the metaphysical may be transposed and made manifest in terms of the historical." He believes that this latter assertion is particularly favorable to a philosophy of history because it postulates "a sort of historical center where the metaphysical and the historical meet."

Berdyaev sharply distinguishes the historical and the metaphysical but does not separate them. The historical manifests the metaphysical, is metaphysical: We have seen (Section B) to how great an extent the *metaphysical* (the "historical") is historical. He says:

But, as I shall attempt to prove, the metaphysical and the historical are really brought together and intimately fused only in the Christian philosophy of history.[3]

The new note that this passage brings in is to be found in the words, *Christian philosophy of history*, and especially in the word, *Christian*. For Berdyaev, Christianity is historical. Christianity gets its historical character from the coming of Christ.[4] It is for Berdyaev also philo-

---

[1] *The Meaning of History*, 26.

[2] This discussion of microcosm and macrocosm is reminiscent of Spengler, whom, we saw, Berdyaev mentions. Cf. *The Decline of the West*, Vol. I, Chapters V and VI.

[3] *The Meaning of History*, 26.

[4] *Ibid.*, 108.

sophical and metaphysical. The metaphysical will have a historical aspect, not only as it relates to terrestrial history, but even as considered completely apart from terrestrial history. There is a celestial history.

What do we understand by celestial history? In it, in the depths of the inner life of the spirit, resides that predetermination which reveals and manifests itself in the terrestrial life, destiny and history of mankind. This heavenly prologue is analogous to that which opens Goethe's *Faust*. Faust's destiny is that of man; and this heavenly prologue pre-determines the terrestrial destiny of mankind.[1]

It is the doctrine of celestial history, a history revealing itself in the terrestrial life, which justifies Berdyaev's positing the fusion of the metaphysical and historical. Celestial history which contains a heavenly prologue, is not the terrestrial history of the cosmos and of man. It is, we will see in Section E, the history within the divine Godhead. It is a predetermination of terrestrial history. We will see, in Chapter II [2] that Berdyaev asserts the illumination of the divine principle, an illumination which is symbolized in the illumination of mankind in terrestrial history.

In our study of Berdyaev's epistemology (Chapter IV), we will find that he justifies his stretching and spiritualizing of such terms as *history* (in *"celestial history"*) by asserting a noetic of symbols and "myths. Celestial history is a true reality, revealed to us and one which we know.

The philosophy of history ought to be the metaphysics of history; it has its origin in that heavenly prologue which predetermines historical destinies, and in the revelation of the inner spiritual history; for heaven is our inner spiritual heaven. Here is to be found that true tie between the historical and the metaphysical in which I see the deepest significance of every Christian philosophy of history.[3]

"Here" (in the heavenly prologue and in the revelation of the inner spiritual history), "is to be found that true tie between the historical and the metaphysical ..." Berdyaev understands the celestial history to be a predetermination, in God, of historical destinies in which human freedom is allowed to operate. When Berdyaev speaks of "the revelation of the inner spiritual history," he means the revelation of the celestial history, both as such and as it is reflected in the terrestrial history.

When Berdyaev says that "here is to be found that true tie between

---

[1] *Ibid.*, 39–40.
[2] Chapter II, Section C.
[3] *The Meaning of History*, 40.

the historical and the metaphysical," he intends that the spiritual history is both historical (as found in history) and metaphysical (in itself). It is celestial and terrestrial, and the philosophy of history ought to be the metaphysics of history because the former has its origin in celestial history, the heavenly prologue, and in the revelation of inner spiritual history, which are metaphysical.

He says that in the "true tie between the historical and the metaphysical" he sees the deepest significance of Christian philosophy of history. He sees, here, the deepest significance because:

> The tie ... transcends cleavage and antithesis; it achieves the maximum union reconciliation and identification; and it brings about the mysterious adaptation and transfiguration of the one into the other, of the heavenly into the terrestrial, of the metaphysical into the historical, of the interior into the exterior.[1]

Hence, in the tie between the historical and the metaphysical is the deepest significance of the Christian philosophy of history because it achieves the maximum union and brings about the transfiguration of history. The truest and deepest intelligibility of Berdyaev's philosophy of history is thus religious; the purpose of philosophy of history is religious, since the tie between the historical and the metaphysical brings about transfiguration of the historical.

Note the direction of the spiritual movement, as Berdyaev understands it. It is not the movement of the terrestrial and historical upward, toward God, but rather of God acting immanently in man and through man in history.[2] Berdyaev thinks in terms of the spiritualization of man and of history. Man is spiritual, already has something of the divine. God is immanent as well as transcendent.[3] Berdyaev says, in concluding the chapter on the metaphysics of history in *The Meaning of History:*

> We draw a sharp line of demarcation between the historical and the metaphysical, between terrestrial and celestial history. But this distinction does not reflect the true reality and but forms an abstraction of our consciousness. ... The metaphysics of history ... approaches man's destiny from the standpoint of the inner intimacy and union subsisting between his celestial and terrestrial destinies.[4]

The truth of philosophy of history is to be found, not in the "abstraction of our consciousness" which divides the historical and the

---

[1] *Ibid.,* 40.

[2] Berdyaev considers the immanent action of God to be gracious in the higher spiritual activity of man. The action of God, immanent in man, is the source of Grace. Cf. *The Realm of Spirit and the Realm of Caesar,* 181. He does not define the exact conditions of Grace.

[3] See Chapter II.

[4] *The Meaning of History,* 42–43.

metaphysical. Philosophy of history finds its truth in the symbolic metaphysics which asserts the inner intimacy and union of man's celestial and terrestrial destinies.[1]

Metaphysics, Berdyaev asserts in a later book, *The Divine and the Human*, is understandable upon condition of its reference to history. In this book he uses a new term which etymologically comprehends both *metaphysics* and *history*; namely, *meta-history*.[2]

My thought ... admits of only one possible metaphysics, and that is meta-history. Everything existential is history, dynamic force, destiny, man, the world, are history, God is history, a drama that is working itself out. ... The philosophy to which I would give expression, is a dramatic philosophy of destiny, of existence which is in time and passes over into eternity, of time which presses on to an end, and which is not death but transfiguration, Everything, therefore, ought to be regarded from the point of view of the philosophy of history. And the philosophy of history can itself be nothing but prophetic, and that which unriddles the secrets of the future.[3]

This passage refers our thought to what we have seen concerning the historical quality of divine celestial history. The mere historical, on the other hand, in whatever degree of spirituality or materiality, is spiritual. "Everything existential is history. ... God is history." [4] That is why Berdyaev's doctrine admits of only one possible metaphysics – meta-history. He sees everything – including all the objects of metaphysics – in respect to history (which is not to say that he asserts only the historical). His is a metaphysics of existence, an existence which has a historical aspect. Meta-history gives rise to philosophy of history because the object of the latter is an existence "which is in time and passes over into eternity." Meta-history brings into being a philosophy of history that is prophetic of the future transfiguration of historical existents, whereby they become solely metaphysical entities.

From the foregoing pages we can see that the philosophy of history is in its essence a metaphysics of history. But while meta-history, or metaphysics, is absolutely spiritual, philosophy of history partakes of

---

[1] *Ibid.*, 52: "This is ... not a philosophy but a mythology. ... Only a mythology, which conceives the divine celestial life as celestial history and as a drama of love and freedom unfolding itself between God and His other self, which He loves and for whose reciprocal love He thirsts, and only an admission of God's longing for His other self, can provide a solution of celestial history and, through it, of the destinies of both man and the world." 54; "... this is the sphere of mythology, in which I find not the negation but the affirmation of reality. And thus mythology may offer a real key to the metaphysics of history."

[2] The term, *meta-history*, appears at least as early as 1940 in Berdyaev's writing, when he wrote *Slavery and Freedom*. It becomes accepted in his philosophical vocabulary from that time onward.

[3] N. Berdyaev, *The Divine and the Human* (Bles, London, 1949), v–vi.

[4] In Section E we study in what sense God is historical.

the material conditions of history. We need only glance at the contents of Berdyaev's books: they have much history, not historical details, but universal history. Berdyaev's philosophy of history attempts to fuse history with metaphysics.

(2) Metaphysics

But this implies that metaphysics can be considered apart from the history to which it gives meaning. Does Berdyaev ever discuss metaphysics as distinct from the historical? One of his last books, *The Beginning and the End*, is an attempt "to write a book in which he should describe his metaphysical position as a whole."[1] He displays a tremendous erudition in the history of philosophy and refers to dozens of metaphysical positions in all periods of Western philosophy. He gives special attention to 19th-century German metaphysical positions.[2] A large section of the book is devoted to the problems of being. He obviously understands the traditional notion of metaphysics; a science which studies transcendental entities, such as Being and Existence.

He defines his own notion of *metaphysics* in the Preface:

I have for a long while wanted to write a book in which I should describe my metaphysical position as a whole. I use the word "metaphysics," but my readers must not give it here its traditional and academic meaning. I am concerned rather with the kind of metaphysics which is disclosed in the spirit of, for instance, Dostoyevsky, Kierkegaard, ... with existential metaphysics. I want to survey all problems in the light of eschatology in the light which streams from the End.[3]

As I deal with the problems of metaphysics I find myself in many respects indebted to Boehme . . . Of all the writers of the ancient world it is Heraclitus with whom I have the greatest affinity. I should describe my book as an essay in the epistemological and metaphysical interpretation of the end of the world, of the end of history, that is to say it is a book on eschatological epistemology and metaphysics. So far as I am aware no interpretation of that kind has been made hitherto. Eschatology has been left as a part of dogmatic theology . . .[4]

Berdyaev is thus claiming eschatology from dogmatic theology, to be used in his own philosophy. Metaphysics, for him, is both philosophical and Christian. He does not intend to change philosophy to religion; indeed, he considers it to be different from religion as well as from science "though standing in . . . intimate relations with science and religion."[5]

---

[1] *The Beginning and the End*, v.
[2] See *ibid.*, Table of Contents.
[3] *Ibid.*, v.
[4] *Ibid.*, vi.
[5] *The Destiny of Man*, 4–5.

"Philosophy is neither religious faith nor science – it is itself." [1] He admits, on the other hand, that his philosophy "goes beyond the accepted limits of philosophy and represents a confession of faith." [2] In his last work, *Truth and Revelation*, he denies the sharp distinction between faith and philosophical knowledge. "If on the one hand religious philosophy . . . presupposes faith, so also on the other . . . does knowledge which is purely philosophical and even scientific knowledge . . ." [3]

The truth which metaphysics seeks is the same truth that religion and even science seek. [4] There is one truth, and "there are degrees in the apprehension of truth." [5]

Metaphysics for Berdyaev, therefore, is distinct and yet not separate from religion. We will study his indebtedness to the Heracleitean metaphysics of the German religious mystic, Boehme, in Chapter II. And in Chapter III, we will see the close relationship of his metaphysics to the existentialism of modern philosophers whose inspiration flows from the religious philosopher, Kierkegaard. His eschatology is treated in both Chapters II and III.

Metaphysics is in its essence associated with philosophy of history through its eschatology and through its existentialism. [6] Berdyaev has said that "Christian metaphysics . . . is above all a philosophy of history." [7] Metaphysics, however, is peculiarly transcendent. [8]

Let us note that Berdyaev's metaphysics is a new kind of metaphysics. The source of it is an attitude which is at once consciously philosophical and yet religious. Metaphysics treats both philosophical first principles and eschatology. Eschatology is religious and therefore prior in importance, and it is the principle of philosophy of history. We may expect to discover in Chapters II and III, therefore, that Berdyaev's metaphysics places philosophical first principles at the service of philosophy of history. And since his eschatology is a messianism, his metaphysics is profoundly influenced by a doctrine of Christ the Godman and Messiah. Christ is a concern of metaphysics. In Chapter III we will consider a personalism and an existentialism which are part of Berdyaev's metaphysics of Godmanhood.

---

[1] *Ibid.*, 5.
[2] *Dream and Reality*, 301–302.
[3] *Truth and Revelation*, 41.
[4] See Chapter IV.
[5] *Truth and Revelation*, 41.
[6] Concerning the affinity of existentialism with philosophy of history, see Chapter III.
[7] *The Divine and the Human*, 168.
[8] Cf. *Dream and Reality*, 127.

D. THE PHILOSOPHY OF HISTORY AND THE END OF HISTORY

We have been dealing with a metaphysics of *historical* existence because it is an existence "which is in time and passes over into eternity, *of time which passes on to an end,* an end which is not death but transfiguration."

The philosophy of history is in its origins intimately allied to eschatology; ... eschatology is the doctrine of the goal of history, its issue and fulfilment. It is absolutely essential for the conception and elaboration of the idea of history, as a significant progression or movement capable of fulfilment. ... it postulates a final solution and issue, it presupposes a catastrophic fulfilment ...[1]

That history and philosophy of history are eschatological is implicit in the doctrine of universal history. Eschatology asserts that history will end at the time of the Second Coming of Christ the Divine Messiah, and it looks toward this event.

Berdyaev frequently refers to the messianism of his philosophy of history, and with good reason. History, considered without reference to the event of the Second Coming, he often says, is inexplicable despite all the partial meanings which can be found in it.

For if we are convinced that history has no immanent solution, then all its failures become imbued with a deep significance that transcends the fulfilment of a given aim in particular epoch. The conception of a transcendent goal gives history a deep significance which it lacks when interpreted as the pursuit of and fulfilment of immediate aims. ... Nor does my interpretation of history as a profound failure imply that it is devoid of significance, for I consider its failure to be sacred. It helps to demonstrate that the higher calling of both man and mankind is super-historical ...[2]

This eschatological viewpoint adds a new note to our considerations of the historical and philosophy of history. We found that, for Berdyaev, historical reality contains intelligible meaning, especially the meaning found in cultural, traditional development. Now, Berdyaev adds that history, if understood without the significance it has when seen in the light of a transcendental principle, has no immanent solution of its own.

The "fulfilment of a given aim in a particular epoch" is incapable of accounting for the failures of history; but, says Berdyaev, "the conception of a transcendent goal" imbues the failures of history with a deep significance. Indeed, Berdyaev interprets history as a "profound

[1] *The Meaning of History*, 32.
[2] *Ibid.*, 182–183.

failure," but it is a sacred failure because it shows that the super-
historical is the "higher calling of man and mankind." [1]

The failure of history does not mean that history is devoid of necessity or relevance. . . . Historical success and achievement do not constitute a valid criterion
of the true. . . . The profound significance of historical destiny and experience
do not depend on any realization. It rests beyond the limits of history.[2]

We now find that Berdyaev sharpens the distinction between the mere
historical and the metaphysical. The mere historical, we see, refers to
something peripheral. There, only the superficial intelligibility of history exists, where historical movements are seen to achieve or miss realization. But philosophy of history employs a messianic perspective
where the solution of history – not merely immanent – is and must be
transcendent over history. There is a divine necessity and relevance
being realized in history and, not being of history, is not subject to
the vicissitudes of history.

We must note that the principle of divine Grace is active in the history and
destiny of both world and man, together with that of natural necessity. . . .
. . . Thus history is made up of the complex interaction of the three principles
of necessity, freedom and transfiguring Grace.[3]

In addition to the principles of natural necessity and freedom, transfiguring Grace interacts with them. *Transfiguring* Grace because it
favors the progress of man towards the transfiguration which will occur
at the end of history.[4]

The failure of history, on the other hand, to provide its own solution
must be understood in terms of Berdyaev's doctrine of freedom. We
will see, in Chapter II, that ultimate Freedom, primal Will, which is
beyond good and evil, is the source of good and evil. The metaphysics

---

[1] The failures of history (which are human) submit to a testing and a self-realization. Cf.
Slavery and Freedom, 263: "History is the failure of spirit, the Kingdom of God is not realized
or expressed in it. But that very failure itself has a meaning. The great testing trials of man
and the experience of the seductive lures through which he lives have a meaning. Without
them the freedom of man would not have been fully tested and proved."

[2] *The Meaning of History*, 201.

[3] *Ibid.*, 60–61.

[4] But let us make no mistake concerning the basic historical pessimism of Berdyaev, even
if he is, on the meta-historical level, a Christian optimist. He says, in *Truth and Revelation*,
80: "History is not the incarnation of Spirit as Hegel and others have taught, it is not a
progressive march and the triumph of reason, nor is it progress along a straight and rising line.
History is a horrible tragedy.
. . . On the one hand I accept history as my path, the past of man, and on the other hand
I indignantly tear the mask from it and rebel against it."
Yet, we will see in Chapter II, Section D, Part 3, that Berdyaev sees a true progress in
history. And he looks forward to greater spirituality in the world, to a new middle ages.

of history applies the light of the Christian doctrine of apocalypse (end of the world):

to those positive Christian forces which culminate in the Coming of Christ together with those negative anti-Christian forces which must culminate in the coming of the Anti-christ.[1]

There are two freedoms and hence two paths taken by men: positive Christian forces which must culminate in the coming of Christ (at the end of the world), and negative, evil forces which must culminate in the coming of the Antichrist (just before the end of the world). The tragic meaning of history is thus seen in the light of sacred Christian doctrine, and the happy meaning of history is seen in the light of the doctrine of the Second Coming at the end of the world. As Berdyaev implies in the foregoing passages, though history by itself could arrive at no solution, yet man, with the aid of meta-history, does progress toward a better consciousness. Berdyaev refers to this when he speaks of "those positive Christian forces which culminate in the Coming of Christ."

E. PHILOSOPHY OF HISTORY IN RESPECT TO TIME

We have seen reference to the idea of celestial history, a doctrine of some kind of history in God. According to celestial history, the destiny of man is predetermined. This theory leads Berdyaev to problems connected with time.

Every metaphysical system ... which regards the "historical" as something essential to the innermost depths of being, is bound to recognize the ontological significance of time, that is, the doctrine that time exists for the very essence of being. And this brings us to the problem of the relation of time and eternity.[2]

Note that he speaks of the "historical" the spiritual significance of history and the mere historical. He is saying, not that the innermost depths of being is historical, but that in some way there is a "historical" quality. Berdyaev associates this "historical" quality with time. If the "historical" is essential to the innermost depths of being, it is necessary for Berdyaev to account for the relation of time to the "historical" and yet continue to respect the meta-physical character of metaphysics. It is a problem, he says, of the relation of time and eternity. "But perhaps time is itself rooted in eternity and forms part of it?" he asks. "This

---

[1] *The Meaning of History*, 204.
[2] *Ibid.*, 63.

is precisely the problem I should like to consider; I regard it as a
fundamental problem of the metaphysics of history ..." [1]

Time therefore is not a finite circle into which nothing eternal can penetrate, but
one that can be extended to comprehend it. This is one aspect of the problem.
The other assumes that time itself is rooted in the depths of eternity. And thus
what we call time in our world historical process, in our world reality, which is a
process in time, is a sort of interior epoch in eternity itself. [2]

Note, first of all, that Berdyaev does not define the notion of time; he
sets out by discussing time as if his readers agree as to what it is. He
seems to understand it to be the measure of change. He will distinguish
kinds of time but will not separate them. Time can be spiritualized so
that the eternal can penetrate it. Time itself has its origin in eternity;
it is an interior epoch in eternity. We will have to examine, presently,
the meaning of *epoch* (or *age*, or *era*, or *aeon*).

... neither Platonism nor ancient Hindoo philosophy provide a tie between time
and the inner essence of being. This latter is generally conceived as timeless and
not as any process possessing its own time and epochs, in other words, as an
immobile eternity opposed to any time process. [3]

His assumption, in the passage above, is that that the metaphysical
existent is itself a process or becoming; hence, eternity is temporal in
some way. God in His inmost depths is a Becoming. [4] We saw (Section
B, Part 3) that the primal depths of God is a will, and we will see in
Chapter II that it is a becoming. And we have seen that the fact of a
freedom from endless cycles (which have no real history) is posited in
universal history. For Berdyaev, universal history is properly a celestial
history, is metaphysical. Hence, for him, the metaphysical partakes
of the temporal character of history. When Berdyaev says:

... time, our world, the whole of our world process, from the moment of its
inception to that of its end, represents a period, an aeon in the life of eternity, a
period or an epoch rooted in it. [5]

he does not mean that our world process is an epoch within an unchanging eternity, but within an eternity out of which occurs a celestial
history.

I believe, therefore, that a real metaphysics of history can be built up only upon

[1] *Ibid.*, 63–64.
[2] *Ibid.*, 64.
[3] *Ibid.*, 65.
[4] See Chapter II, Section C.
[5] *The Meaning of History*, 66.

the basis of a dynamic and not a static interpretation of the nature of the world process.[1]

That is, the inner intelligibility of the world process, which is to be in celestial history, must be dynamic in order to have a true metaphysics of history. This means that the "historical," even in its least historical and most spiritual and metaphysical aspect, is dynamic and changeful, partaking of freedom's changefulness.

Berdyaev worked over and reconsidered the problem of time and eternity for nearly twenty years after he wrote *The Meaning of History* before he discovered a doctrine of time which explains the temporal character of celestial history.[2] We find the new doctrine first presented in the book, *Slavery and Freedom*, first published in 1940.

The philosophy of history is to a considerable extent the philosophy of time. . . . Time has a variety of meanings and it is needful to make distinctions. There are three times: cosmic time, historical time, and existential time, and every man lives in these three forms of time. Cosmic time . . . is nature's time, and as natural beings we live in this time. Cosmic time is objectivized time, and it is subject to mathematical calculation. . . . Man is not only a cosmic being, . . . Man is also a historical being. . . . The time of history is also objectivized time, but there is also a break-through in it from a deeper stratum of human existence. . . .

In addition to cosmic time and historical time, which are objectivized and subordinated to number, though in different ways, there is existential time, profound time. Existential time must not be thought of in complete isolation from cosmic and historical time, it is a break through of one time into the other. . . . the irruption of eternity into time, and interruption in cosmic and historical time . . .

This is inward time, not exteriorized in extension, nor objectivized. It is the time of the world of subjectivity, not objectivity. It is not computed mathematically . . . the infinity of existential time is a qualitative infinity, not a quantitative. . . . A moment of existential time is an emergence into eternity. *It would be untrue to say that existential time is identical with eternity, but it may be said that it is a participant in several moments of eternity.*[3] (my italics)

Man lives in all three times, cosmic, historical and existential time. Cosmic and historical time are both objectified, and both are subject to mathematical calculation. But cosmic time is only nature's time.

[1] *Ibid.*, 66.
[2] Berdyaev's theory of time follows very properly out of his doctrine. It is very possible that Berdyaev was influenced by a scheme of three times which was published by Alexeyev a few years before *The Meaning of History* was written. N. O. Lossky, in his *History of Russian Philosophy* (International Universities Press, New York, 1951), 381, mentions Alexeyev's *Thought and Reality*, written 1914. In the article on "Time," Alexeyev distinguishes between ontological, psychological and physical time. Ontological time is cognized by thought apart from connection with movement in space; in that time there exists a "now" univalent for all world systems.
[3] *Slavery and Freedom*, 257-261.

Historical time, however, refers, not only to nature's time (time measured by the astronomical movements) but also to historical epochs known by memory and tradition. In tradition and in the suggestiveness of tradition historical time is at once conservative and revolutionary.[1]

Existential time is a break-through of eternity into historical and cosmic time. It is subjective and inward and cannot be externalized mathematically. Though it is not exactly eternity, it is a participant in eternity. Every creative act of man (such as a metaphysical insight or an artistic creation), is performed in existential time and projected in historical time.[2]

We find Berdyaev's answer to the problem of the temporality of celestial history, the "history" within the divine. It is "temporal," but its temporality cannot be understood at all in the mathematical way in which cosmic and historical times are understood. Neither can the duration of culture, which is grasped by the memory, though beyond the reach of mathematical extension, define the temporality of existential time. The temporality of celestial history, Berdyaev seems to mean, consists in its dynamism and creativity, in its ability to spiritualize measurable times, and in its power to contain eternally all historical and cosmic histories. The "several moments" of eternity that existential time participates in are celestial history.

Berdyaev's theory of time, besides explaining his doctrine of the temporality of celestial history, by the same token, shows the close spiritual relationship of the merely historical with celestial history, and yet the definite distinction between them.

The existential breaks through in the historical and the historical in return acts upon the existential. ... Within history there is meta-history, which is not a product of historical evolution. ... The revelation of God in history is also this irruption of events belonging to existential time. *The full significance of an event in the life of Christ moved in existential time;* in historical time it only shines through the burdensome environment of objectivization. The meta-historical is never contained in the historical, history always distorts meta-history in adjusting it to itself. [3] (my italics)

The mere historical is not the existential; the existential only breaks through in the historical, and history acts upon and distorts this revelation in adjusting it to itself.[4] When Berdyaev says, above, that "the

[1] *Ibid.*, 259.
[2] See Chapter II, Section C.
[3] *Slavery and Freedom*, 262.
[4] We will see, in Chapter III, that the existential, so far as we know it, concerns man in his spiritual subjectivity.

meta-historical is never contained in the historical," he means that this revelation, in history, is not historical. Philosophy of history understands the *intelligibility* of history in enabling the philosopher to know the existential as such. But for Berdyaev, philosophy of history does not assert *history* to be an existential reality. We see, in the example Berdyaev uses; namely "an event in the life of Christ"; that the existential reality (which occurs, really, only in celestial history) is not historical, is not of history. Berdyaev, we will see in Chapter III, tends to be unhistorical. He does not recognize an autonomous existence of terrestrial history. We will find that he wants mankind to divest itself of the conditions of life which are historical in order to prepare itself for the transfiguration of history.[1]

He next considers the relationship of historical time to cosmic time:

> There are two ways out of historical time, in two opposite directions, towards cosmic time and towards existential time. The submersion of historical time in cosmic time is the way out for naturalism ... History returns to nature and enters into the cosmic cycle.[2]

Since historical time includes cosmic time, it is possible for historical time to be submerged in cosmic time if man's outlook became exclusively cosmic. This would happen if men forgot the "historical" and forgot themselves and considered only the cosmic world.

> The other way is the submersion of historical time in existential time. This is the way out taken by eschatology. History passes into the realm of the freedom of the spirit. And a philosophy of history is always in the last resort either naturalistic, even though it makes use of the categories of spirit, or it is eschatological.[3]

Indeed, there could be a philosophy of history dominated by the cosmic outlook.[4] The other alternative is Berdyaev's philosophy of history, which, he says, is eschatological, "the submersion of historical time in existential time." Eschatological, because the eternity of existential time contains the apocalypse of history.

Berdyaev takes only two alternatives (ignoring the possibility of a philosophy of history which would remain in historical time),[5] because

---

[1] See Chapter II, Section D, Part 3.
[2] *Slavery and Freedom*, 262.
[3] *Ibid.*, 262–263.
[4] See Spengler, *Decline of the West*, Volume II, Chapter I.
[5] Berdyaev ignores the possibility of a philosophy of history which would remain in historical time because, for him, it would not be philosophical. It would be a relativism, lacking the intelligibility which occurs in a cosmic or an eschatological philosophy of history. He accuses Hegel of such a relativism, precisely because Hegel remains in the historical. (*Slavery and Freedom*, 256) "In History, Hegel subordinated not only man, but God – God is the creation of history – The above view – inevitably asserts relativity ..."
But Hegel, for Berdyaev (and for anybody), has truly a philosophy of history. Berdyaev

both alternatives set themselves outside the relativity of terrestrial history. The cosmic alternative would find an intelligibility beyond history in natural laws. The eschatological alternative would find an intelligibility beyond history in the spiritual realm.

Can Berdyaev's philosophy be called historical because the intelligibility of terrestrial history that he finds is in celestial *history*? No, not if we define his philosophy in his own terms; for it is clear that he believes celestial history is not historical. It is meta-historical. We may call his philosophy historical if we mean that it is very much concerned with terrestrial history, but, properly speaking, we must say it is not historical. Its light is metaphysical and religious, not natural or historical; its interest is predominantly meta-historical all the time; and it must be termed a mystical philosophy.[1] We will encounter its mysticism in Chapter IV. Berdyaev continues:

Historical time with everything that happens in it has a meaning, but that meaning lies outside the limits of historical time itself, it is to be seen in an eschatological perspective.[2]

And the meaning of history breaks through into the mere historical through the freedom or free creativity of man:

is referring to Hegel in the text above cited (Cf. . . . .) when he speaks of a naturalistic philosophy of history which yet uses the categories of spirit. For Berdyaev, Hegel has a naturalistic philosophy of history because he makes the historical into a law, relative though it may be. "A philosophy of history, *in the last resort*, is either naturalistic, even though it makes use of the categories of spirit, or it is eschatological." (*Slavery and Freedom*, 263).

He says, in *Truth and Revelation*, 88: "And revelation must be freed from the power of the historical, or, to speak more truly, *from the power of historism, from the process of making what is relative absolute*." (my italics)

[1] It is a temptation to call Berdyaev's philosophy merely historical because a philosophy of celestial history partakes of the metaphorical or unscientific knowledge, of the historical that is found in a great work of history. That is, it uses the same epistemological approach and often-times diverts itself with a purely historical study. And if one were not on guard, in defining the philosophy of Berdyaev, he might believe there is an essential historicism in his philosophy or theology of history. He says, concerning his mysticism of history, in *Freedom and the Spirit*, 268: "Mysticism is the opposite of historical realism. Yet there is, nevertheless, a mysticism of history. The whole history of the world is the history of my spirit, for in the spirit these two histories cease to be externally opposed to one another. This, however, does not mean that reality of myself is destroyed or that I lose my identity by being merged into all other objects. It means, rather, that I acquire being, reality, and personality when everything about me has ceased to be external, strange, impenetrable, or lifeless, and when the kingdom of love is realized."

For Berdyaev, therefore, what we may call a historical metaphor becomes identified in the knower with a mystical knowledge of one's spirit. And, since a mystical knowledge of one's spirit is at the same time mystical knowledge of the highest religious reality, the metaphor becomes identical, in the knower, with a mysticism of meta-history, but there is not a historicism in this mysticism of history, because the whole history of the world is spiritualized into meta-history in joining with the mysticism of one's spirit. In short, in a mysticism of history, history is transfigured, eternity, the end of the world, is at that moment apprehended.

[2] *Slavery and Freedom*, 263.

... this break-through from the depths is the work of man and God, it is the combined work of man and God, a divine-human action. ... The whole mystery here lies in the fact that God does not act in the determined arrangement of things which belongs to objectivized nature. He acts only in freedom, only through the freedom of man.[1]

The key to understanding "the combined work of man and God" is found in the phrase: "a divine-human action." Berdyaev means, not two actions in transfiguring history, God's and man's, but the action of a divine-human man in whom God and man act. It is an implicit reference to the doctrine of Godmanhood, where, we will find, man is said to be divine, as well as human. This is why the meta-historical can break through into history by means of man; man is divine. Consequently, Berdyaev says:

... the end of history is thought of as taking place in time, while at the same time the end of history is the end of time, that is to say, the end of historical time. The end of history is an event of existential time. And at the same time we must not think of this event as being outside history.[2]

And thus Berdyaev solves the problem of the relation of time and eternity which he sets himself in *The Meaning of History*. Celestial time, the end of history, must take place in history (though not as historical time), because it is brought about by the divine-human action occuring in man. And this brings us to a consideration of Berdyaev's doctrine of Godmanhood.

F. PHILOSOPHY OF HISTORY
AND THE DOCTRINE OF GODMANHOOD

Berdyaev says in *The Meaning of History*:

Christ, the Absolute Man, the Son of both God and man, stands in the center of both celestial and terrestrial history. He is the inner spiritual tie between these two destinies. Without His help the tie between the human and the absolute reality, could not exist. In fact, history owes its existence entirely to the presence of Christ at its very heart. He represents the deepest mystical and metaphysical foundation and source of history and of its tragic destiny. Both the divine and the human energy flow towards and away from Him. Without Him this energy would neither exist nor possess any significance.

... The coming of Christ put an end to the cleavage between the metaphysical and the historical which become united and identified in Him. Thus, the meta-

---

[1] *Ibid.*, 263.
[2] *Ibid.*, 263–264.

physical becomes the historical and vice-versa; and celestial becomes terrestrial history which can be apprehended as a stage of the former.[1]

Christ is the Absolute Man because, as we shall see in Chapter II, He is absolutely True Man. He "stands in the center of both celestial and terrestrial history" in the sense that He dominates both "Histories," and also in the sense that His activity in both histories occurs neither at the first moment nor at the last moment of the historical progress. He is the inner spiritual tie between these two destinies because, while he is ineffably God, and a divine celestial history, he is also the Godman, the Existent, Who is the metaphysical destiny of history. The divine and the human energy flow towards Him and away from Him because it is an energy grounded in an irrational and absolute freedom. So far as it is illuminated by Him (in God and, sporadically, in man) it is good. So far as it is not illuminated by Him, it is evil. Without Him (Who is God) this (divine) energy would not exist; this energy would not possess any significance, because only the divine Word, or Meaning, can give it (irrational freedom) significance.

This is why Christ's coming put an end to the cleavage between the religious, the metaphysical and the historical; the participation of pre-Christian man in this energy or irrational freedom before Christ's coming was unilluminated by the revelation of Christ. The historical, therefore, before His coming was separated from the metaphysical. The two are identified in Him and, as a result of His coming, they progressively became identified with one another. Berdyaev implies that the "historical" is most properly the divine Logos. In Him, celestial history becomes terrestrial history; and terrestrial history can be apprehended as a stage of the celestial history.

G. SUMMARY

1. The reality with which philosophy of history is primarily concerned is not the superficial history studied by historical science; but a spiritual reality which Berdyaev terms the *"historical."* And philosophy of history is a spiritual knowledge known by the human spirit. The spirituality of the "historical" is such, that the "historical" is both the reality which is known and also is identical with the knower through his knowledge of it. The "historical" is especially known through the

---

[1] *The Meaning of History*, 58–59.

category of historical tradition. Historical tradition is itself a reality, even though it is the mode of knowing the "historical." The "historical" is organic and a coherent spiritual unity.

The "historical" (with quotation marks) refers to something beyond history. It is the spiritual meaning of history and does not partake of the material conditions of history. The "historical" also refers to man in the concrete fullness of the spiritual being, that is, in his most existential reality. It refers both to the ultimate Reality, so far as it is the meaning of history, and to man through whom the diffusion of meaning into history occurs. Hence, there is no separation between the "historical," the human spirit, or the mere historical. The mere historical itself is more or less spiritual (as are, for example, historical traditions or the "historical nation.") And philosophy of history studies the mere historical in the light of the "historical" in order to find the spiritual meaning materialized in history.

The "historical," the spiritual meaning of history is identical with the true spiritual being of man. The True Man is the Godman, the divine Logos. Christ, the Godman is the true meaning of history. For Berdyaev, it seems, He is the "historical" which the philosopher of history seeks. And each man is a microcosm in whom the "historical" is sought; a microcosm in which all the past historical epochs coexist. The "historical" is thus grasped by the historical memory of man. The historical memory is a spiritual activity and the ontological basis of history. It is through the historical memory that the philosopher approaches history and existentially identifies his destiny with its destiny. This is an existential philosophy. And the memory, which is also spiritually related to the "historical," transfigures history and brings it closer to reality, to the "historical." It does this by means of the symbols it creates, the historical myths and traditions. They symbolize historical destinies.

Berdyaev exhorts the reader to recognize and experience the unity of his own destiny with that of all mankind. This is necessary in order to attain the "historical." Berdyaev thus asserts the religious and moral doctrine of universal history. His philosophy is religious; it is about an after-world, the "historical," the goal of history. All history is a unique history, with a beginning and an end. There is one historical culture, of which all other cultures are parts. The philosopher of history studies historical cultures in order to understand the meaning of history. It is incarnated in them and in the single culture of all history. Christianity posits a universal history, without which a philosophy of history is impossible. Christian consciousness asserts that events are unique and non-recurrent, participating in a single history, whose course is known in Christian revelation. The Christian world is therefore dynamic and purposeful. The condition of this dynamism is freedom, a radical freedom that Christianity finds in man and in God. Indeed, universal history is the story of the interaction between the free human spirit and necessitarian and fallen nature. Fallen nature, which enslaves man, needs to be spiritualized so that it will be transfigured, with man, at the end of the world.

Berdyaev sees five epochs of terrestrial history, during which the divine-human action gradually frees man from the cosmos and fallen nature in a progress towards the end of history. Historical epochs are seen to culminate in a future age, a New Middle Ages; which is nigh and will be a final spiritual preparation of man for the end of the world.

Berdyaev asserts the unity of history and the "historical," and, consequently, the unity of universal history, both in its terrestrial aspect and in its divine aspect. Terrestrial history of man is determined by a celestial "history" within the Godhead, of which the Incarnation of Christ is one moment. Celestial history, the divine development, is the true reality, while terrestrial history is not fully true.

2. There is a metaphysics of history, a meta-history which is about the existential reality found in celestial history. Philosophy of history is meta-history (or metaphysics) in its truest essence. But meta-history is more spiritual and not so concerned with the mere historical. Philosophy of history is less spiritual, more concerned with the mere historical.

Metaphysics itself is a philosophical discipline in Berdyaev's doctrine; it is Christian, but Berdyaev does not intend to change philosophy to religion. There is no sharp distinction between faith and philosophical knowledge; both are concerned with the same truth. Metaphysics treats both philosophical first principles and eschatology; it is existential, personalist and is concerned with Christ, the Godman and Messiah.

3. Philosophy of history is eschatological. It looks forward to the Second Coming of the Messiah and the end of the world. History is explainable only in the light of eschatology. It has no immanent solution but a transcendent one. Its failure (which will culminate in the coming of the Anti-Christ) can only be overcome beyond the limits of history. Man is free and the working of Divine Grace in history transfigures his freedom.

4. The doctrine of celestial history, through which the unity of universal history is asserted, requires a philosophy of time. There is a *cosmic* time of the fallen cosmos. There is a *historical* time of the past and the present, which, in tradition, reaches towards the future. An there is an *existential* time, which is the irruption of eternity into time. Celestial history, which consists of several moments of existential time, is "temporal" in the sense of being dynamic and in its power to spiritualize terrestrial history as an eternal epoch within itself. This celestial "history," then, is not historical in the usual sense of the word; and we will find that Berdyaev does not recognize an autonomous existence of terrestrial history. Furthermore, his philosophy is mystical. The spiritualization of historical time in existential time which is to occur, will be the combined work of God and of man, a divine-human action. Man himself is properly unhistorical and, in his true reality, divine.

5. Christ, the absolute Man, is the inner spiritual tie between celestial history and terrestrial history. Both the divine and human energy flow towards and away from Him. The Coming of Christ put an end to the the cleavage between the metaphysical and the historical which become united and identified in Him. Thus, celestial becomes terrestrial history which can be apprehended as a stage of the former.

GODMANHOOD,
FREEDOM AND PHILOSOPHY OF HISTORY

A. INTRODUCTION

We saw in Chapter I that the principle of philosophy of history, for Berdyaev, is Christ, Godmanhood. We observed, too, that the free will of man figures importantly. By studying Berdyaev's doctrine of Godmanhood and his voluntarism we will be able to understand his philosophy of history. The present chapter studies the metaphysical subject-matter of philosophy of history especially as it is divine or religious.

First, we will consider the doctrine of Godmanhood, that is, of Christ Who is the Principle and Term of Berdyaev's philosophy of history. Then we will study Berdyaev's voluntarism and the all-important function of the free will of man in the philosophy of history. The voluntaristic philosophy, we will find, is a philosophy of spirit and a philosophy of beauty. Next, we will investigate three important consequences which follow from the doctrine of Godmanhood. First to be seen is the doctrine of *Sobornost'* or alltogetherness of mankind. Second to be studied, is the place of cosmology in the philosophy of history, a cosmology which is inseparable from the doctrine of Godmanhood. Finally to be investigated is the eschatological doctrine of the age of the Spirit. It is a Christian doctrine of a goal of history which discovers and strengthens the purposiveness that exists in human history.

B. THE DOCTRINE OF GODMANHOOD

Berdyaev says in *Freedom and the Spirit:*

The Christian conception of man is hierarchical and not evolutionist. Man is not a transitory fragment of the cosmos, a mere step in its evolution; he is superior to the cosmos, independent of its infinity, and in principle embraces it completely.[1]

[1] *Freedom and the Spirit*, 275.

The Christian conception of man is hierarchical. Man is superior to the cosmos by virtue of a pre-ordained hierarchical supremacy, not by virtue of a natural evolution to the summit of the universe. He is independent of the cosmic infinity because he is above it. As we will see in Chapter III, Section F, he embraces the cosmos *in principle* because Christ, the True Man, the Eternal Man, is the principle from whom men and the cosmos come (and to whom they will return).

> The time has come to write a justification of man, an anthropodicy. Perhaps an anthropodicy is the only way to a theodicy ... A religion of man is being born.[1]

The problem of Godmanhood for Berdyaev, at least, comes from contemporary Russian thought.[2]

> The idea of God-manhood, the development of which was principally due to Vladimir Soloviev, and the religious philosophy of the beginning of the twentieth century, means the mutual penetration and the union of two natures, the Divine and the human, while the distinction between them and their independence is preserved.

> The doctrine of God-manhood presupposes commensurability between God and man, the presence of the divine principle in man, and at the same time it does not admit monistic identity.[3]

Berdyaev refers to Solovyev, the founder of the doctrine of Godmanhood who formulated his theory shortly before the twentieth century.[4] The movement of religious philosophy Berdyaev mentions is Russian. The mystical quality of Berdyaev's philosophy is clearly seen, particularly in the phrase, "the mutual penetration and the union of two natures, the Divine and the human." [5] This is why Berdyaev's philosophy of history is primarily a metaphysics of history in which the light of revelation and Sacred Doctrine is stronger than the light of reason. Man is considered to be divine. His philosophy of history is seen to be divine rather than historical.[6] True knowledge is mystical and divine.

---

[1] *The Meaning of the Creative Act*, 19.

[2] Berdyaev leaves no doubt of the origin of the doctrine of Godmanhood in his book, *The Origin of Russian Communism* (Bles, London, 1948), 180: "Russian creative religious thought has introduced the idea of God-Humanity"; 172: "There is nothing of this doctrine in such a form either in Schelling or in other representatives of Western thought."

[3] *The Beginning and the End*, 36.

[4] Cf. V. Solovyev, *Lectures on Godmanhood* (Dobson, London, 1948).

[5] The human and the divine (in every man) are distinct however. See Chapter III, Section F.

[6] We find the following statement in *The Meaning of History*, 44, concerning the divinity of man's knowledge: "For heaven is not a remote transcendental and unattainable sphere: it is a part of the inmost depths of our spiritual life. When we dive below the surface and penetrate into these depths we then readily commune with celestial life. ... in this interior spiritual reality ... lies the source of history. And in it, too, is revealed the drama of the mutual relations between God and man."

The doctrine of Godmanhood is the principle by which Berdyaev's philosophy states that human history is an epoch in a divine and mystical celestial history. Man and his history are more or less divine, symbols of God and His history.

Though the immediate origin of Berdyaev's doctrine of Godmanhood is in contemporary Russian thought, it is inspired by an ancient outlook of Eastern Orthodoxy.

For the idea of the divinization of man is the fundamental concept of Orthodox mysticism, the object of which is the transfiguration of everything created.[1]

The gulf between the natural and the supernatural does not exist for mystical and patristic writers of the East in the same sense as it does for Catholics...

The Eastern Fathers, who were steeped in the spirit of Platonism, have never regarded the non-divinity of the natural as absolute.[2]

These are the thoughts that are always present with Berdyaev, and when he considers history, the basic reality he seeks in historical events is the divinization of man and the transfiguration of everything created. His philosophy both attempts to reveal this in history and strives to make it an ethical and mystical norm. God is seen to be both immanent in man as well as transcendent over man.

Pure transcendence involves a complete dualism between the divine and the human and makes impossible any real union between them. This is the reason why both theology and philosophy must refuse to take either God or man as their starting point, but must rather begin with the God-Man whose theandric nature is beyond and above this antithesis.[3]

If a philosopher starts his philosophy with Christ the God-Man, then he will avoid the danger of separating God and man or of identifying God and terrestrial man. (The word, *theandric*, originating in the Greek *theos* god, plus *andros* man, refers to the union of the divine and the human.)

Berdyaev because he is a philosopher of history, is interested in the divinity of man as well as in the divinity of Christ the Second Person of the Blessed Trinity. He says in a later work, *The Divine and the Human*:

The birth of man in God is a theogonic process. In the eternal idea of him, man is rooted in God-manhood and linked with the God-man ... Humanity exists in eternity and ought to be realized in time.[4]

---

[1] *Freedom and the Spirit*, 254–255.
[2] *Ibid.*, 256.
[3] *Ibid.*, 95.
[4] *The Divine and the Human*, 111–112.

The Birth of man in God is a theogonic process, a process within God, because it is the birth of the God-man, Christ, in the birth of the Trinity, out of the primordial depths of God.[1] Eternal Man is the eternal idea of man, Christ, Godmanhood. Humanity exists in eternity, in Christ.[2] Humanity ought to be realized in time says Berdyaev; that is, the divine idea of humanity should be attained by men.[3] It is a metaphysical doctrine of redemption of mankind by Christ that Berdyaev stresses in his philosophy. He opposes a notion of attainment through legality or good works.[4] "Man is redeemed from the power of the law."[5] In Berdyaev's theory, God historically became man in order to raise him to divinity but not, primarily in order to redeem him morally. Christ is our revelation, not primarily our ransom.[6]

Berdyaev understands "eternal idea of man" in the light of his metaphysics. It is not an idea in which man is created, but an idea in which man eternally exists.[7] For Berdyaev this idea is not merely intelligible but also imaginable. The mind knows by means of images and ideas in which there is no sharp distinction between intelligence and imagination. Berdyaev's doctrine of Eternal Man and the theory of knowledge that goes with it is especially favorable to the philosophy of history that we find in Berdyaev.[8]

Berdyaev often calls his philosophy a prophetic philosophy. We saw in Chapter I how the (prophesied) future events of universal history are both future and eternal.[9] The knowledge of the future, which must be peculiar to prophecy and to universal history, requires an imaginative component. Hence, Berdyaev's philosophy can easily conceive of a universal history which manifests an Eternal Manhood; for his imagi-

---

[1] "Out of the Divine Nothing, the Gottheit or the *Ungrund*, the Holy Trinity, God the Creator is born," *The Destiny of Man*, 25. Berdyaev says, in *The Beginning and the End*, 107; "The divine *Ungrund*, before its emergence, is in the eternity of the Divine Trinity. God gives birth to himself, realizes himself out of the Divine Nothingness."

[2] Cf. *Dream and Reality*, 182, See Chapter III, Section C.

[3] *Dream and Reality*, 182.

[4] Indeed the Fall of man is considered metaphysically rather than morally. The Fall cannot be considered juridically as a formal transgression of God's will and an act of disobedience: It is simply a wrong orientation by which man loses the idea of himself as a microcosm and separates himself from the inner radiance. *Freedom and the Spirit*, 20, 21–23; 131–133; 148, 199–201.

[5] *The Destiny of Man*, 105.

[6] "The moral end of life is for it not the salvation of one's soul or the redemption of guilt but creative realization of righteousness and of values which need not belong to the moral order. ... This is the basis of the ethics of creativeness." *The Destiny of Man*, 133.

[7] See Chapter III, Section D.

[8] See Chapter IV, Section G, Part 4.

[9] See Chapter I, Section D, which concerns eschatology. Thus the prophesied return of the world to God is a metahistorical event, occuring in eternity; yet it will occur in the future also as a goal of history.

native noetic is adaptable to a universal history and suited to a mysticism of Eternal Man.

We will see [1] that Berdyaev's mystical doctrine of an Eternal Man, considers terrestrial man an image, a metaphor of the Proto-type. The image improves and there occurs the return of all men to God. That is why a *mystique* and metaphoricism of history are amalgamated with a mysticism of history in Berdyaev. We should understand in this light the closing sentence of the above-quoted passage which says, "Humanity exists in eternity and ought to be realized in time." [2] Terrestrial man is an image of Absolute Man and therefore is capable of realizing and ought to realize, his Proto-type.[3] The "ought" is a mystical and also a mythical or metaphorical "ought." That is, Eternal Man can be realized, not absolutely but only in a metaphorical approximation, in time.[4] With this limitation, eternal humanity ought to be realized in time. Berdyaev's philosophy of history sees, in its metaphoricism and in its Christian mysticism, that the image of the Eternal Man, of Christ, is improving throughout history. For example, man passes from an era dominated by the cosmos to an era in which the natural is ruled by man.[5]

Berdyaev says in his last (and posthumous) work, *Truth and Revelation*:

Pure humanity, however, actually is the divine in man.[6]

It is not man, but God who is human.[7]

... the Son is not only God but man in the absolute and spiritual sense of the word, that is the Eternal Man.[8]

And Eternal Man is mystically and metaphorically revealed in man and in the various historical myths and particular cultures. It is the problem of philosophy of history, along with the other parts of philosophy, to bring forth this revelation of the Eternal Man.[9]

[1] Chapter III.

[2] To say the image of the Eternal man is improving throughout history is a way of referring to the progressive incarnation of spirit. See Chapter IV, Section G, Part 3, notes.

[3] See Chapter III, Section F.

[4] See Chapter IV, Section G.

[5] Berdyaev refers to the passage of man from an era dominated by the cosmos to an era in which the natural is ruled by man, He describes this in terms of spirit, i.e., "spirit's active conquest of nature." *The Bourgeois Mind and Other Essays* (Sheed and Ward, London, 1934), 35.

[6] *Truth and Revelation*, 50.

[7] *The Divine and the Human*, 110. Concerning Berdyaev's idea of Grace, see Chapter I, p. 31, note 2.

[8] *Freedom and the Spirit*, 137.

[9] *Solitude and Society*, 22.

In order to understand distinctly Berdyaev's Principle of Godmanhood let us turn to his doctrine of freedom. For, while Berdyaev has given us the principle by which the *patterns* of events and entities may be explained, we have not yet seen the way in which he accounts for the *freedom* of man and of God. There are two reasons why the role of freedom in Berdyaev's doctrine will interest us. First, terrestrial history needs to be an epoch of celestial history because freedom allowed the Fall of man. Second, Berdyaev asserts on the one hand, an existential metaphysics, and on the other hand, a metaphorical theory of the participation of man in Godmanhood. (a) The primacy of freedom does allow the supremacy of existentialism over objective philosophy. (b) The primacy of freedom is the condition of the metaphorical theory of participation.

C. GODMANHOOD AND THE FREEDOM OF MAN

Berdyaev understands his own idea of freedom in relation to the philosophy of some Russian predecessors and contemporaries. They have taken over the cosmologies and cosmogonies of German Idealist philosophers, particularly those of Schelling.[1] And the question that Berdyaev has brought to these philosophers is: how well is the primacy of freedom accounted for?

Vladimir Solovyev (1853–1900), a Russian philosopher, set forth the doctrine of Sophia (the supreme Wisdom) and Godmanhood and attempted to synthesize the cosmogonical and cosmological doctrines to which he fell heir.[2] Sophia for Solovyev is the pan-human organism (all mankind), the eternal world-soul. It is also the divine Logos, Christ.[3] This sophiology (as it is called) is added to the doctrine of Godmanhood by Solovyev. Godmanhood is the source of Solovyev's philosophical inspiration.[4]

His followers (and Berdyaev's contemporaries) [5] set forth a sophiology in their own doctrines and thus kept the views of Solovyev alive in Berdyaev's own day. Berdyaev has found the primacy of freedom so ill accounted for or neglected in their writings that he has defined his own

---

[1] See Chapter III, notes.

[2] V. V. Zenkovsky, *A History of Russian Philosophy* (Routledge and Kegan Paul, London, 1953), 529–531. Solovyev, *Lectures on Godmanhood*, 154, 159, 163.

[3] *Lectures on Goodmanhood*, 163.

[4] Zankovsky's *History of Russian Philosophy*, 483.

[5] P. A. Florenski (1882–c. 1941) and S. N. Bulgakov (1871–1944) are Sophiologists following Solovyev. Cf. Zenkovsky's *History of Russian Philosophy*, 480, 875, 890.

philosophical position in contrast to theirs. By so defining his doctrine, he is able to assert a free Christian cosmogony, and can establish the reality of history itself. History and historical movements tend to be generalized and slighted in the intellectualist system. Their unique quality is recognized in a doctrine which emphasizes the freedom of God and of man.[1]

His anti-intellectualist approach may be viewed through a criticism he makes of a fellow Russian emigré, Sergei Bulgakov, a professional theologian and a sophiologist. Berdyaev says, in Bulgakov's doctrine:

There is no absolute division between the Creator and His creation. The uncreated Sophia exists in God for all eternity, it is the world of Platonic ideas. Through Sophia our world was created, and there exists a created Sophia which permeates creation. ... The chief difficulty for Sophiology arises from the problem of evil which is indeed inadequately stated and left unsolved. It is an optimistic system; the fundamental idea is not that of freedom but the idea of Sophia. ... the lack of clarity in defining what Sophia is gives rise to criticism. Sophia appears to be the Holy Trinity and the cosmos and humanity and the Mother of God. The question arises: does there not result too great a multiplication of intermediaries? ... it remains doubtful how the eschatological expectation is to be reconciled with sophiological optimism. There is an identification of the Church with the Kingdom of God and that contradicts eschatological expectation. I do not myself share the view of the sophiological school, but I place a high value on Bulgakov's line of thought in Orthodoxy and upon his statement of new problems. His philosophy does not belong to the existential type; he is an objectivist and a universalist and fundamentally a platonist. He has too great a belief in the possibility of arriving at the knowledge of God through intellectual concepts.[2]

And, as Berdyaev states in his last book, *Truth and Revelation*:

In spite of everything, (Bulgakov's) religious metaphysics is a metaphysics of an ontological datum not of an act. His nature philosophy is not free from sophiological determinism. The problem of freedom in such a system is full of difficulty and it finds no solution, and the same is true of the problem of evil.[3]

Berdyaev is critical of Bulgakov's stand that there is no absolute division between the Creator and His Creation. But, for Berdyaev, too, so far as the intelligibility of the world and of history is concerned, there is no absolute division between them and God. The division which Berdyaev asserts must be seen with respect to willing and in the order of freedom; and the doctrine of freedom is uppermost in his mind when he criticizes the sophiological doctrine.

---

[1] But though Berdyaev recognizes the reality of history, he believes that human history is not completely real or true. Only celestial history – that of God – is completely true. This unhistorical attitude is due to Berdyaev's mystical outlook.

[2] *The Russian Idea*, 240–241.

[3] *Truth and Revelation*, 64.

Berdyaev mentions the various meanings of Sophia in Bulgakov's doctrine and complains of a lack of clarity. He says there are too many intermediaries posited in Bulgakov's sophiology. He means, that, since Bulgakov makes no absolute division between the Creator and the world, the cosmos, humanity and the Mother of God become divine intermediaries instead of something less.

Berdyaev says, "I do not share the view of the sophiological school." The sophiological doctrine amalgamates intellectual notions such as the doctrines of the world-soul, humanity, and the cosmos with the Ineffable. It seeks the knowledge of God through intellectual concepts. Berdyaev does not like this objective, universal and rational approach to knowing God, and he calls it Platonic. It intellectualizes God. It is in this light that he criticizes the objectivism, universalism and platonism of Bulgakov. In Bulgakov, then, Berdyaev is criticizing the "sophiological determinism" of the school. There is, he believes, no solution to the question of freedom in such a system. He associates freedom with a metaphysics of act, and determinism with a metaphysics of essence ("an ontological datum.") Hence, the doctrine of freedom is connected with an existentialism, here.

The nature of this doctrine of freedom reveals itself when Berdyaev criticizes another sophiologist, Vladimir Solovyev. Berdyaev says, in *The Russian Idea*:

Solovyev was an intellectualist not a voluntarist. For that reason freedom does not play such a part with him as it does with the voluntarist Khomyakov. His world outlook belongs rather to the type of universal determinism, but the determinism is spiritual. . . . The attainment of the all-embracing, both social and cosmic, is for him of an intellectual character. There is no irrational freedom with him. The falling away from God is the acceptance of principles which are hostile to God.[1]

Berdyaev frequently says that he himself is a voluntarist; and he here opposes a voluntarism which insures freedom to Solovyev's intellectualism. He modifies the criticism by admitting that Solovyev's determinism is spiritual (that is to say, it is not a determinism of pure essential intelligibility, but a determinism by the Divine Logos, spiritual and ineffable). Berdyaev's philosophy, in fact, has an aspect of "spiritual determinism"; for he accepts the Christian prophecy of the destiny of history and of man and goes so far as to predict the beatitude of every man. This is a "spiritual determinism," and his philosophy of history therefore posits a "spiritual determinism."

[1] *The Russian Idea*, 168–169.

Berdyaev says there is no irrational Freedom with Solovyev, but, in Berdyaev's doctrine, we will see, irrational freedom is at the basis of God and operates in man. In Berdyaev's eyes, Solovyev's attainment of the all-embracing unity is intellectual. Berdyaev asserts that, for Solovyev, the Fall occurs by virtue of intelligible principles; but in his own doctrine, the Fall occurs because of the irrational Freedom.

We cannot, however, study the difference between Berdyaev's position and the outlook he opposes without noting the compatibility of the two doctrines. As we have seen, the voluntarism does not at all nullify the "spiritual determinism" but attempts to clarify some events in terrestrial and celestial history. In brief, voluntarism is compatible in the same doctrine with "spiritual determinism." [1]

Solovyev's philosophy tends towards the existentialism of Berdyaev. Berdyaev says:

... he, so to speak, approaches existential philosophy, but his own philosophical thought does not belong to the existential type. At the basis of his philosophy there lies the living intuition of the concrete existent ... But his philosophy remains abstract and rationalist. In it the existent is overwhelmed by his schemes. He all the while insists upon the necessity of the mystical element in philosophy. ... But as a philosopher, Solovyev certainly was not an existentialist. [2]

Like Solovyev, who indeed is his true predecessor in the doctrine of Godmanhood, Berdyaev finds at the basis of his own philosophy the concrete existent; namely, the Godman, Christ. And that is why he says Solovyev approaches existential philosophy; for the concrete Godman, the metaphysical object of both philosophers, is not an essence. He is an existent. Yet, adds Berdyaev, Solovyev overwhelms the existent in his philosophy with abstract rational schemes. The mystical element is existential; nevertheless Solovyev was not truly an existential philosopher.

Berdyaev contrasts a doctrine of Sophia asserted by the 16th-century mystic, Jacob Boehme, with the doctrine of his own Russian contemporaries. "Sophiology in Boehme is chiefly of an anthropological character. In Solovyev it is mainly cosmological." [3] Berdyaev, we have seen, denies the sophiological doctrine is true. He presents the sophiological doctrine of Boehme in *Freedom and the Spirit*,[4] not as his own doctrine

---

[1] The compatibility of a voluntarism with "spiritual determinism" seems clear in Professor Gilson's discussions on the subject of voluntarism in his book, *Jean Duns Scot* (Vrin, Paris, 1952), 606. Cf. Index: "Volontarisme."

[2] *The Russian Idea*, 171.

[3] *Ibid.*, 176.

[4] *Freedom and the Spirit*, 300, ff.

but to contrast it with the Russian kind. After showing that man instead of the cosmos rules, in Boehme's doctrine, he concludes as follows: "Russian sophiology seems to deny that man is at the center of the world and that the cosmos is in him..." [1]

Boehme's formulation of the primary metaphysical principle in God and in man is the model of Berdyaev's primary doctrine. The primacy of freedom, as it is conceived by Boehme, is reasserted by Berdyaev.

In a chapter on celestial history in *The Meaning of History*, Berdyaev attempts to show a connection between the dynamism of history and that of the divine life. He says:

... it is impossible to assert the tragic destiny of the Son of God and His expiatory death without at the same time admitting movement in the divine life. [2]

That is, there is a movement, and a tragic one, in the divine life. A few pages further, he says:

... the origins of history lie in the inmost depths of the Absolute and in the tragic potential of divine life itself (and this constitutes the true hypothesis of the esoteric Christian philosophy of history) ...

I am thinking of Boehme. ... and particularly of his *The Dark Nature of God*. Somewhere, in immeasurably greater depths, there exists a state which may be called *Ungrund* or "groundlessness" to which neither human words nor the categories of good and evil nor those of being or non-being are applicable. *Ungrund* is deeper than anything else ... In the nature of God, deeper than Him, lies a sort of primal dark abyss, and in its inmost depths occurs a theogonic process or that of divine genesis.

This process is secondary when compared with that primal "groundlessness" ... [3]

The origins of history, according to the passage, lie beyond the Triune existence of God, in the *Ungrund*, the dark abyss from which the Trinity is born. When Berdyaev says this is "the true hypothesis of the *esoteric* Christian philosophy of history," he intends several things. He says "hypothesis" in order to indicate that the doctrine cannot be demonstrated; and "true hypothesis" in order to indicate its truth can be known with certitude. It introduces us, mystically, into an esoteric knowledge of the divine life. It is esoteric because it is mystical, abstruse, secret and knowable only to the initiates in such matters.

This irrational force, *Ungrund* or dark abyss, is beyond the distinctions between good and evil. Good and evil, the Holy Trinity and

---

[1] *Ibid.*, 301.
[2] *The Meaning of History*, 48.
[3] *Ibid.*, 54–55.

potentially everything else, come from this source through a divine genesis. When Berdyaev says that the process itself is secondary when compared with the primal groundlessness, he gives the basis for his doctrine of a celestial history. For the *Ungrund* is the condition of a movement in the divine life the passage tells us.

He continues:

for the fact of such a dark primal source and nature implies the possibility of tragic destiny for the divine life . . . the passion of God Himself and His Son . . . [1]

That is, the evil of the tragic passion of Christ the Godman on Calvary originates, along with the good, in the *Ungrund*. And now Berdyaev is ready to remark the voluntarism of this doctrine. The evil, the tragedy, originates in the primordial Will.

. . . the primal foundations of being rest upon a certain irrational and wilful principle, and the whole significance and essence of the world process consists in the illumination of this dark irrational principle in cosmogony and theogony. And this is the hypothesis of my metaphysics of history, that the terrestrial destiny is predetermined by the celestial, in which the tragedy of illumination and Redemption take place through the divine passion, and that tragedy determines the process of illuminating world history.[2]

Here occurs the explicit voluntarism of this doctrine.[3] Berdyaev calls this irrational principle "wilful." [4] It is a primordial Will. The purpose, not merely of history but of the world process, is to illuminate this dark principle, both in a theogony (in a celestial history) and in a cosmogony (in a terrestrial history). When Berdyaev says that the terrestrial destiny is predetermined by the celestial, he assumes that the tragedy of the passion of Christ is primarily celestial destiny, a necessary part of celestial history, in order to illuminate the Primal Abyss. And the tragedy determine the process of illuminating world history (that is, the passion of Christ illuminates world history). The *Ungrund* is not only the primal basis of God, but it is also the primal basis of man, a basis which gives man an absolute freedom to will good or evil.[5] This must be understood, not rationally, but mystically.[6] The history of the world

---

[1] *Ibid.*, 55.

[2] *Ibid.*, 56.

[3] Cf. *The Beginning and the End*, 107: "Will, that is, freedom, is the beginning of everything. . . . The *Ungrund*, . . . the abyss, the free nothingness . . . The divine *Ungrund*, before its emergence, is in the eternity of the Divine Trinity."

[4] Berdyaev has accepted Boehme's doctrine of *Ungrund* as primordial freedom early in his career. Cf. *Dream and Reality*, his autobiography, 179. He asserts the doctrine of primordial Will in his posthumous book, *The Beginning and the End*, 107, 108, 109. Always remember, however, that Berdyaev does not posit the Will as other than God. Cf. *Ibid.*, 105.

[5] *The Destiny of Man*, 25, ff.

[6] *The Beginning and the End*, 107. See Chapter IV, Section G.

must serve as an epoch within celestial history in order to complete the illumination of the *Ungrund*.

It was no merely poetic thing for Berdyaev to assert: that the terrestrial history is an epoch within celestial history. He writes, indeed, a little further on in *The Meaning of History* of the need of God for the revelation of man. He says:

In the Image of Christ is brought about the genesis of God in man and of man in God ... Thus for the first time, in response to God's movement and longing, a perfect man is revealed to Him. This mysterious process occurs in the interior depths of the divine reality itself; it is a sort of divine history of mankind. History is, indeed, not only the revelation of God, but also the reciprocal revelation of man in God.

... History would not be tragic if it were only the revelation of God and its gradual apprehension. Its drama and tragedy are not only determined in the divine life itself, but also by the fact that they are based upon the mystery of freedom, which is not only a divine, but also a human revelation – that longed for by God in the depths of the divine life.[1]

There is a real and actual drama and history in God because the *Ungrund*, which does not lie outside of God, has to be illuminated; and the dialectic of this doctrine leads to the assertion that God Himself needs to be illuminated. Man shares in illuminating the *Ungrund* and, consequently, man shares in illuminating God. This is why Berdyaev says that God needs man, and there is a revelation of man to God, as well as a revelation of God to man.

In Berdyaev's philosophy, history is therefore the revelation of man in God (as well as the revelation of God).[2] Hence, history – both celestial and terrestrial – orientates itself by the perfect Man, Christ, Who illuminates the *Ungrund*.

We can now see where the doctrine of Godmanhood is joined to the voluntarism of Boehme. The *Ungrund*, the primal Will, is illuminated both by terrestrial man and by the God-man. The complexity of history arises from the relation of the two revelations (of God and of man). The tragedy and chaos of history occurs because the divine voluntary principle allows, in the hierarchy of being, the freedom of man to operate untrammelled by intelligibility.

Berdyaev, in the next paragraph, reveals a certain stress in his phi-

---

[1] *The Meaning of History*, 57–58.

[2] Berdyaev does not consider history to be identical with revelation. He says history is a revelation, but history for him may be said to contain revelation. Human and terrestrial history are not a completely true reality. History is a revelation only in the sense that it reveals meta-history, the true reality. See Chapter I, 9–10.

losophy of history, caused by the doctrine of Godmanhood and his voluntarism. He begins, saying:

There would be no᷄ history without freedom. It is the mataphysical basis of history;[1]

He does not mean that it is the one and only absolute metaphysical basis of history; he continues:

The revelation of history can be apprehended only through Christ as perfect man and God ... in fact, history owes its existence entirely to the presence of Christ at its very heart. He represents the deepest mystical and metaphysical foundation and source of history and of its tragic destiny.[2]

Christ, the perfect Man, represents "the *deepest* metaphysical foundation and source of history." Now, where are we? Berdyaev has just said that freedom is *the* metaphysical basis of history. Yet, we have to interpret the paragraph to mean that Christ, the Godman, is a more important metaphysical foundation of history than freedom.

We must conclude that there is a structural flaw and a stress in Berdyaev's doctrine, or there would be if his philosophy were rationalistic instead of mystical. He is a voluntarist; that is, he does not merely assert that God is free – along with most Christians – but that the freedom is absolutely prior to God's intelligibility. This is Berdyaev's doctrine, there is not the slightest doubt of it. And yet, he says that Christ, the divine Logos, is the deepest metaphysical basis of history.

Berdyaev is not so careless as to contradict himself; he is fond of expressing himself in antinomies, such as the one we have seen. He knows that there is a contradictory quality in what he says; this life, for him as for Hegel,[3] is antinomic, must be understood by antinomies.[4] It is his Heraclitean way; he considers himself to be in a tradition which stems from Heraclitus.[5] Heraclitus is "one of the greatest of philosophers." [6] He often says he has a paradoxical philosophy, expressed in paradoxes. The paradoxes are supposed to be reconcilable. Berdyaev has some reconciliation of the paradox of freedom and divine Logos in mind. Christ, according to Berdyaev is perfect illuminated freedom,[7]

---

[1] *The Meaning of History*, 58.

[2] *Ibid.*, 58–59.

[3] *Dream and Reality*, 87.

[4] *The Meaning of History*, 51.

[5] *The Beginning and the End*, 24.

[6] *The Meaning of History*, 49–50.

[7] Berdyaev discusses the relation of freedom to Christ in *Freedom and the Spirit*. He says: "How ... can freedom be separated from the evil it brings in its train except by the destruction of freedom itself?"

"To this universal problem there is no solution save in the coming of Christ ... The

the freedom of the God-man is the true, the best freedom. Thus it is that Berdyaev, very probably, resolves the antinomy in his own mind. The reconciliation is "historical," there is a celestial history, a theogony. It is the mystical pattern of human history:

The explanation of history as an interior metaphysical and spiritual, and not an antimetaphysical, principle can be based only on a tie between the theogonic, cosmogonic and anthropogonic processes. This tie unites and integrates our spiritual experience.[1]

By introducing a historical process into the profoundest reality, Berdyaev is able to posit a voluntarism in which Will is supreme, and yet Logos, intelligibility, is supreme, too, because it illuminates Will completely at the end of the history. Mystical intelligibility wins out as it were over irrationality when universal history is viewed. This, indeed, seems to be the explanation of history according to Berdyaev.[2] He says, in *The Destiny of Man:*

Victory over meonic freedom is impossible for God, since that freedom is not created by Him and is rooted in non-being; it is equally impossible for man, since man has become the slave of that dark freedom and is not free in his freedom. It is possible only for the God-man Christ Who descends into the abysmal darkness of meonic freedom ... Apart from Christ, the tragic antinomy of freedom and necessity is insoluble ... [3]

mystery of Christianity, the religion of God made man, is above all the mystery of liberty. ... the Christian doctrine of grace is the true doctrine of freedom." *Freedom and the Spirit,* 135.
   "The source of man's freedom is in God, and that, not in God the Father, but in God the Son." *Ibid.,* 137.
   There is a movement in Berdyaev's doctrine of freedom which is particularly discernible when his posthumous works are read after all his other books. At the end of his life, he asserts Trinitarian Christian Doctrine more strongly than before. Thus freedom becomes more Christianized.
   In *The Beginning and the End,* Berdyaev discusses the role of freedom in the creative act of man. Something new breaks through out of freedom, he says, "and not out of a dark freedom, but out of an illuminated freedom." *The Beginning and the End,* 171.
   [1] *The Meaning of History,* 61.
   [2] In fact, in his posthumous papers, gathered into the book, *The Realm of Spirit and the Realm of Caesar,* 102. Berdyaev says that a metaphysics of the Will or of Freedom, taken in itself, would be inadequate. He says: "Of the two types of metaphysics, the intellectual and the voluntary, the former is always unfavorable, and the latter favorable, to freedom. But voluntary metaphysics, taken by itself, is not yet a philosophy of freedom. What we must decisively affirm is this, that freedom is spirit..." That is, the complete metaphysics is concerned with a spiritually illuminated freedom, not the irrational alone.
   [3] *The Destiny of Man,* 281. In *The Beginning and the End,* 106, Berdyaev says: "The *Ungrund,* then, is nothingness, the groundless eye of eternity; and at the same time it is will, not grounded upon anything; bottomless, indeterminate will. ... at the same time the *Ungrund* is freedom. In the darkness of the *Ungrund* a fire flames up and this is freedom, meonic, potential freedom." He says on the preceding page: "Free will in God is the *Ungrund* in God, the nothingness in him."

Berdyaev states most strongly God's need of man.[1] *Meonic* in "meonic freedom," is an adaptation of the Greek word for non-being. So Berdyaev next says, freedom is vested in non-being. The notion of God's need of man is significant in his philosophy of history because it shows that human history is a real and necessary epoch within celestial history. In Christ, the Godman, the tragic antinomy of freedom and intelligibility is solved.

The affiliation which Berdyaev establishes between the divine intelligibility and the primal Will is set forth in two metaphysical doctrines; the doctrine of Spirit and the doctrine of beauty. His philosophy can be called a philosophy of beauty and a philosophy of spirit. Beauty is a metaphysical entity in Berdyaev's theory, and Spirit is likewise a metaphysical entity.

Firstly, spirit is treated by Berdyaev in distinction from the Holy Spirit. He says, in *Freedom and the Spirit*:

Spirit cannot be identified simply with the Holy Spirit, the third Hypostasis of the Trinity. Spirit is the sphere in which the divine and the human are united. . . [2]

Spirit cannot be identified with the Holy Spirit because the Holy Spirit is born out of the *Ungrund* in the theogonic process, but Spirit is wilful, the primordial will acts in it. Berdyaev, in his last book, *Truth and Revelation*, clarifies the relation of Spirit and the Holy Spirit. He says:

The divine element in man is not a special act of grace communicated to him, neither is it a natural element. It is the spiritual element in him, a reality of a special kind.

There is a difference between Spirit and the Holy Spirit, but they are one and the same reality in different degrees.[3]

Spirit is not Holy Spirit, yet they differ only in degree and are really the same reality. And the divine element is the spiritual element in man. The human spirit is not divine by nature, but in virtue of being spirit. There is no natural divinity here. Berdyaev explains his notion of spirit in a work devoted to the philosophy of spirit; namely, *Spirit and Reality*:

Spirit emanates from God but it is not a Divine creation like nature; it is a Divine infusion, an inspiration. That is the biblical image. But spirit emanates from not only the Deity but also from the primal pre-existential freedom from the

[1] Cf. *The Meaning of History*, 57-58.
[2] *Freedom and the Spirit*, 47.
[3] *Truth and Revelation*, 141.

Ungrund. That is, indeed, the fundamental paradox of spirit: it is a Divine emanation, and at the same time it can reply to the Deity in terms not dictated by it. ... it is freedom in God and from God. ... The Logos is akin to spirit, it informs everything with purpose. But at the same time spirit is irrational, extra-rational, supra-rational.[1]

This doctrine of spirit, since spirit is different from God, is not a doctrine of the Holy Spirit, but of something less.[2] Inasmuch as Berdyaev's doctrine of man holds that man is an incarnate spirit, this passage shows us that it is through spirit that the primordial freedom is communicated to man (the human spirit). Moreover, in Berdyaev's philosophy, man, an incarnate spirit, receives everything else through spirit; imagination, intelligence and all the powers of the soul.[3] Spirit, therefore, communicates both the mind and the will to man from the Logos and the *Ungrund.*[4] This is why Berdyaev says the Logos is akin to spirit, because the spirit informs everything with purpose. But spirit differs from the Logos, from the perfect God-man because spirit is also irrational. This is mysterious, and the mystery of the irrationality of spirit remains in Berdyaev's writings.

Spirit is incarnated in the cosmos. Berdyaev says, in *Spirit and Reality:*

Spirit is incarnated ... not only in the human body but also in the ... historical bodies, in natural life, tradition and so forth.[5]

Berdyaev goes on to show that the incarnation of spirit is the progress of the world through historical epochs. Thus, spirit has progressed from organic incarnation, where man was the slave of the cosmos, to technical incarnation, where man rules the cosmos.[6]

Berdyaev calls his philosophy a philosophy of the spirit more often than he calls it a philosophy of Godmanhood. (He has many names for his philosophy.) He devotes far more time to the theory of the spirit (as it is in itself and as man) than to the doctrine of man as the image of the perfect Man, Christ.[7] The doctrine of spirit becomes a vehicle of his voluntarism; and the doctrine is the means of reconciling intelligibility

---

[1] *Spirit and Reality*, 34.

[2] See p.69, note 1 below.

[3] *Freedom and the Spirit*, 27; *Slavery and Freedom*, 32.

[4] How rational powers ensue ultimately from an irrational basis is an unanswered mystery in Berdyaev's philosophy.

[5] *Spirit and Reality*, 66.

[6] *Ibid.*, 68.

[7] Berdyaev, however, devotes considerable space in his writings to the doctrine of Godmanhood.

and purpose with voluntarism. Rational intelligibility, however is slighted in his mystical doctrine.[1]

This doctrine of spirit should be understood in the light of the meaning of the Russian word for *will: velya*. It is the Russian word, both for *will* and also for *freedom*. The will, in Berdyaev's doctrine means principally non-compulsion, freedom not *for* something but *from* something, and particularly from compulsion to personal doing. Free will is seen as a condition in which no one else can command it.

Berdyaev asserts not so much a spirit, an *esprit*, a *Geist*, which aspires heavenward in search of God. He rather describes a spirit, *duch* is the Russian word, which descends as it were from heaven to man, a spirit which incarnates itself. The free will of the human spirit does not seek supplicatingly, like the steeples of Gothic cathedrals, towards God.[2] The free will of the human spirit participates in the incarnation of spirit, in which man experiences freedom from the objectivizations of the fallen world. It is a spirit which diffuses itself like the many domes of Russian churches, freeing and divinizing the world. Indeed, the Russian word for *spirit, duch,* is etymologically associated with the Russian word for *breath*; the relation suggests the divine breath bringing life to man.[3]

The doctrine of will which is found here is like the will of Western voluntarists: that is, both wills are conceived of as freedom *from* something, as well as for something. Berdyaev finds Western voluntarism (as that of Boehme) suitable to his own Russian outlook. His philosophy of history is seeking, through the spirit, freedom from the objectivization of the world and man.

Secondly, Berdyaev's philosophy is a philosophy of beauty. He says, in a later work, *The Destiny of Man:*

The real transfiguration and enlightenment of human nature means the attainment of beauty. The good realized actually, and not formally and symbolically, is beauty. The highest end is beauty and not goodness, which always bears a stamp of the law. ... The transfiguration of the world is the attainment

[1] See Chapter IV.

[2] To understand how very much opposed Berdyaev is to the typically Western and ascetic type of spirituality, see *Spirit and Reality*, Chapter VII. Ascetism (as, for example, that of St. Simon Stylites), is not asserted in this doctrine, but opposed. See the ethical work, *The Destiny of Man*.

[3] Berdyaev, however, does not entirely reject the aspect of spiritualism which he finds in Latin Christendom: rather, it is a difference of emphasis. "Love is the path to the realization of personality and there are two types of love, there is a love which ascends and a love which descends, love which is *eros* and love which is *agape*." *Slavery and Freedom*, 55.

He criticizes Nygren, who has written *Agape and Eros* (S.P.C.K., London, 1953), for rejecting the "*eros*" type of love. *The Divine and the Human*, 137.

of beauty. The kingdom of God is beauty. ... Beauty is God's idea of the creature, of man and of the world.[1]

We could guess this philosophy of beauty from Berdyaev's doctrine of creativity. The philosopher of history, like every other thinker, is creative, as we saw in Chapter I. The historical memory is creative, and it creates historical tradition and culture.[2]

Berdyaev is speaking here of the highest beauty, not of the beautiful symbols in this world. When he says "The highest end is beauty and not goodness, which always bears a stamp of the law," he is showing us how Beauty provides a mystical reconciliation of the doctrines of *Ungrund* and *Godmanhood*, of voluntarism and intelligibility. The good cannot be the highest end because it bears the stamp of the law; it would disallow freedom and the primacy of freedom. Berdyaev has a doctrine of something that is beyond good and evil; namely the *Ungrund*, primal and irrational Will, that which is deepest in God. It is illuminated by the Godman, the divine Logos. Beauty is Berdyaev's goal because beauty is, I think, sought and discovered in an intellectual quest which is creative. The will and the intellect work so closely together that the reason does not hesitate to conform itself to the guidance of volition. I believe this may be said of every artistic creativity where transcendental Beauty is sought.

He says, finally, that Beauty is God's idea of the world.[3] This doctrine is very amenable to the prophetic philosophy of history we find in Berdyaev's universal history. Indeed, Berdyaev's prophecy is concerned with the future, as such, as well as with the present. Prophecy, therefore, requires the use of the imagination, as well as the intellect; because the future, as such, can only be known through the singular knowledge of the imagination. A philosopher of beauty such as Berdyaev, is disposed to prophetic philosophizing. The imagination plays an important role in prophecy.

Berdyaev's philosophy of history is a philosophy of beauty, and the theory of knowledge set forth in his doctrine explans knowing the beautiful. The imagination will play an important role, and the will or desire will predominate over the intellect. The mystical doctrine of Godmanhood can be synthesized with voluntarism by means of a phi-

---

[1] *The Destiny of Man*, 247.

[2] See Chapter I, Section B, Part 2 and Chapter III, Section F.

[3] When Berdyaev says Beauty is God's *idea* of the world, he is not referring to ideas as humans rationally have them. He is probably influenced by Schopenhauer's notion of divine Idea (See 140, n, above). He is describing the Divine Idea as Beauty.

losophy of beauty. And we will find in chapter IV, the same synthesis of intelligibility and irrationalism in the doctrine of knowledge.

D. SOME CONSEQUENCES OF THE DOCTRINE OF GODMANHOOD

(1) *Sobornost' – Unity of the World*

Sobornost' is a Russian word which cannot be translated into English. O. F. Clarke, who has translated many of Berdyaev's books, says:

> In Russian the adjective *soborny* corresponding to the noun, *sobornost,'* translates the word "Catholic" as applied to the Church in the Creed. As *sobernost'* and *soborny* have a wealth of meaning not found in any equivalent English words, I have used them where even the symphonic character of Catholic consciousness seems to be indicated.[1]

Sobornost' means symphonic character of Catholic consciousness, communion, alltogetherness of the people. It distinguishes the Russian communal outlook from the Western individualism. Berdyaev says:

> An individualist form of humanism could not be imported into Russia. Only a communal form of humanism is possible there, a form of *sobornost'*, to use a religious term.[2]

Sobornost' is a commonalty, and it is typically Russian. R. M. French, another translator of Berdyaev, says:

> "Altogetherness" would come near to its meaning. It is the dynamic life of the collective body.[3]

N. O. Lossky, a Russian contemporary of Berdyaev, an emigré, an eminent philosopher, and a good historian of philosophy, says in his *History of Russian Philosophy* (written in English):

> *Sobornost'* means the combination of freedom and unity of many persons on the basis of their common love for the same absolute values.[4]

Sobornost', we may say, is an altogetherness, a communal life, a religious communion, the combination of freedom and unity of many persons on the basis of their common love for the same absolute values. How does the theory come from the doctrine of Godmanhood? What is the use of the idea of *Sobornost'* in Berdyaev's philosophy of history?

---

[1] *Freedom and the Spirit*, xiv, note.
[2] N. Berdyaev, *Towards a New Epoch* (Bles, London, 1949), 67.
[3] *Slavery and Freedom*, title page.
[4] *A History of Russian Philosophy*, 41.

Sobornost', a doctrine of simplicity, and of altogetherness, characterizes Berdyaev's philosophy. It is an ethical norm according to his ethics; it is a condition of knowledge according to his noetic (and we will consider this in our chapter on epistemology). At present, we are merely seeking the philosophical foundation of the doctrine of *Sobornost'* and its place in philosophy of history.

The doctrine follows from the doctrine of Godmanhood. Berdyaev says, in *Spirit and Reality*:

> Spirit – the Holy Spirit – is incarnated in human life, but it assumes the form of a *whole humanity* rather than that of authority.[1]

Not only individual men but society – *"whole humanity"* – are incarnated Spirit. "A *whole humanity*, rather than that of authority," because, as we will see, it is a communion in love, a *Sobornost'*. This incarnation of spirit (ultimately, of the Holy Spirit), is not completed at the beginning of the world-process. Berdyaev says, in *Spirit and Reality:*

> Spirit is historically incarnated in hierarchical authority, in historical bodies, in authority whereas spirit is really incarnated in truth, in man's creative emancipation from slavery. The symbolical incarnation of spirit is merely a way determined by the fallen world, while the real incarnation of spirit is the goal, the supreme achievement.[2]

When Berdyaev says that Spirit is historically incarnated in historical bodies, he is referring to the fallen world; "historically incarnated" assumes the condition of fallen world. And just as spirit is incarnated in an individual man through the soul, so spirit is incarnated in history through the world-soul and through the historical memory of men. The organic doctrine of spirit is here extended to historical entities. Historical entities are created and preserved in the historical memory, and this process is a "symbolical incarnation of spirit."

The passage closes in stating the real incarnation of spirit (distinguished from the symbols of incarnation that are at hand) as a norm, a religious goal. Now, the basis of the doctrine of *Sobornost'* is making its appearance. The real incarnation of spirit is in truth; and truth, here, is the Divine Truth, Christ, the God-man; this is the real incarnation of spirit. Thus we can see that spirit provides a unity of the cosmos and of man and history, both in their fallen state and in their true and perfect state.

Sobornost' indicates the communion of all persons in history, both

---

[1] *Spirit and Reality*, 167.
[2] *Ibid.*, 64.

directly and through the medium of historical institutions and entities; it also means the communion of humanity with the cosmos. The notion of *Sobornost'* shows the unity of history. It gives significance to historical symbols. It lays down a norm, a perfect goal to be sought after. Berdyaev, in his last book, *Truth and Revelation*, speaks of *Sobornost'* as it will exist at the end of the world, when the world and mankind is returned to perfect integrity:

The era of the Spirit can be nothing but a revelation of a sense of community which is not merely social but also cosmic, not only a brotherhood of men, but a brotherhood of man with all cosmic life, with the whole creation.[1]

We will soon see why Berdyaev calls the final age "the era of the Spirit"; it is the adaptation and spiritualization of a terminology which has also been used by the proponents of the doctrine of "the Ages of the World" (such as Schelling and Slavic thinkers.)[2] The sense of community, the brotherhood of man with all creation, is *Sobornost'* taken in its most inclusive sense. And yet, it is a personal community, a communion, not an impersonal collectivism. The individual personality is preserved:

The significance of communion as a goal of human life is essentially religious. . . . This participation must take place in the very heart of the Ego's union with the Thou. The inter-penetration of the Ego and the Thou is consummated in God.[3]

The brotherhood of man with the cosmos and with all creation must therefore be understood in view of the fact that man is a microcosm; for it is by virtue of each individual man containing the whole creation in himself that this personal union of the Ego and the Thou is attained. Berdyaev says, in the same text:

. . . one Ego is accessible to another, to the Thou. As a corollary, the Ego also postulates the We, in whose depths the communion of the Ego and the Thou is achieved.[4]

How vividly the personalism of this philosophy comes to light when Berdyaev postulates the We, the *Sobornost'*, from the communion of an Ego and a Thou. Philosophy of history postulates a We, whether it is only symbolically realized in a stage of history, or truly realized beyond history. In the communal doctrine of the We, Berdyaev's anthro-

---

[1] *Truth and Revelation*, 149. Did Spinoza suggest this to Berdyaev? Who knows? At least the sentiment follows from Berdyaev's cosmogony.
[2] See Part 3 of this Section.
[3] *Solitude and Society*, 141.
[4] *Ibid.*, 140.

pocentrism is clearly seen to have replaced the cosmocentrism of his predecessors.[1]

Berdyaev says, in his last book:

That to which Khomyakov gave the name of *Sobornost'* and which is difficult to define in rational terms, is not an "objective" collective reality, it is an interior quality ... an existential subjectivity ...[2]

The doctrine of *Sobornost'* shows us that Berdyaev's philosophy of history neither sees a collectivism or blind cosmic togetherness at the root of history, nor posits it as the goal of history. The true altogetherness or communion is subjective, not impersonal. It is existential, not merely ideal. We will investigate, in the next chapter, how it is possible to have an existentialism which, properly speaking, refers only to the human subject. For the present, we will consider the cosmological aspect of this doctrine.

---

[1] Quite possibly the doctrine of the We is inspired by passages in Spengler's *Decline of the West*.

Spengler says, Vol. II, 295, note 1: "That '*All*' *are responsible for* 'all' – the 'it' for the 'it' in this boundlessly extended plain – is the metaphysical fundament of all Dostoyevski's creation. ... Mystical Russian love is love of the plain, the love of brothers under equal pressure all along the earth, ever along and along; the love of the poor tortured beasts that wander on it, the love of plants – never of birds and clouds and stars."

And, as if to inspire Berdyaev, if he read it, Spengler concludes the note saying: "What sort of a Christianity will come forth one day from this world-feeling?" (of the Russians).

Spengler's use of the word, *we*, occurs in a discussion of the spiritualism of a school of thought which he terms *Magian*. He says, 234–235:

"But still more important than all this is the opposition of Spirit and Soul (Hebrew *Ruach* and *nephesh*, Persian *ahu* and *urvan*, Mandaean *monuhmed* and *gyan*, Greek *pneuma* and *psyche*) ... Philo ... Plotinus, Gnostics .. Islam and the Kabbalah.

"But souls are at bottom discrete entities, whereas the Pneuma is one and ever the same. The man *possesses* a soul, but he only participates in the spirit of the Light and the Good; the divine descends into him, thus binding all the individuals of the Below together with the one in the Above. This primary feeling, which dominates the beliefs and opinions of all Magian men, is something perfectly singular, and not only characterizes their world-view, but marks off the essence and kernel of their religiousness in all its forms from that of every other kind of man. ...

"Whereas the Faustian (i.e. Western, Latin) man is an 'I' that in the last resort draws its own conclusions about the Infinite; whereas the ... Magian man, with his spiritual kind of being is only a *part of a pneumatic* '*We*' that, descending from above, is one and the same in all believers."

I am certain Berdyaev has studied *The Decline of the West*. The work has an index. The reader can find many subjects that would fascinate Berdyaev. Joachim of Flora, for example, is much revered by Spengler (see index: "Joachim of Flora.") Both Spengler and Berdyaev are philosophers of history; both owe a tremendous debt to German Idealism. Berdyaev is vitally interested in much of the subject matter of the book. Berdyaev may well have taken his notion of the We from Spengler. He mentions Spengler in his last work, *Truth and Revelation*, 148: "I use the words 'culture' and 'civilization' in a sense which is closely akin to the meaning that Spengler attaches to them."

[2] *Truth and Revelation*, 39–46.

(2) *Cosmology and the Unity of the World*

We just saw that the *Sobornost'* of mankind which Berdyaev seeks is also "brotherhood of man with all cosmic life, with the whole creation." Indeed, Berdyaev's philosophy of history requires a very definite cosmic consciousness. The reason for an emphasis upon cosmology is found in his doctrine of Godmanhood. He asserts the return of the Cosmos to a unity within man and the return of man to a unity within God. The doctrine is one of the main themes of his philosophy of history.

This doctrine of cosmology interests us because Berdyaev himself makes a point of stressing a cosmic consciousness. We want to see the place of cosmology in his philosophy of history.

He says, in *Freedom and the Spirit:*

> We must return in some entirely new way to a sense of the cosmos. The task of Christian gnosis is to establish an ideal balance between theosophy, cosmosophy, and anthroposophy. For mysticism, occultism, and religion do exist side by side in human consciousness. Mysticism is immediate communion with God, the contemplation of God and union with Him. Occultism is union with the secret forces of the cosmos and it is also cosmic development. Religion is the attitude of man towards God in an organized form, it is the hierarchical and normative method of communion with Him. Boehme ... knew how to unite in himself the mystical, occult, and religious moments; thus his gnosis, in spite of certain errors, is nearest to a true Christian gnosis.[1]

Berdyaev means that we need a doctrine of the cosmos, comparable in importance to that of the scholastics, a doctrine which finds the temporal unity and order of the cosmos and its significance in the philosophical and religious world outlook. And this is why Berdyaev's cosmology is one of the principles of his philosophy of history; fot it is a necessary condition of a universal history.

A Christian gnosis (a body of philosophical and religious knowledge), should contain theosophical, cosmosophical and anthroposophical elements. Theosophy, for Berdyaev, pertains to the mystical knowledge of divine things.[2] Cosmosophy refers to an occult knowledge of the secret forces of the cosmos.[3] And anthroposophy refers to the pre-eminence of man in the universe and to organized Christian religion.[4] Boehme is

---

[1] *Freedom and the Spirit*, 301–302.

[2] Cf. *Ibid.*, Chapter Eight: "Theosophy and Gnosis."

[3] Cf. *Ibid.*, 271: "cosmosophy ... deals with ... the composition and development of the cosmos."

[4] Berdyaev uses the term, *anthroposophy*, to add the distinguishing mark that shows the advance of his philosophy beyond that of the Russian Sophiologists. He says: "...today, the main religious problem is that of man, not of *Sophia* or the cosmos. Sophiology must be linked to the problem of anthropology. ... Russian sophiology seems to deny that man is at the center of the world and that the cosmos is in him ..." *Ibid.*, 271.

praised for combining the three elements of a Christian gnosis. Berdyaev combines than also.

Why is he so interested in cosmology and cosmogony and their relations to philosophy of history? Why does he say that "the main theme of universal history ... is that of man's destiny seen in the light of the interaction between the human spirit and nature?" [1] Why does he define the ages of the world in terms of man and the cosmos? [2]

Berdyaev's approach to his philosophical problems gives rise to these questions. It is a way of viewing the problems which he has found in his predecessor, Vladimir Solovyev.[3] It is an approach which characterizes such German predecessors of Russian philosophy as Schelling and Hegel.[4] This cosmogonical and cosmological way of defining the philosophic attitude is one of the genera of philosophic positions. One of the most outstanding examples is the theology of John Scotus Erigena (9th century). Indeed, the similarities between his doctrine and Berdyaev's are numerous and far-reaching.[5]

---

[1] *The Meaning of History*, 112, quoted in Chapter I, Section B, Part 4.

[2] Cf. Chapter I, Section B, Part 5.

[3] Cf. V. Solovyev, *Lectures on Godmanhood*, 192, ff; Cf. present chapter, Section C.

[4] Cf. F. W. J. Schelling, *The Ages of the World*, tr. F. Bolman, Jr. (Columbia Univ., New York, 1942); G. W. F. Hegel, *The Phenomenology of Mind* (Allen & Unwin, London, 1949), "Reason," 271–453; *The Logic of Hegel*, tr. from *The Encyclopaedia of the Philosophical Sciences* by W. Wallace (Oxford Univ., Oxford, 1950), 70–71.

[5] The following doctrines, which Berdyaev also holds, have been asserted by Scotus Erigena:

1. The meaning of the world is above and beyond being. De Divisione Naturae, in J. Migne, *Patrologia Latina* (Paris, 1853), Vol. CXXII, Col. 443B. ("*Patrologia Latina*, Vol. CXXII," will subsequently be indicated as: "*P.L.*"). *The Beginning and the End*, 98.

2. Essences are not supreme, but God is above essential intelligibility; consequently, a negative or apophatic theology, is preferred to an affirmative, or catophatic theology. *P.L.*, 458A. Both philosophers take pains to show that the Aristotelian categories must not be applied to God. *P.L.*, 469A, *Liber Primus in passim*. *The Beginning and the End*, 102–103.

3. There is a true revelation of God in the hierarchy of creation; to grasp the revelation contained in created beings is to ascend to God. *P.L.* 449C. *Truth and Revelation* 143, ff.

4. The doctrine of the Trinity is not merely a mysterious truth of revelation relating to the nature of the Deity, but a fundamental fact in the organization of the universe. *P.L.* 456. *The Meaning of History*, 58–59.

5. The act of knowledge is an act of creation; to understand is to create. *P.L.* 579D. *The Beginning and the End*, 38.

6. Man is the microcosm in the strictest sense of the word. He is the summary of all existence. *P.L.* 530. *Dream and Reality*, X–XI.

7. The whole of man is made in the image of God. *P.L.* 790D. *The Realm of the Spirit and the Realm of Caesar*, 170.

8. Both thinkers give a mystical interpretation of the Fall. Everything is spiritualized. Paradise is human nature in its first state, not a place but a state. (Much like Berdyaev's doctrine of Godmanhood.) *P.L.* 822A. See 49, n6; 51, m4 above.

9. Evil cannot be perpetual, but must come to an end, altogether abolished (*et omnino abolebitur*). *P.L.* 918. *Truth and Revelation*, 136.

Berdyaev differs from Erigena where voluntarism occurs. N. Lossky, in his *History of Russian Philosophy*, says: "Berdyaev is wrong in thinking that his *Ungrund* is identical

Note, however, that I do not distinguish this doctrinal position by first principles which are peculiar to it. I simply find that these doctrines all have the peculiarity of making an outstanding study of the place of cosmogony and an attendant cosmology in human wisdom.

with the 'Divine Nothing' of Dionysius the Areopagite. The Divine Nothing in every respect transcends all possible determinations ..." 148.

Creation is out of nothing for Erigena, which is to say, it is out of God's ineffable self. (P.L. 634B) But Berdyaev asserts that the *Ungrund* is the divine Nothingness. Hence, God is born from the irrational *Ungrund,* and He creates out of the *Ungrund. The Beginning and the End,* 105–106.

The problem of evil is therefore viewed differently. Erigena says, like Berdyaev, that evil is caused by an irrational will. (P.L. 975), but that there is no origin of evil. P.L. 976; 944. Berdyaev, however, says that the irrational *Ungrund* is the origin of evil. *The Divine and the Human,* 90–91.

If we compare Berdyaev with Erigena, it helps to answer the question: How much is Berdyaev's philosophy affected by his voluntarism?

Berdyaev shares many principles with Erigena. Yet, the addition of voluntarism causes Berdyaev to bring the irrational ineffability, which Erigena found in God, down into the creation, from the lowest to the highest level. The ultimate metaphysical principle in any created object is irrational; it is a Heraclitean becoming, a flux. Berdyaev says, of the irrational ineffability, on the highest level: "Parmenides ... conceived the deepest ... reality ... as something that was unique and immobile. But Heraclitus ... conceived it as fiery movement." *The Meaning of History,* 49. Berdyaev, like Boehme, identifies the Heraclitean "fiery movement," or "becoming," with the irrational *Ungrund.*

Berdyaev calls the reader's attention to the similarity of Heraclitus' doctrine and that of his and Boehme. He says, in *Spirit and Reality:* "Boehme stands out as the first voluntarist in European thought ... In the dark void, anterior to being, freedom is kindled. Boehme's vision discloses being and dynamic depths of being, much vaster probably, than being itself. There is an affinity between Boehme and Heraclitus. ... Boehme's vision is dynamic ..." *Spirit and Reality,* 130.

In the definitive (and posthumous) work on his metaphysics, *The Beginning and the End,* Berdyaev writes of the irrational ineffability, on the lowest level: "What is the source of movement and change? Is it potency or act? Pure act is unmoved and unchanged, for it is a completed condition, whereas movement and change indicate incompleteness ..."

"... it is possible to adopt a point of view which differs in principle from the Aristotelean and scholastic position ... there is more in potency than in act, more in movement than in immovability and there are greater spiritual riches in freedom than in being." *The Beginning and the End,* 157.

Along with the voluntarism, the meaning of history is found in the mystical doctrine of Godmanhood. True, the doctrine of voluntarism is added in order to account for the presence of change, tragedy and evil, and to explain the freedom of man. Yet – and this is important – the meaning of history, the meta-historical meaning of history, is intelligible; and, at the end, it completely illuminates the irrational *Ungrund.* History consists in the illumination, and philosophy of history shows what the illumination is and how it occurs. It is in this part of Berdyaev's philosophy, above all, that the doctrine of Godmanhood is stressed. And if the voluntarism were taken away, a philosophy of history would still remain. Berdyaev's voluntarism dominates the picture when he discusses the problems of evil, love, ethics, freedom, being and existence, potency and act; but Godmanhood rules in his philosophy of history. And Godmanhood therefore rules in all his philosophy, since all his philosophy is guided by philosophy of history. Christ, the source of intelligibility, is the meaning of history.

Berdyaev points out that the doctrine of *Ungrund* is figurative rather than literal. "Free will in God is the *Ungrund* in God, the nothingness in him." *The Beginning and the End,* 108–109. The *Ungrund* is really identical with God. Berdyaev takes Boehme's distinction between God and Ungrund only in a symbolic sense. He means that if he is to understand in any way whatever how will is primary in God and in man, than the theogonic myth is very helpful.

Such a study is placed at the service of philosophy of history in Berdyaev's doctrine.

In Chapter III we will find Berdyaev asserts that man in his true depths is at the center of the world and the cosmos is in him.[1] And the world, the cosmos (which has fallen away from man as well as from God) is properly in Man. The Divine Principle, from which the world has fallen, is Integral Man. Indeed, Berdyaev says, in the chapter quoted from above:

> The cosmos can only be conceived as a living organism. We must be able to see the spirit in nature and nature in the spirit, the objective in the subjective, the natural in the spiritual, and the cosmic in the anthropological. Cosmology has always been based on the inner identity of spirit and nature, that is to say, on a conception of nature which regards it as a spiritual phenomenon.[2]

The key of Berdyaev's cosmology is the inner identity of spirit and nature. Nature is a spiritual phenomenon. The cosmos is natural because it has fallen; nevertheless, it is spiritual because it originates in man (and ultimately in Godman), who is spiritual. It is spiritual, also, because its spiritualization is being prepared for in the progress of mankind.[3] This is the cosmological outlook that Berdyaev is attempting to teach. He says in an earlier chapter:

> The world is an organic hierarchy in which every part is linked to another and in which everything that takes place in the upper regions affects the lower. The separation from God of one part involved the separation of the whole soul of the world with it, including all humanity and indeed all creation. ... Man, together with all creation and the whole hierarchy of the universe, became separated from God ...[4]

The separation of the highest part of the world, man, from God involved the separation of the soul of the world and of the whole of creation from God. The notion of a world-soul is not stressed or elaborated in Berdyaev's doctrine. The above is the only assertion of it I have found. Berdyaev refers to the organic unity of the world, especially as it is unified in man at the beginning and the end of history. World-soul should not be considered apart from the human soul. This interpretation does not betray Berdyaev.[5]

We see the cosmological and cosmosophical aspects of Berdyaev's doctrine of time. When he says, "everything that takes place in the

---

[1] Chapter III, Section F.
[2] *Freedom and the Spirit*, 299–300.
[3] See Chapter III, especially Section F.
[4] *Freedom and the Spirit*, 162.
[5] See Chapter I, 12, where we find mention of a soul of history.

upper regions also affects the lower," he means that celestial history, which is spiritual, affects terrestrial history; because terrestrial history is an epoch within celestial history.

Cosmic consciousness in Berdyaev is an attitude which does not see visible nature and the visible world except in relation to the higher reality. He says, in the same work:

> The problem that disturbs me may be expressed in the following manner, in the terms which I have adopted; how can the natural world be transfigured and brought into the spiritual world as something real and not illusory? How can the "psychical" be related to the spiritual? ... Man, the cosmos, and the divine creation are not merely for time but also for eternity. The deification of creation does not mean any loss in its significance, still less its extinction. Man and the world are not annihilated in God, but illuminated and transfigured.[1]

In the line, "how can the 'psychical' be related to the spiritual?" when Berdyaev says, "psychical," he has in mind the trasfiguration of the soul of man by the spirit; and this brings about the transfiguration of the cosmos. The deification of man will involve the deification of the cosmos, its return to unity with man, and the return of mankind to unity with the Godman.[2] The relation of the psychical to the spiritual is one where the psychical in all its distinct multiplicity preserves its identity in transfiguration. The Godman principle is a spiritual terminus where all the individuals of creation will maintain their being and identity when united with Godmanhood.

We can see the significance of Berdyaev's rejection of the Greek cycle theory of histories in favor of the Augustinian doctrine of a single and unique Universal History.[3] In accordance with his cosmic theory, Berdyaev prophesies deification of the whole creation in its absolute integrity and identity; that is, in its truth. If a Christian philosopher brings the doctrine of a single universal history into prominence, the doctrine of historical cycles is of secondary importance.[4] It is possible to draw historical rules from the recurrence of certain historical patterns over a greath length of time. But if Berdyaev explained history this way, the unity of his universal history would become very mysterious. Indeed, it is just the unity of celestial history with temporal history (universal history) that Berdyaev is seeking to illuminate. He preserves the *unity* of celestial and temporal history by forbidding the

[1] *Freedom and the Spirit*, 264–265.
[2] See Chapter III, Section F.
[3] See *The Meaning of History*, 113–115.
[4] See Chapter III, Section F.

intelligibility of history to be explained and dismissed [he thinks] by rules of eternal cyclical recurrences. He acknowledges cycles of recurrences in history, but he is not interested in this part of philosophy of history.[1] He emphasizes the overall psychic and spiritual unity of history – in the human and divine spirit.[2] The unity presupposes the termination of history and final transfiguration.

And though he seems to take the historical culture as the unit of history, it is not a numerical unit, identical with other units, but primarily a step in the progress of universal history. Berdyaev does not ever abstract from the image of a culture in order to examine its intelligibility. History, with its concrete cultures, is seen in the light of cosmic doctrine which (along with anthropological and theosophical doctrine) shows the integrity of history within the unity of Godmanhood. "History has a meaning simply because meaning, the Logos, appeared in it; the God-man became incarnate, and it has meaning because it is moving towards the realm of Godmanhood."[3]

The main observation that we have made is to see the positive purpose of cosmology, rather than to view the attempt of Berdyaev's anthropocentrism to escape the slavery of the cosmos. He says in a late work, *Slavery and Freedom*:

Behind the call of the "natural," of the "organic," there lies hidden the need to get free from the disuniting multiplicity of the world of civilization, and to pass over to the completeness and unity of the divine life. Man feels himself crushed by this intolerable multiplicity, disintegration, and relativeness and conventionality of the civilized world.[4]

Berdyaev wants to bring a doctrine of organic unity into his philosophy of history, so that history and the activities of man can be understood as parts of a divine unity. He therefore recognizes the legitimacy of the call of the organic cosmos, a call which is answered in historical cultures and in the one culture of universal history. And Berdyaev sees a relativity, an "intolerable multiplicity," in the modern historical outlook which views history and civilization without the illumination of a cosmology.

Berdyaev, in the same work, relates this personalist philosophy to his view of the world.

---

[1] Berdyaev acknowledges cycles of recurrences of history, "a periodical return of similar stages." *The Meaning of History*, 179. But he mentions this only in passing. Such a doctrine is rational, abstract and scientific and therefore does not interest Berdyaev as something to be studied in itself.

[2] See Chapter III, Section F.

[3] *The Beginning and the End*, 115.

[4] *Slavery and Freedom*, 119.

There is no hierarchical unity of the cosmos, in relation to which personality would be a part. . . . That the world is partial, that the world as a whole and a unity does not exist, is entirely in accord with the revolution in contemporary physics. A whole, and a unity, can be sought only in spirit which is not alienated from itself and not objectivized. But in that case the whole and the unity acquire a different meaning, and do not imply the suppression of the "partial," the multiple, the personal.[1]

Berdyaev states again the doctrine of a living and organic principle which provides a unity. He opposes the mechanical outlook. It has argued from the assumed isolation of natural events to the isolation of historical events and entities. He asserts a principle of unity which is above and beyond the cosmic. It is the spirit, where not only the multiple is organically preserved, but also the personal. This personalist doctrine is investigated in the next chapter. Before turning to the personalism, however, let us attempt to find out why it is that Berdyaev's philosophy so vitally concerns itself with the Second Coming of the Messiah. Does his messianic doctrine order and divinize the anthropocentric cast of his philosophy?

(3) Eschatology and the Age of the Spirit

Berdyaev's mysticism, which is based on the Godman doctrine, is necessarily eschatological or messianic: it looks forward to the Second Coming of the Messiah and to the end of the world, and the New Jerusalem. In nearly all Berdyaev's books, messianism is very important. In *The Meaning of History* (1923), messianism and eschatology occur at the beginning of the book in the definition of philosophy of history, and at the end of the book. In *The Destiny of Man* (1931), he entitles Part III, the last division of the book: "Of the Last Things, Eschatological Ethics." He turns, in the final pages of *Spirit and Reality* (1937), to the theme of the Second Coming. In *Slavery and Freedom*, he closes with a section entitled "Active-Creative Eschatology." *The Beginning and the End* has the subtitle in the Russian edition: "An Essay in Eschatological Metaphysics." In his spiritual autobiography, *Dream and Reality* (1950), he devotes some pages (294, ff) to eschatology and says that Russian thought has always been preoccupied with the problems of philosophy of history and with eschatology.

History has meaning because it comes to an end. . . . the historical process ought to be understood in the light of the end. The philosopher of history, therefore, speaks as a prophet . . .[2]

[1] *Ibid.*, 98.
[2] *Dream and Reality*, 294.

The Realm of Spirit and the Realm of Caesar (1952), closes with a page which expounds his own kind of mysticism:

... prophetic and messianic mysticism; that is, super-historical and eschatological ...

In his last book, *Truth and Revelation* (1953), he devotes the last chapter to describing the age of the Spirit and the Eternal Man. It will occur after the Second Coming and the End of the World. He never tires of reminding the reader of his books that his is a "prophetic philosophy of history," an "eschatological metaphysics," "philosophy of the end of history," etc.

Berdyaev's philosophy looks to the future because the future is given in universal history. Since the goal will be realized in the future, Berdyaev treats it, not as a transcendent and ever-present norm, but as a future event.

Further, his metaphysics rules philosophy of history through the doctrine of Godmanhood. Metaphysics is eschatological.

Eschatology, in Berdyaev, is a practico-theoretical norm (which he teaches because of his religious principles).[1] He is himself absolutely preoccupied with the messianic expectations.

Eschatology, for him, is a description and also an ethical norm. It describes a kind of progress towards the end of history which develops through historical epochs. This progress is itself an eschatology; it is bringing history towards the Second Coming and the end of history. And this is also the object of the philosophy of history. Berdyaev says, in *The Beginning and the End*:

The end of history is not only a truth of religious revelation but also a moral postulate of existential philosophy. That is why it is so important to grasp the fact that the objective world does not exist as a whole, as a cosmos; it is partial. The cosmos is a regulative idea. The cosmos is still to be created; it will make its appearance as a result of the transformation of the world.[2]

Berdyaev shows, in this passage, the interdependence of his doctrines of cosmology and messianism. The return of the Messiah and the end of the world is the attainment of perfect integrity of man and the cosmos. He says in the above-quoted passage:

... the objective world does not exist as a whole, as a cosmos; it is partial. The cosmos is a regulative idea.

[1] Cf. *The Destiny of Man*, Part III: ' Eschatological Ethics."
[2] *The Beginning and the End*, 148.

The world is objectified, bound in natural laws (it is the world discovered by Isaac Newton).[1] because it has fallen, with man, from cosmic integrity in man. The cosmos is a regulative idea; that is, a norm, a goal, because the true cosmos will be in the Godman. The cosmos is to be created (created, because this philosophy asserts the creativity of man, the microcosm, and the primacy of beauty which is the object of human creativity). Finally, the true cosmos will appear as a result of the transfiguration of the world. For, unlike man, who gradually escapes from objectivization during the course of history, the visible world of space and time is transformed into the true cosmos only at the end of time.

Berdyaev says, later, in the same book:

A genuine act of love is eschatological, it makes an end of this world, this world of hatred and enmity, and the beginning of a new world.[2]

This expresses not merely a conclusion from the cosmological doctrine but also a persistent attitude of Berdyaev. It is part of his eschatological preoccupation. Every good or beautiful act or event takes the world towards the end of the world; therefore, every such act or event is eschatological.

But when we read this passage, we can find a difficult and momentous problem; namely, what sort of a beginning does the future world of Integral Man, which is beyond history, have in the fallen world? It is a momentous problem because Berdyaev's Slavic and German predecessors and his Slavic contemporaries have indulged in a nationalistic futurism of earthly paradise.[3]

He approaches the problem of futurism in *The Meaning of History*, via the notion of time. He says:

---

[1] The Newtonian world-outlook is presented in Kant's *Critique of Pure Reason*, and Berdyaev, without mentioning Newton, accepts this view of the natural world. *Immanuel Kant's Critique of Pure Reason*, tr. N. K. Smith (MacMillan, London, 1950). See Chapter IV, Section B, notes.

[2] *The Beginning and the End*, 184.

[3] On eartly paradise see 81, ff., below. D. Merejkowski, the Russian novelist writes in his book, *The Menace of the Mob* (Nicholas L. Brown, New York, 1921), 105: "In this land of ours, rather than in any other, will the Glorious Resurrection of Christ be celebrated. Is that a dream? But why does this dream come to no one else but the Russian?" See also 83, 84. On 47, Merejkowski describes the three Joachite Dispensations. See also Merejowski's *Peter and Alexis* (Modern Library, New York, 1931), 582. "there shall be a new Church of Joann." *Ibid.*, 58, "... the third Rome ..." (Moscow).

Concerning the significance of this outlook to the Slavic consciousness, see: F. Baldensperger, *Mélanges d'Histoire Littéraire Générale et Comparée offerts à Fernand Baldensperger* (Librairie Ancienne Honoré Champion, Paris, 1930), Vol. II, 365–366. "*C'est dans cette réalization de la troisième époque que la part de la race élane – et, parmi les nations slavic, celle de la Pologne – doit avoir, selon Cjeszkoski, une importance toute spéciale. La tendence messianiste apparait ici avec netteté ...*".

The fundamental weakness of the idea of progress lies in its attitude to the insoluble problem of time. The only possible solution of universal history and its anti-thesis is in terms of a victory over time ... The theory of progress is not concerned with the solution of human destiny and history in timeless eternity, beyond the limits of history itself. It is concerned solely with a solution within the time torrent of history ...[1]

Berdyaev rejects futurism if it means everlasting progress in time, because the goal of history is beyond time.[2] The theory of everlasting progress is historical, instead of meta-historical. Berdyaev, however, is faced with the problem of the link between history and the end of history; how will the transition occur, gradually or suddenly? He discusses the link between time and eternity in a late book, and says:

... the process which goes on in the world is inwardly linked with the process which goes on in God, in eternity not in time ...[3]

This indicates the answer. If the world process is linked with the process which goes on in God, but in eternity, not in time, then the age of the Spirit cannot occur in the world epoch. Societies, cultures and civilizations belong to the historical, not to the meta-historical. A future age of history – a splendid new civilization – could not be the age of the Spirit nor the beginning of the age.[4]

But the question: what kind of an earthly beginning of the age of the Spirit will there be? has not been answered. For, though the link between our epoch and the future (and eternal) epoch of the Spirit is in eternity and not in time; yet, time may conceivably become saturated, as it were, with the eternal, and thus provide the beginning. To see Berdyaev's answer, we must study his philosophy of revelation.

He says, in a chapter of *The Divine and the Human*, entitled, "Religion of the Spirit":

The Eastern doctors of the Church were of great importance in their contribution to the interpretation of Christianity as the reign of the Spirit, especially Origen and St. Gregory of Nyssa ... Further, the religious movement in Italy at the end of the twelfth and the beginning of the thirteenth centuries, which was a quest for the Christianity of the Holy Spirit, is of enormous importance. Its central figures were St. Francis of Assisi ... Joachim of Flora ... ... The German mystical movement ... Eckhardt, Tauler ... Jacob Boehme and later Angelus Selesius ...

---

[1] *The Meaning of History*, 190.
[2] See Chapter I, Section E.
[3] *The Divine and the Human*, 47.
[4] See Chapter I, Section E. Berdyaev has developed a theory of three times: cosmic, historical and existential time. He leaves no chance that the reader or himself will mistake God's "time" for historical time. Reality (the past, the present and the future), has been disrupted and shattered into pieces by fallen time. And fallen time itself is distinguished into cosmic time and historical time.

German idealistic metaphysics of the beginning of the nineteenth century, also constituted a most outstanding event in the history of the European spirit ... German mysticism, as a whole, however, inclines to be hostile to eschatological thought. It was in Russia that eschatological aspiration, with its expectation of a new epoch of the Spirit, and belief in the possibility of a crowning revelation, was most forcibly expressed. ... Dostoyevsky, Vladimir Solovyev ... [1]

This is a good summary of the history of the doctrine of the Church of the Holy Spirit, as Berdyaev understands it. He finds the origin of the doctrine in the Eastern, Greek Fathers of the Church. Then he mentions Joachim of Flora who lived just before 1200. The movement that took place "is of immense importance," he says. He singles out this 12th century movement above all the others in importance, though he does not give an explanation here or elsewhere of the doctrine of Joachim.

He seems to be justified in singling out the age of Joachim of Flora, because the modern notion of the ages of the world (which are consummated in the age of the Spirit) was first set forth by Joachim. Joachim was an Italian monk and an exegete of Sacred Scriptures. [2]

He asserted three great dispensations,[3] three ages of the world, respectively associated with the Father, the Son and the Holy Ghost The first age reaches from Adam to Christ. The second age (overlapping

---

[1] *The Divine and the Human*, 186–188.

[2] The work of Joachim which develops his doctrine of the ages of the world is not available to me. H. Bett presents the theory in *Joachim of Flora* (Methuen, London, 1931), 44–46. Bett refers to the *Concordia novi ac veteris* of Joachim, printed at Venice in 1519. "This appears to be the only edition in existence ... The excessive scarcity of copies makes it difficult for a student to have access to the volume ..." *Ibid.*, 26.

Bett says: "... the three great dispensations which are respectively identified with God the Father, God the Son, and God the Holy Spirit. The first age reaches from Adam to Christ ... age of those who marry and give in marriage. The second age reaches from Uzziah, fructified from Zacharias to the forty-second generation following, and consummated, therefore, in the year 1260. During this age men live a mixed life, between the flesh and the spirit; it is the age of clerics. The third age reaches from St. Benedict to the end of the world. It is initiated in St. Benedict, and fructified from the twenty-second generation after St. Benedict, i.e., about 1200, to the end of the dispensation. During this age men live a spiritual life; it is the age of monks. The three ages therefore overlap. The age of the Son begins to appear in the age of the Father, and reaches on into Joachim's own lifetime. The age of the Spirit begins to appear in the age of the Son, some centuries before Joachim's time, and reaches on to the end of the world. ... The three ages therefore represent a spiritual progress. Truth is revealed dimly in the first age of the Old Covenant, more clearly in the second age of the New Covenant, and fully and finally in the last age, the dispensation of the Spirit." 44–46.

"Thus Joachim has really one theme in all his books. It is the thought of the three dispensations – the progress of revelation through an age of God the Father, an age of God the Son, and a final age of God the Spirit." *Ibid.*, 48.

"... Joachim's general doctrine came to be known later as *the Eternal Gospel*. ... he does expressly say that this everlasting gospel is the gospel of the Holy Spirit. And he speaks of the gospel of Christ as transitory and temporal, but of the spiritual significance of it as eternal." (my italics)

"Again, Peter, Paul, and John represent the Father, the Son and the Spirit, and also the three ages ..." *Ibid.*, 38.

[3] See preceding note.

with the first and the third) reaches from Uziah to the year 1260. The third age, the age of the Spirit, reaches from St. Benedict to the end of the world. The three ages represent a spiritual progress, a progress of revelation. There is a gospel of the Holy Spirit which is finally revealed in the age of the Spirit, and the gospel of Christ is only transitory and temporal. Joachim's doctrine came to be known as the "Eternal Gospel."

Berdyaev, in the above quotation, says the German idealistic metaphysics was a "most outstanding event" in the history of philosophy of the spirit. There has been, we may remind ourselves, a whole tradition of philosophy of the Spirit in German Idealism. Berdyaev's philosophy of revelation is akin to that of the German Idealists. The influence of the German philosophers upon Berdyaev has probably been both direct and indirect. His Russian predecessors were strongly influenced by the German Idealists, particularly by Schelling.[1] I am not concerned to establish the exact sources of the parts of Berdyaev's philosophy of revelation. Berdyaev displays a tremendous philosophical erudition, and particularly in 19th-century German thought. The exact sources of his doctrine probably could never be determined, even by himself. But we can note some similarities between his theory and that of Schelling. We may observe the way in which Berdyaev participates in a doctrinal complex or current of thought which has been in existence at least since the time of Schelling. Schelling wrote a late work entitled *Philosophy of Revelation*,[2] and other German philosophers, especially Hegel, approached Christian Revelation in the same philosophical way.[3] This current of thought is affiliated with a certain religious outlook, an outlook which is interested in the Church of the Spirit. It considers Divine Revelation to be unfinished, and revelation of Christ is to be followed by a revelation of the Spirit which is to occur in the Church of the Spirit.

Schelling followed the general scheme first set forth by Joachim of

---

[1] Berdyaev states, in *The Russian Idea*, 72, that Hegel's philosophy was of immense importance in Russis. See Chapter III, notes. See Lossky's *History of Russian philosophy*, 13' 23, 51, 53.

[2] Cf. F. W. J. Schelling, *Sämmtliche Werke* (Stuttgart and Augsburg, 1856 seq.), II, Vol. 3 and 4.

[3] Indeed Hegel's *Philosophy of History* attests that other philosophers or theologians are familiar with the Joachite doctrine of the ages of the world. Cf. G. W. F. Hegel, *The Philosophy of History* (The Colonial Press, New York, 1900), Part IV. "The German World – The Principle of Spiritual Freedom," 345. "We may distinguish these periods and Kingdoms of the Father, the Son and the Spirit. The Kingdom of the Father . . . . The Kingdom of the Son is the manifestation of God merely in a *relation* to secular existence – shining upon it as upon an alien object. The Kingdom of the Spirit is the harmonizing of the antithesis."

Hegel adds, in a footnote: "The conception of a mystical *regnum Patris, regnum Filii* and *regnum Spiritus Sancti* is perfectly familiar to metaphysical theologians . . ."

Flora and wrote an important work entitled *The Ages of the World*. He proposed to present a philosophy of revelation divided into three parts concerning the age of the Father, the age of the Son, and the age of the Spirit.[1] The Apostles, Peter, Paul and John represent, as in Joachim, the three ages, and the third age is known as the Joannine age, or the age of the Joannine Church.[2]

Berdyaev, however, has criticized Schelling (and Fichte and Hegel) for not being Christian enough in their philosophy. Schelling,[3] I find, asserts an overlapping of the three ages. For Schelling, a large-scale beginning of the age of the Spirit occurs in human history; he looks forward to an earthly Church of the Spirit, to be devoted to St. John (a

---

[1] See 71, note 4.

[2] See next note. See also K. Löwith, *Meaning in History* (Univ. Chicago, Chicago, 1949), Appendix I.

[3] *Dream and Reality*, 94. Indeed, Schelling's theogony, cosmogony and phlilosophy of revelation are ordered by a doctrine of three potencies in God; he constantly refers to the three potencies in *The Ages of the World* and in his *Philosophy of Revelation*, and the three potencies replace, to a large extent, the Trinitarian doctrine of Christianity.

The ages of the world, in Schelling's view, are adapted to his cosmology. He devises a number of three-fold divisions of reality (Cf. Translator's Introduction, *The Ages of the World*), but, in *The Ages of the World*, he has the Joachite division of Father, Son and Spirit in mind. This division seems to be associated in his mind with three cosmological ages of time; namely pre-temporal eternity; the present time of creation; and the future eternity to be attained. They are non-continuous with each other, and their relation is supra-historical, because between the ages an act of freedom intervenes. Cf. Translator's Introduction, *The Ages of the World*, 58, also 75.

The age of the Father, Schelling seems to believe, merges in time and in eternity with the pre-temporal eternity; and the age of the Son is identical with history as it has been since the time of the Incarnation. The age of the Spirit merges with the future eternity to be attained; that is, the age of the Spirit is to begin sooner or later (*früher oder später*). See following passage.

He says: "*Hätte ich in unserer Zeit eine Kirche zu bauen, ich würde sie dem heil. Johannes widmen. Aber, früher oder später wird eine gebaut werden, die die drei Apostelfürsten vereinigt, da die letzte Potenz die frühere nicht aufhebt oder ausschlieszt, sonder sie verklärend in sich aufnimmt. Diese würde dann das wahre Pantheon der Christlichen Kirchen-geschichte sehn.*" *Sämmtliche Werke*, II, 4, 332.

This passage follows a statement of Schelling of the threefold dispensation of Christianity: that of Peter, that of Paul and that of John. It indicates that Schelling's position is this: the age of the Spirit will begin in historical time; for Schelling says that if "he were to found a Church in our time, he would dedicate it to St. John. But sooner or later one will be built ... Then the true Pantheon of the history of the Christian Church will be seen."

Karl Löwith, in his *Meaning in History*, Appendix I, refers to Schelling's philosophy of history. His words confirm the above-mentioned finding. He shows that Schelling's age of the Spirit has an earthly beginning. He says, 209–210:

"The most profound and original attempt to establish the reign of the spirit philosophically is that of Schelling, in the thirty-sixth lecture of his *Philosophy of Revelation*. Schelling, like Joachim, refers to St. Paul (I Cor. 13: 8, ff.) and to St. John as the apostles of the future, in order to justify his elaboration of a spiritual religion of the human race; 'for only thus can Christianity remain the religion of the Germans after the Reformation.' ... Schelling's thesis was, that the work of Christ could only lay foundations but could not survive in its contemporary settings. ... in place of himself Christ proclaims the Spirit which is independent of the ecstatic gifts of the apostolic age."

Joannine Church.) [1] Berdyaev criticizes this outlook, along with the philosophical approach of German mysticism, in the passage from *The Divine and the Human*, quoted above, when he says:

German mysticism, as a whole inclines to be hostile to eschatological thought, It was in Russia that eschatological aspiration, with its expectation of a new epoch of the Spirit, and belief in the possibility of a crowning revelation, was most forcibly expressed.

Yet, Berdyaev participates in the Joachite tradition of philosophy of revelation so far as it is Christian. He says, in *The Divine and the Human*:

The Church of the New Testament was a symbolic image of the eternal Church of the spirit. In the Church of the Spirit the eternal Gospel will be read.[2]

This might have been lifted from Joachim. Indeed, earlier in the same chapter (entitled "Religion of the Spirit"), Berdyaev speaks approvingly of Joachim of Flora: "There are always spiritually-minded people who live before their time ... Joachim of Flora ..." [3]

There is an affinity between the spiritualism of the German Idealists and that of Berdyaev. But when he says "eternal Church of the Spirit," he means something different from the national Church of Schelling. His Russian mysticism transforms the notion.

His mystical preoccupation causes him to place a low value on nature in his doctrine. There is not, as we find in Schelling,[4] an interest in the natural as well as the supernatural. Rather, he sees from his mystical viewpoint the transfiguration of the natural in the supernatural. For a western proponent of philosophy of revelation, such as Schelling, who is interested in the natural for its own sake, it is all right for the visible Church to have natural manifestations, and for the future Church of the Spirit to have a beginning on earth. The trouble is, Schelling's Church would no longer be Christian. For Berdyaev, the visible Church can only be a symbol of the True Church; and revelation, so far as it is historicized, is symbolic and falls short of the complete revelation of the Eternal Gospel. Therefore, the "Church of the Spirit," according to

---

[1] *The Divine and the Human*, 202. See *The meaning of the Creative Act*, 320: "The world is passing through three epochs of divine revelation: the revelation of the law (the Father), the revelation of redemption (the Son) and the revelation of Creativity (the Spirit). ... It is not given to us to know the definite chronological limits of these three epochs: they are all co-existent. Today we have not fully lived out the law, and redemption from sin has not yet been completed, although the world is entering a new religious epoch. Even in the epoch of the law the world had a premonition of new religious epochs ..."

[2] *Ibid.*, 186–187.

[3] See *The Divine and the Human*, 47.

[4] Cf. *The Ages of the World*, 141–142.

Berdyaev, cannot be established, as a historical church, on earth. He remains consistent and true to his key doctrine: transfiguration of mankind by the Godman, Christ.

Berdyaev uses the phrases of a philosopher of revelation – "Eternal Gospel," "Church of the Spirit." The terms represent what has been imperfectly revealed in the Gospel and in the Church. They have, consequently, a signification in his mystical doctrine which differs from that of Schelling. Furthermore, Berdyaev needs phrases such as these to help him define the age of the Spirit. The age of the Spirit is completely out of this historical world. Yet, it is the termination of the progress which the world has made during universal history. This presupposes the doctrine that the cosmos, along with man, will return to unity within Godmanhood. Man will take this world – spiritualized – with him. The futuristic earthly and spiritual Utopias of his German and Slavic predecessors [1] provide Berdyaev with material to define the age of the Spirit. And he wants to define the age of the Spirit in order to lay down a goal which will guide men in their progress towards the day of the transfiguration of the world.

His concern with the inadequacy of man's understanding of revelation does not assume that the second dispensation, that of Christ, has been inadequate, but rather that it would be inadequate by itself in the present age.

The Christian renaissance of a new humanity, matured in the Spirit, moving out of the epoch of fearfulness and guardianship, can take place only under the sign not of the Church of Peter but of John and of the mystic Joannine tradition. ... The historic Church of Peter is unable to satisfy the modern man; it cannot cope with his religious tragedy; it is always answering the questions which have not been asked; it soothes the wrong suffering, heals the wrong wounds; it is helping to save men from childish sins, but is powerless to help with the sins of maturity ... in the Christian world humility and obedience have long since been transformed into servitude and opportunism ... To overcome this religious servility, this heteronomic consciousness, is the first task of a Christian renaissance. Man must know himself religiously not as the slave of God but as a free participant in the divine process. [2]

Nevertheless, Berdyaev holds that the Christian Church is not to be superseded by the Church of the Spirit:

The new revelation is certainly not to be thought of as a new religion distinct from Christianity, but as the fulfilment and crowning of the Christian revelation ... [3]

---

[1] See *The Beginning and the End*, 115; *The Divine ann Human*, 47.
[2] *The Meaning of the Creative Act*, 332–334.
[3] *The Divine and the Human*, 183.

We can understand Berdyaev's outlook only if we recall that he is intensely eschatological, the Second Coming of the Messiah is always in his mind. The whole world will be saved, not just a few persons. It is as if the City of New York and all its citizens were going to be saved. Berdyaev does not make the break between the concrete aspect of history and metahistory,[1] or between man and the divine that we Westerners do. History will be transfigured in its concreteness and in its *entirety*,[2] and Berdyaev describes this transfiguration as if *it* is the true revelation, "the fulfilment and crowning of the Christian revelation."

He continues:

The revelation of the Spirit cannot just be simply waited for; it depends also upon the creative activity of man; it cannot be understood simply as a new revelation of man to God. This means that it will be a divine human revelation.[3]

Man must creatively help to bring on the end. This new revelation of the Spirit— which needs the efforts of man, as well as of God, to be achieved – is the "fulfilment and crowning of the Christian revelation."

The age of the Spirit will not occur in *history*, even though it is a human, as well as a divine, revelation. It will have only a beginning in history. There will be certain men who are *forerunners:*

We are not yet entering into the era of the Spirit; we are entering into the dark era. There have been forerunners of the new revelation of the Spirit throughout the whole extent of the history of Christianity, and such there are also now.[4]

There, we have found the answer to our question: how the world can progress towards the age of the Spirit and what sort of a beginning the age of the Spirit will have in history? The age of the Spirit has certain great men who are forerunners. Berdyaev names many men, starting with some Eastern Doctors of the Church and ending with some moderns, as, for example, Leon Bloy and Vladimir Solovyev.[5]

Berdyaev has not cheated the reader of a promise to remain spiritual and other-worldly in his philosophy of history. No, he has, on the contrary, remained true to his spiritualism. In particular, the world has a tragic history as well as a happy history, and the reign of Anti-Christ will precede the end and glorification of the world. Of the people in

---

[1] See Chapter IV, Section G.
[2] *Ibid.*; Chapter III, Section F.
[3] *The Divine and the Human*, 183.
[4] *Ibid.*, 186.
[5] *Ibid.*, 186, ff.

the world, there are only forerunners, few in numbers, of the age of the Spirit. And yet through them (and their influence on society) the progress of history towards the end of history is realized.

Berdyaev has worked out an elaborate doctrine of the age of the Spirit in which he shows how progress towards it has been made, and is to be made in the New Middle Ages. To investigate this is beyond the economy of my study; it would take us to the periphery of Berdyaev's doctrine. We are investigating the principles and method of his philosophy of history, which need more clarification than do his conclusions.

Here, we must rest content to have determined that Berdyaev's eschatology has remained metaphysical and spiritual, that the old theory of the ages of the world, which has been an earthly futurism in Berdyaev's predecessors and contemporaries, has been given an new meaning in Berdyaev's doctrine.

E. SUMMARY

1. According to Berdyaev's doctrine of Godmanhood, man in principle contains the cosmos completely and is superior to it. The idea of Godmanhood, upon which this theory is based, means the mutual sharing of two natures, the Divine and the human, while the distinction between them is preserved. Every man is a distinct creation, but he is, in principle, divine; hence Berdyaev's philosophy of history is ruled far more by the light of revelation than by the light of reason. His outlook is that of ancient Eastern Orthodoxy; it is mystical, and its object is the transfiguration of everything created. And the basic reality Berdyaev seeks in his philosophy of history is the divinization of man and creation. There is an Eternal Humanity which ought to be realized in time. Terrestrial man is metaphorically related to the Proto-type; hence, a metaphoricism of history is subordinated to a mysticism of history. Philosophy of history seeks, metaphorically, and also mystically, the revealtion of the Eternal Man.

2. To understand Berdyaev's use of the doctrine of Godmanhood in his philosophy of history, it was necessary to see the role of freedom. Berdyaev, in the light of an existential doctrine of freedom, rejects the Sophia theory of the Russians, Bulgakov and Solovyev. Russian Sophiologists are not existentialists, but intellectualists; their philosophies are bound by an essentialistic determinism. Berdyaev, inspired

by the voluntarism of Boehme, observes that they are not voluntarists. An irrational Freedom is not the ultimate principle of their philosophies. Berdyaev's difference with the Russian Sophiologists defines his own cosmogony; it prevents his cosmogony from being completely unhistorical and his philosophy of history from being enslaved by essences.

The fall of man has its roots in freedom, not in an intelligible principle. The freedom of the will and the tragedy of history have their roots in the *Ungrund*, an irrational and primordial Will, a groundlessness which is the deepest force in God. This irrational principle needs to be illuminated by Christ. The tragic destiny of the Son of God and His expiatory death is part of a movement in the divine life of God. The movement in the divine life is a theogonic process, or divine genesis, in which the Holy Trinity is born. And it is the condition which allows Berdyaev to assert there is a celestial history, a history of God in His theogonic process. Hence, the whole significance and essence of history and the world process consists in the illumination of the dark irrational principle in cosmogony and theogony. And this is the hypothesis of metaphysics of history, that the terrestrial destiny is predetermined by the celestial, in which the tragedy of illumination and Redemption take place through the divine passion, and that tragedy determines the illumination of world history.

A terrestrial history, as an epoch of celestial history, is needed, because God Himself needs to be illuminated, and man shares in the illumination of the *Ungrund*. The God-man, the perfect man, is the principle of this doctrine. The *Ungrund*, however, is the basis of divine and world processes. A stress between Berdyaev's voluntarism and his intelligibility arises, due to the twofold primacies of irrational freedom (*Ungrund*) and of Godmanhood in Christ (intelligible Logos). The stress is overcome in Berdyaev's universal history. The process begins with irrational freedom and ends with freedom being perfectly illuminated by the divine Logos.

The reconciliation of voluntarism and intelligibility is seen in two metaphysical doctrines: the doctrine of Spirit and the doctrine of beauty. Spirit is the sphere in which the divine and human are united; at the same time, Spirit emanates from both God (Godmanhood) and from primordial Freedom (*Ungrund*). And Spirit is incarnated, not only in the human body but also in the cosmos and even in historical bodies and traditions. The incarnation of Spirit is progressive in universal history, diffusing itself more and more completely, so that man experiences more and more freedom from the objectivizations of the fallen world.

Beauty, in the same way, is a principle of reconciliation. That is, the transfiguration of human nature and of the world is the attainment of beauty. Universal history progresses towards beautification as towards spiritualization. Beauty is a principle of reconciliation because the intellectual quest of man is creative and artistic, and the will is prior to the intellect. Yet, beauty is God's idea of the world, and, hence, beauty is finally perfect illumination of the irrational will.

Berdyaev's philosophy of history is a philosophy of beauty, where beauty is known imaginatively and voluntarily, as well as intellectually. Such a doctrine serves his prophetic philosophy.

3. One of the consequences of the doctrine of Godmanhood is Berdyaev's theory of *Sobornost'*. *Sobornost'* is an alltogetherness, a communal life of many persons, properly, of all mankind. It is achieved in the incarnation of Spirit; attained symbolically in historical bodies and actually in a free brotherhood of men. True and complete *Sobornost'* is attained in the transfiguration of the world and the cosmos when there will be a brotherhood of men with the whole creation. It is a subjective communion or brotherhood.

Another aspect of the doctrine of Godmanhood is an emphasis upon a cosmic consciousness. Berdyaev belongs to that group of philosopher who make an outstanding study of the place of cosmogony and an attendant cosmology in human wisdom. Like Scotus Erigena, he asserts the return of the cosmos to a spiritual unity within man and the return of man to a unity within God. The cosmos is a living organism because it belongs to the anthropological; it is a spiritual phenomenon because it originates in the Godman, Christ, and because its future spiritualization is being prepared in the progress of mankind. The world is an organic hierarchy, and the separation of man from God involves the separation of the whole creation from God. Thus, celestial history is seen to affect terrestrial history, itself an epoch within celestial history.

Berdyaev wants to show that the psychical – both the world, so far as it participates in the human soul, and also the souls of men – can be brought into the spiritual world without being destroyed. The psychical, in all its distinct multiplicity, preserves its identity in transfiguration.

Such a cosmology predisposes Berdyaev to set forth a philosophy of history in terms of an Augustinian Universal History rather than in terms of historical cycles. He is interested in the unity of universal history, not in the rules of historical cycles. He sees history as a progress rather than as the manifestation of laws and consequently does not ever abstract from the images of cultures. He wants to assert a doctrine of organic unity, and the unity is ultimately spiritual.

A further consequences of the doctrine of Godmanhood is the notion of the age of the Spirit, a theory that was first formulated by Joachim of Flora. Berdyaev's mystical theory looks forward to the coming of the Messiah and the end of the world. He posits an age of the Spirit much in the same way that Schelling and other thinkers have done. Berdyaev does not, as they do, posit an earthly futurism as the goal of history. Unlike Schelling, Berdyaev looks forward, not to a Church of the Spirit to supplant the Christian dispensation, but to a Church of the Spirit which will completely reveal the Christian dispensation after the end of the world. Berdyaev's Orthodox messianism and mysticism sees that, though the world does and should progress towards the age of Spirit, the latter has only a modest beginning in this world. There are forerunners, great and spiritual men, through whose influence the progress of history towards the end of history is realized.

CHAPTER III

EXISTENTIALISM:
A PERSONALIST PHILOSOPHY OF HISTORY

A. INTRODUCTION

I seek in this chapter to discover the way in which Berdyaev's Existentialism fulfills a need in his philosophy of history. What relation does his Existentialism have to his doctrine of the "historical?" In this connection, we will have to study a Personalist doctrine which is inspired by religious thought and stems from certain philosophical currents.

We saw in Chapter I that "his thought ... admits of only one possible metaphysics, and that is meta-history. Everything existential is history; dynamic force, destiny, man, the world, are history, God is history. ... The philosophy to which he would give expression, is a dramatic philosophy of destiny, of existence which is in time and passes over into eternity ... Everything, therefore, ought to be regarded from the point of view of the philosophy of history." [1]

We saw, too, in Chapter I that history is transformed and transfigured in the historical memory,[2] that every man is a sort of microcosm "in which the whole world of reality and all the great historical epochs combine and coexist. He ... is a world in his own right ..." [3] In Chapter II, we studied the pre-eminent place of personal freedom in the doctrine. We noted the mutual dependency of a voluntarism and an anti-intellectualist Existentialism. We saw how the pre-eminence of the Will and of Freedom made it possible for Berdyaev to assert an Existentialism in which the primary existent is the person.[4]

Thus we have witnessed a Personalist philosophy of history which holds that man should go outside himself and enter history in order to bring it within the unity of his personality. We observed the outstanding place of cosmogony in this philosophy,[5] according to which the freedom

---

[1] *The Divine and the Human*, v–vi, quoted on 32, above.
[2] *The Meaning of History*, 17–18, quoted on 11, above.
[3] Cf. *ibid.*, 22–23, quoted on 15, above.
[4] Cf. *The Russian Idea*, 171, quoted on 56, above.
[5] Cf. Chapter II, Section D, Part 2.

and worth of every person was asserted, where the Existential is most truly approached through personal and mystical creativity, and where the world and history is seen to be taken up into the divine and human unity of the person.

The Existentialism of Berdyaev's philosophy of history is therefore in some sense a Personalism; indeed, we want to find out whether or not the philosophy may be characterized as a peculiarly Personalist doctrine; and we seek to know the way in which it articulates its need for a Personalism. We know, from our study of his doctrine of the microcosm,[1] that "the personality is a biography ... a 'history'. Existence is invariably 'historical,'" [2] and the human Ego – as we may term it – realizes its personality through the historical memory which indeed is "attuned to the *primal wisdom* of man ... of the earliest epochs (and which) persists ... throughout the history of the human spirit"; [3] and it is attuned as well to the later epochs of history.

In Section B the first principles of Berdyaev's philosophy of history with respect to Existentialism will be studied. We seek to know whether or not these principles require a peculiarly Personalist doctrine. In Section C, Berdyaev's spiritual philosophy of personality will be studied. We enquire there whether the spiritualism is irrational, rational or mystical. In Section D, the question of a spiritual personality and its connection with the concrete (and "historical") existent will be investigated. The connection of the existent with universality, the relation of the imaginableness of reality with concreteness and the relation of human creativity with concrete existence must all be studied. This study will uncover further the Personalism of Berdyaev's philosophy of history. In Section E, the metaphysics of the communion of the person with the Thou and the We will be studied. How necessary is this Personalist doctrine of communion to Berdyaev's philosophy of history and universal history? Finally, in Section F the doctrine of human microcosm will be investigated; namely, the theory of the inclusion of the cosmos, mankind and all history in the personality. We will then be able to decide how greatly Berdyaev's philosophy of history needs a Personalism and Existentialism.

---

[1] Chapter I, Section B, Part 2.
[2] Cf. *Solitude and Society*, 124, quoted on 7.
[3] Cf. *The Meaning of History*, 7, on 11. (my italics).

B. PERSONALISM: THE EXISTENT AND THE EGO

Berdyaev says, in *Truth and Revelation*:

He who creates is a microcosm. ... The world is my creative act. Another man is my creative act. God is my creative act. ... Beauty in the world is a creative act not an objective reality. Creative transformation must therefore go on all the time.[1]

This doctrine of creativity is very important to Berdyaev's philosophy because it explains how the person knows the transcendent Truth and yet takes it existentially into his own subjectivity. It is both immanent and transcendent. We saw, in Berdyaev's voluntarism, that he asserts a philosophy of beauty. And he finds that beauty is both to be known and to be created by the historical memory.

The idea of beauty, which is so necessary to his metaphysics is necessary to his philosophy of history. The historical and the entities which are known in Berdyaev's philosophy are known as symbols, as true myths.[2] Philosophy of history is not historical, it is meta-historical; and this requires that the myth or symbol, by which the philosopher sees meaning in history, is a symbol of a higher entity (not a lower, historical, entity). The *reality* which the philosopher of history seeks to know by his true myths is the "historical," the divine meaning of history, the Truth of history.

But note: a myth or a symbol – true myth, too, as Berdyaev has it – is a fiction (and a true fiction). A fiction is a work of art, in Berdyaev's doctrine a thing of beauty. When his philosopher of history forms historical myths (such as "historical culture") he is a creator of beauty, seeking after beauty. His myths serve to bring him in his mystical philosophy to the reality, the true meaning of history. The reality, consequently, is beauty; his philosophy is a philosophy of beauty. The philosopher both creates beauty and knows beauty. Philosophically speaking, Berdyaev is interested in the divine Beauty of history.

These considerations about the beauty of history are closely related to Berdyaev's Personalism and Existentialism. When he says the world, another man, or God, is my creative act, he means that we create myths or symbols by means of which we attain higher and higher approximations to the realities which our creations symbolize. The philosopher, here, obviously takes them into his own subjectivity while at the same

---

[1] *Truth and Revelation*, 75–76. See *The Meaning of the Creative Act*, 138: "The world-process is the eighth day of creation, it is continuing creation."
[2] Cf. Chapter IV, Section G, Part I.

time approximating to a knowledge of them in their transcendent Truth.

This is a mystical philosophy to which Berdyaev's definition of spirit is suited. His notion of spirit, where the wilful principle predominates over the intellectual, and yet where the wilful principle is finally all illuminated by the intellectual, is correlative with a philosophy of beauty. For beauty is not humanly attained, except under spiritual conditions where the will predominates over the reason. And beauty is known under the same conditions.

The philosophy is an Existentialism because the human spirit, in knowing the world, other men and God – by symbols – is creating, discovering and knowing *himself*. We saw, in Chapter I, that Berdyaev posits a doctrine of creative reminiscence. A person recalls and creates what he is, a spirit eternally created by God, an image of the Godman and a microcosm in whom world history is spiritualized. This is an Existentialism because man is a microcosm, and all the things he knows and the history he creates become himself by truly revealing him to himself. His knowledge becomes the existent which he is, the microcosm in whom true existence is finally attained.

Indeed Berdyaev recognizes the Existentialism of the cognitive mind. He says first, in *Truth and Revelation*:

Existentialism may be defined in various ways, but the most important in my opinion is the description of existentialism which regards it as a philosophy which will not accept objectifying knowledge. Existence cannot be the object of knowledge.[1]

This first and most important definition defines negatively in respect to objectified knowledge. He then takes up another definition:

Another definition of existential philosophy is this. Existential philosophy is expressionist. In other words, it seeks to express the existentiality of the cognitive mind rather than something abstracted from that existentiality, which is what objectifying philosophy seeks to do. In this sense an element of existentialism behind the process of objectivization may be discovered in all great philosophers.[2]

Berdyaev so connects his Existentialism with the creative knowing of the world, other men and God, that he finds an Existential element in another part of the human spirit, as well as in its freedom and its spirituality; namely, in its knowing mind. When he says that Existential philosophy is expressionist, he is getting at the cognitive part of the existent. Existential philosophy is expressionist, and seeks to express

[1] *Truth and Revelation*, 11.
[2] *Ibid.*, 12.

the existentiality of the cognitive mind (which is the existentiality of the spirit, the existent, to whom the mind belongs). And he even discovers an element of Existentialism in the objectivization which would set up an essence as an existent, because even the objectivization participates in the existentiality of the cognitive mind. We will see, in the following chapter, that the existentiality of the cognitive mind consists in the existentiality of the concrete human spirit.[1]

The two definitions of Existentialism, in fact, are the only ones that Berdyaev offers in *Truth and Revelation,* and both refer to knowledge, to the subjective knowledge of man the microcosm. Thus the spiritual and human principles of Berdyaev's philosophy of history are explained by a philosophy of beauty and by an Existentialism which asserts the primacy of the knowing person.[2]

At the same time beauty is not only the invented symbol, but the reality which Berdyaev's Existential doctrine seeks.

... the subject can orientate himself by means of Existential philosophy, which dispenses with objectivization:
the human subject does not apprehend the object, but the revelation of human existence and, through it, that of the divine world. Thus in the light of Existential philosophy, knowledge is both active and creative, though in a somewhat different way, I can illuminate the objective world wherein *meaning* is revealed, the meaning of human existence and of the universe as part of the Divine Being.[3]

Thus beauty is not only subjective in this Existential philosophy, but, through beauty, human existence and the universe *reveal* the Divine Being. Note that, for Berdyaev, there are two principal moments of this revelation: there occurs the revelation of human existence and through it that of the divine world. Thus Berdyaev seeks to express the existentiality of the cognitive mind. This reveals human existence and, thereby, the existence of the divine world.

How does Berdyaev further conceive of the relationship between the "existential" and the "personal" in his philosophy? Does he identify them? Is the person one and the same as the existent, or the act of

---

[1] Chapter IV, Section G.

[2] Berdyaev offers a description of his Existentialism in *Dream and Reality,* 102, which is as follows:

"I was an existentialist even before I came to know Kierkegaard's writings ... I believe that Russian thought has always been marked by an existentialist tendency. This applies, evidently, above all to Dostoevsky, but is also true of Leo Shestov. Existentialism is, indeed, not a new phenomenon: we may discern its vivifying theme throughout the whole history of thought. The emphasis on the subject as against the object, of the will as against the general and universal; the antithesis between intuitive and conceptual knowledge, between existence and essence, were understood by some medieval thinkers and, in some measure, even in Greek thought ..."

[3] *Solitude and Society,* 53.

existence, at the origin of reality? To find an answer to these questions will enable us to know whether Berdyaev's philosophy is primarily a Personalism or primarily an Existentialism or equally a Personalism and Existentialism. And this will throw some light on his philosophy of history. If the personal *is* supreme in his doctrine, this will emphasize the personal quality of the subject-matter of philosophy of history, namely, the "historical," and, therefore, of philosophy of history itself. Further, if the personal is prior, if the creative Existentialism is predominately personal, then the unity of Berdyaev's universal history will be preserved.

Outside personality there is no absolute unity and totality in the world, to which personality would be subordinate ... An existential center, and a suffering destiny are to be found in subjectivity, not in objectivity. ... And everything which is existential in the objectivized ranks of the world, in mankind, in the cosmos, etc. belongs to the inward being of personality ...[1]

Berdyaev thus conceives his idea of man the microcosm in Existential terms.[2] *Existential* is the predicate, in this text, and *personality* is the implied subject. Thus he also is discussing a Personalist doctrine in Existentialist terms. He refers to the existential reality of the external world, but relates this in its existentiality to the human personality. The personality is not only superior to the external world, but the reality of the world belongs to the personality. "Personality is a microcosm, a complete universe. ... Personality is not a part and cannot be a part in relation to any kind of whole, not even to an immense whole, or to the entire world. This is the essential principle of personality and its mystery. ... For personality ... in its self-revelation is directed towards an infinite content. And at the same time personality presupposes form and limit ... it is the universal in an individually unrepeatable form."[3] Later in the chapter in *Slavery and Freedom* where personality is defined, Berdyaev indicates that personality most properly speaking is the Godman, Christ, insofar as He is reflected in every individual man.[4]

The individually personal for Berdyaev is the most Existential of all things.[5] We saw, in Chapter I, that through the historical memory, the

---

[1] *Slavery and Freedom*, 41.
[2] Cf. Chapter I, Section B, Part 2.
[3] *Slavery and Freedom*, 21–22. The Russian word for *personality*, *lichnost*, is very similar in meaning to the English term. *Lichnost* connotes the quality of having form and separate distinguishable features. *Lich* means face, *gestalt*. *Razlichat* means to discern, distinguish; *razluka* means separation, partition.
[4] *Ibid.*, 28.
[5] *The Beginning and the End*, 45.

person experiences the world and history as part of himself.[1] "My own existence is the most 'existential' of all. ... I have experienced the world around me and all the historical processes and events of my time as part of myself, as my spiritual biography. At the deepest mystical level, everything that has happened to the world happened to me." [2]

Indeed, "Existence," he says, "is not fully realized until we can pass from the subject to the human personality. Existential philosophy is a Personalist philosophy; the human personality is the real subject of knowledge." [3] He understands his Existential doctrine in terms of modern Existentialism.

Existence (*Existenz*) is not essence, it is not substance, it is a free act. *Existentia* takes supremacy over *essentia*. From this point of view existential philosophy is akin to every philosophy of action and all philosophies of freedom. ... *Existenz* in its depths is freedom. This is to be seen both in Jaspers, who allied himself with Kant, and again in Sartre who has very little in common with him. The events which take place in the existential sphere lie outside any causal sequence. ... It cannot, therefore, be said, for example, that God is the cause of the world. There can be no causal relations between God and man.[4]

We will see below how Berdyaev relates the Existentialism of Jaspers and Sartre to his own. Existence, which is supreme over essence, is a free act. He points out the voluntarism of an Existential philosophy, and speaks of philosophy of freedom. This is why he denies a principle of causality in an Existential philosophy. Causality, Kant has shown him, belongs to the natural and necessary realm, not to the realm of freedom.[5] Because existence is voluntary, wilful – that is, intimately related to primordial will and freedom [6] – existence in its depths cannot be a cause. The world is not an *effect* of God but an *image* of the true Christian world.

A little later Berdyaev says:

Freedom, that is to say, the act of freedom, is in fact *Existenz*.[7]

Note how carefully Berdyaev relates *Existenz* to freedom. He does not say freedom is exactly *Existenz*, but freedom, *that is to say, the act of freedom, is in fact Existenz*. Later in the same work he says:

---

[1] Chapter I, Section B, Part 2.
[2] *Dream and Reality*, X–XI.
[3] *Solitude and Society*, 51.
[4] *Truth and Revelation*, 12–13.
[5] See Chapter IV, Section A, concerning the Kantian notion of freedom and nature which is found in Berdyaev.
[6] Concerning the connection of will and freedom, see Chapter II, Section C.
[7] *Truth and Revelation*, 14.

Primary existence is freedom and act, it is creative power.[1]

Note, again, that he does not identify existence and freedom. He speaks, instead, of a *primary* existence which is freedom. By "primary existence," he means the ultimate aspect of existence; and this ultimate aspect of existence is freedom. He adds, "it is creative *power*." The ultimate in existence, namely freedom, is a creative power. He understands by *creative power a* principle which is a creative potentiality. He continues in the same text and adds: "The primary thing is movement."[2]

I do indeed love freedom above all else. Man came forth out of freedom and issues into freedom. Freedom is a primordial source and condition of existence . . .[3]

This passage confirms the hints given above; namely, that existence follows freedom; that *Existenz* is freedom only as the act of freedom, or is freedom with respect only to its own ultimate reality. Berdyaev is careful in defining the relation of existence to freedom; it is not a causal relation. He speaks, not of the *cause* of existence, but of the *"primordial source and condition"* of existence. And this primordial source, which is here called "freedom," may also be called "will," because the primordial freedom is one and the same as the primordial will. The Russian word for *will, velya,* is also the Russian word for *freedom.*[4] The *Ungrund*, the primordial source and depth of God and of man, is "at the same time will . . . and freedom." "In the darkness of the *Ungrund* a fire flames up and this is freedom, *meonic*, potential freedom."[5] It is *meonic*, Berdyaev says, using a word taken from the Greek which means non-being, a sort of nothingness.[6] This is a potential principle, a principle which is potency. The source of movement and of change is potency, not act; there is more in potency than in act.[7]

We saw, in the text quoted above, that "primary existence is freedom and *act*, it is creative power." And we have just seen that *potency* is prior to act, according to Berdyaev. *Act* refers more properly to existence and *potency* refers more properly to primary freedom or will.

The *Ungrund*, the dark abyss, the primordial source is *meonic*.[8] This is the dark will,[9]

---

[1] *Ibid.*, 70.
[2] *Ibid.*, 70.
[3] *Dream and Reality*, 46.
[4] Concerning the identification of primordial will and primordial freedom in Berdyaev's philosophy, see 71, n 5 above.
[5] *The Beginning and the End*, 106.
[6] *Ibid.*, 106.
[7] *Ibid.*, 157.
[8] 71, n 5 above.
[9] *The Beginning and the End*, 144.

... the non-being ... the dark abyss ... This non-being ... does not exist, but has an existential significance.[1]

The primordial will or freedom does not exist; it is prior to existence. *Existenz*, for Berdyaev, is not identical with the ultimate principle because the ultimate will and freedom is prior to existence.

As always, however, when he discusses *Existenz* and freedom, he asserts the close relationship between them. We have seen in past pages that existence in its depths is freedom; now we see that the dark abyss, the primordial freedom, though it does not exist, "has an existential significance."

Thus, in Berdyaev's doctrine, freedom or will is prior, absolutely speaking, to existence. And this may be said of God and man; for he says it of God and sometimes of man. Man in his truth is the True Man, the Godman, Christ;[2] that is, true man is God. The *Ungrund*, the primordial freedom, is the deepest reality, both in man and in God.[3]

Berdyaev's Existentialism posits something deeper than existence; namely, the primordial will which operates in man as well as in God. Berdyaev's philosophy is more properly called a Personalism than an Existentialism. It is an Existential commonplace that God in His depths *is*, but does not *exist*.[4] In Berdyaev's doctrine this is a Person-

---

[1] *Ibid.*, 143.

[2] See Section F of the present chapter.

[3] Cf. Chapter II, Section C and notes. Berdyaev says, in *Freedom and the Spirit*, 165: "The void (the *Ungrund* of Boehme) is not evil, it is the source of every kind of life and every actualization of being. It conceals within itself the possibility of both evil and of good. And initial, irrational, and mysterious void lies at the heart of the whole life of the universe, but it is a mystery beyond the reach of logic."

Yet, although the *Ungrund* (primal Freedom) is the profoundest reality it is not the dominating reality in God. We have seen the Trinitarian doctrine of Berdyaev in Chapter II. Nor is the *Ungrund* the dominating reality in man, even though it is the primal freedom. Berdyaev speaks, in *The Beginning and the End*, 171, of: "an illuminated freedom" (not a dark freedom), which is introduced in creative activity. He means the illumination of Christ.

[4] James Collins in his book, *The Existentialist, A Critical Study* (Regnery, Chicago, 1952), 15, writes of the primacy of the personal in Kierkegaard's Existentialism. He says:

"... Kierkegaard has associated existence exclusively with the exercise of human freedom in the formation of self. For the same reason, he is prevented from applying existence to God. He is the fountainhead of the existential commonplace that God *is*, but does not *exist*. Existence cannot be predicated of the eternal, immutable being, since to exist means to be engaged in becoming, time, freedom, and history. This has given rise to the existentialist quandary of how to relate existential thinking to the divine Being, who is by definition placed beyond the existential order. Man is not only central in existence: he is the only truly existential being.

... His own answer to the problem of man's relationship to God was formulated in terms of faith in the Incarnation. In the person of Christ, God Himself enters into the zone of the existential."

We can now understand how Berdyaev's Existentialism differs from Kierkegaard's. For Kierkegaard, God does not exist (God is); and existence pertains to the merely historical. For him, it is an unexplanable paradox how existence and Godhead meet in the Person of Christ. For Berdyaev, however, God does exist in a certain sense, though the deepest ground of God,

alism, according to which God *in His depths* is the *Ungrund*. Not only is the primary principle a personal one (for the *will* pertains to the personal in contra-distinction from merely natural and external objects). What is more, the primary principle is asserted in a philosophy which holds that man is a microcosm.[1] The reality of anything in this world is human and the ultimate principle is personal. Since existence in its depths is freedom and will, the existence of any external natural thing cannot be, except in its relationship to man.

We find in Berdyaev's philosophy that the metaphysical principles of will or freedom and existence are treated in a doctrine of the human Ego. The scheme, we will find, is similar to that of the German Idealists, particularly Fichte and Schelling.

Indeed, Berdyaev has always attempted to relate his philosophy to 19th-century European currents of speculation.[2] He refers to the points of agreement and disagreement between his philosophy and the outlooks of German Idealism. But he has turned to German Idealism in most cases, not for doctrine, but for confirmation of his own theories. Thus he notes the turning of philosophy from objectivism to subjectivism in German philosophy, but adds that the followers of Kant betrayed him by objectifying the human subject.[3]

Kant's philosophy is a source in his Personalism and Existentialism. Berdyaev says that "his true master in philosophy was Kant." [4] Fichte

---

the *Ungrund*, is prior to existence. We have seen, in the present Section the Existentiality of the *Ungrund* and the willfulness of *Existenz*. *Ungrund* and *Existenz* are very close, though distinct. On the other hand, Berdyaev seems to accept the "historicity" of existence. But he overcomes the paradox of history and meta-history by making God Himself "historical," by asserting a celestial history. Berdyaev is therefore better able than Kierkegaard to relate Existential thinking to the divine Being, to relate the existentiality of Christ to His divinity. Existence, for Berdyaev, has more metaphysical meaning than it does for Kierkegaard. However, though Berdyaev gets closer to a metaphysics of existence in his Existentialism, Kierkegaard respects the reality of history more than Berdyaev does. See III,n 3 below.

[1] See Chapter I, Section B, Part 2; Section F of the present chapter.

[2] Berdyaev says (*Dream and Reality*, 121 and 122) that in his first book, *Subjectivism and Individualism in Social Philosophy*, he "endeavoured to show the possibility of a synthesis of critical Marxism and the Idealist philosophy of Kant and partly of *Fichte*." (my italics). We find, in *Solitude and Society*, 36, ff, a treatment of the influence of German Idealism on the history of philosophy. Berdyaev indicates both the work of German Idealism that he thinks should survive and the work that should not. "The work done in this sphere (the subject's deliverance from the external tyranny of the objective world) by Kant and the German Idealists ... precludes any return to the ancient metaphysical system of the substantialist type which identified Being with object. Henceforth Being could only be apprehended subjectively ... but in the process they interpreted the subject in an objective and non-existential way." In Chapter I of *The Beginning and the End* Berdyaev discusses both the desirable and undesirable accomplishments of German Idealism in metaphysics and anthropology.

[3] See preceding note.

[4] *Dream and Reality*, 93.

also has been an influence. Indeed Berdyaev's first book attempted a synthesis of Marxism with the idealism of Kant and partly that of Fichte.[1] In the works, however, that are referred to in this book (those published since 1916), he has never referred to himself as a follower of Fichte but has criticized the latter for betraying Kant's philosophy.[2] Indeed "Anti-personalism" he says, "is a property of all German idealistic metaphysics, with the exception of Kant ..." [3]

The exact influence of Kant and Fichte upon Berdyaev cannot be determined. We can only note certain parallels between Berdyaev's doctrine of the human Ego and Kant's and Fichte's. Like Kant, Berdyaev believes that man as a noumenon, an absolute reality, is beyond the category of causality.[4] Like Fichte, he develops a doctrine of the human Ego, according to which an irrational and ungrounded wilful principle in man is the source of consciousness, and it is illuminated during the course of history.[5]

The following passage occurs in a section in *Solitude and Society* entitled, "The Ego and the Personality":

> The fundamental problem of Existential philosophy is that of the personality. I am an Ego before I become a personality. The Ego is primary and undifferentiated; it does not postulate a doctrine of the personality. The Ego is postulated *ab initio;* the personality is propounded. The Ego's purpose is to realize its personality, and this involves it in incessant struggle. The consciousness of the personality and the endeavor to realzie it are fraught with pain. Many would rather renounce their personality than endure the suffering which its realization involves.[6]

We have seen in the foregoing pages what Berdyaev means by "Existential philosophy"; namely, a philosophy which states the primacy of existence and the priority in existence of a personal principle: primordial and wilful freedom. To see, however, why Berdyaev says the fundamental problem of Existential philosophy is that of the personality will require further investigation. We must know how, in history, the Ego can realize its personality. And we must see the role of suffering in Berdyaev's Existentialism. For we want to know the Personalism of his universal history and the tragic element of his philosophy of history.

When he says the Ego is primary and undifferentiated, he means that the Ego occurs prior to the differentiation contained within personality:

[1] See 99, n 2 above.
[2] *Ibid.*
[3] *The Divine and the Human*, 26.
[4] See 141, n 6; 142, n 2, below.
[5] See 101, n 2, below.
[6] *Solitude and Society*, 121.

spirit, soul and corporeal body. The Ego does not postulate a doctrine of the personality because the personality flows out of it.

The Ego is primitive; it can neither be deduced from nor reduced to anything. ... It is not true to say, "I think, therefore I am"; but rather "I am surrounded on all sides by impenetrable infinity, and therefore I think." I am, in the first place. The Ego belongs to the sphere of existence.

The Ego is primarily existential ... it is synonymous with freedom.[1]

Berdyaev rejects an idealism which would derive existence (I am) from thought (I think). The word, *existence*, is not quite as good as *freedom* as a word in this text. The Ego is existential, he says. But, what is more, it is synonymous with freedom. In this description of the Ego *freedom* expresses his intention better than *existence*.

His doctrine is similar in some respects to that of Fichte, if not in its Existentialism and Personalism, at least in its voluntarism. Like Fichte, he asserts that the basic Ego of a person is freedom.[2] This means, we

---

[1] *Ibid.*, 65.

[2] Concerning the primacy of will in Fichte's philosophy of man, see J. G. Fichte, "The Vocation of Man," translated by W. Smith in *Modern Classical Philosophers*, edited by B. Rand (Houghton Mifflin, Boston, 1908), 516. Fichte says: "I am a member of two orders: the one purely spiritual, in which I rule by my will alone, the other sensuous, in which I operate by my deed. ... The will is the living principle of reason." 517: "My will, which is directed by no foreign agency in the order of the super-sensual world, but by myself alone, is this source of true life, and of eternity ... an absolutely *first*, primary and original power, before which there is no preceding influence by which it may be governed ..."

Schelling, in *Of Human Freedom*, tr. J. Gutmann (Opencourt, Chicago, 1936), 62, describes the voluntarism of Fichte's doctrine. "The Ego, said Fichte, is its own deed ... this Being (the being underlying the concious Ego) which is assumed as prior to knowledge is no being, even if it is not knowledge either; it is real self-positing, it is a primal and basic willing which makes itself into something and is the basis and foundation of all essence."

Fichte, hoewever, associates with the will, the *reason* as an intelligible principle. Cf. *Modern Classical Philosophers*, 516. His philosophy asserts a rationalism, even though it is voluntaristic. Berdyaev's philosophy is not a rationalism. The principle of intelligibility is concrete. For him, it is Christ, the Godman, not Reason. Berdyaev does not teach a rationalistic approach but (1) a Personalistic way which would attain knowledge and intelligibility through a communion of the knower with other persons (see Section E of this chapter); and (2) a symbolic and metaphorical approach. (See Chapter IV, Section G.) Berdyaev says, in *The Beginning and the End*, 42:

"The depth of my ego is steeped in infinity and eternity and it is only a superficial layer of my ego which is illuminated by the mind, rationalized, and recognized on the basis of the antithesis between subject and object." Rationalization and generality are only a superficial aspect of the Ego, for Berdyaev. Indeed he criticizes Fichte on this score, in *Solitude and Society*, 67:

"Fichte's Ego is not authentic, because it is universal rather than individual, and because it postulates the non-Ego rather than another Ego or the Thou. The Ego becomes conscious of itself as the product of its own activity; but this activity is based upon the existence of something and of someone else as well as upon that of the active Ego. But we are primarily concerned here with the existence of another Ego, of the Thou."

That is, according to Berdyaev, Fichte asserts a non-Ego, in this scheme, which is known rationally and universally, but not other Egos (persons), known in communion. (See the present section of the present chapter.) See following note.

have seen, that the Ego participates in the *Ungrund*, primordial freedom, the deepest principle in man. The mode of discussion is similar in Fichte's and Berdyaev's philosophies, insofar as it is descriptive of the Ego's realization of itself.[1] And for both Fichte and Berdyaev a universal history is posited in the scheme.[2] That is, the *Ungrund*, the primordial will of the Ego, is illuminated in both doctrines and personalized in Berdyaev's theory; and the illumination is understood and propounded in nothing less sweeping than a universal history. This scheme seems to originate in German Idealism (Schelling also subscribed to it as it was developed by Fichte).[3] The characteristic assertion is: the pure willing, which is the basic Ego, is not consciousness, nor a self-apprehension; but is the fecundating source which freely seeks illumination. The notion is personalized and etherialized in Berdyaev's philosophy.

We have seen that the Ego is "primarily existential ... it is synonymous with freedom." Berdyaev intends that existence is a principle almost as primary as freedom; and he is refering to his Existential doctrine.

Originally there was not a line of demarcation between the Ego and the "totality"; later, when the existence of the non-Ego was revealed, the Ego developed in contact with it a particularly acute and anguished sensibility. ... The stages

[1] The scheme of development of the Ego, according to Fichte's theory is presented in his "Science of Knowledge." Cf. *Modern Classical Philosophers*, 497, ff. Fichte says that to the Ego (1) the non-Ego (2) is opposed; and thus it is posited in the Ego. And the non-Ego is united (3) with the Ego.

In Berdyaev's doctrine there are also three stages, *Solitude and Society*, 66: "firstly, the undifferentiated unity of the Ego with the universe; secondly the dualist opposition of the Ego and the non-Ego; thirdly and finally, the achievement of the concrete union of every Ego with the Thou, a union which preserves plurality in a transfigured form."

The schemes are apparently similar. But the conclusion of both dialectics are different. First, Fichte's rationalistic philosophy considers the relationship between the individual man and divine Providence. And from this follows a co-operation with other persons in the race. *Modern Classical Philosophers*, 532. Berdyaev's Personalist philosophy always considers, rather, the communion between men and through it communion with God. See Section E of this chapter. Second, Fichte asserts a naturalistic rationalism: "All that happens in this world is subservient to the improvement and culture of man, and, by means of this, to the promotion of the purpose of his earthly existence. It is *this higher world-plan which we call Nature*, when we say, – Nature leads men ... to industry ... to a just constitution ... to *endless peace on earth*. Thy will, O Infinite One! thy Providence alone, is this higher Nature. ... all things must work together for the good of those who love their duty and who know thee." (my italics) *Modern Classical Philosophers*, 533. We may contrast what we have seen of Berdyaev's opposition to Nature: Chapter I, Section B, Part 4; Cf. Chapter IV, Section B. And as for a world-plan which leads to an endless peace on earth, we may contrast what we know of Berdyaev's unworldliness and his historical pessimism: Chapter II, Section D, Part 3.

[2] See note preceding, concerning the universal history that is posited by the respective schemes.

[3] Cf. *Of Human Freedom*, 62. Schelling summarizes Fichte's scheme, here, and states that it is his own scheme, too.

of its development are as follows: firstly, the undifferentiated unity of the Ego with the universe; secondly the dualist opposition of the Ego and the non-Ego; thirdly and finally, the achievement of the concrete union of every Ego with the Thou, a union which preserves plurality in a transfigured form.[1]

This is a short history of the Ego. Berdyaev means one man's Ego and even more the development of human consciousness through the epochs of history.

"The concrete union of every Ego with the Thou" refers primarily to the perfect state of man after the end of the world and secondarily to the Ego of a person still living in this world. The Ego develops an anguished sensibility in contact with the non-Ego because it has to overcome its submersion in the non-Ego (in cosmic nature, for example, or in technocracy).[2]

His reference to the final union of the Ego with the Thou, "a union which preserves plurality in a transfigured form," gives us a hint of a Personalism and an Existentialism which are, at the same time, part of philosophy of history. He is here speaking of the union of *every* Thou with the Ego (every person in history) and of a union which preserves plurality (that is, preserves, ultimately, all of history) in a transfigured form.

Despite the grand potentialities of the Ego and of the person, the most important thing about the Ego is that it is a principle of enduring self-identity in the process of change:

for unless there existed a subject of mutation, a subject capable of preserving his identity in the process of change, the Ego could not suffer a temporal change or actualize itself. But the Ego does preserve its identity and uniqueness despite its ever changing aspect. . . . The Ego may, therefore, be defined as the constant unity underlying all change . . . It is self determining; it determines itself from within when responding actively to all external influences.[3]

The Ego, at one and the same time, provides the unity of the person, underlying all change, and determines the change and development of the person in responding to external influences.

It is the principle of the change and development of the personality because:

The personality postulates further (besides the principle of self-identity) the existence of a dark, violent and irrational principle . . .[4]

[2] *Solitude and Society*, 66.
[2] Cf. *The Realm of Spirit and the Realm of Caesar*, 48.
[3] *Solitude and Society*, 66–67.
[4] *Ibid.*, 122.

Berdyaev refers to the self-determining principle, the primitive will which is at the basis of the Ego and the personality.

The personality . . . also postulates the soul's ultimate and everlasting triumph over this irrational principle. But although it is rooted in the unconsciousness, the personality implies an acute self-consciousness of its unity in the midst of change. It is sensitive to all the currents of social and cosmic life and open to a variety of experience, but it takes care not to lose its identity in society or in the cosmos.[1] (my italics)

Thus as soon as Berdyaev sets forth the primordial foundation of the person, just as quickly, he asserts the soul's ultimate victory over this irrational principle. He seems to associate this victory with the self-consciousness, with a sensitivity to the currents of social and cosmic life.

This, then, is a philosophy of history which holds that social and cosmic life are revealed in history and that this figures importantly in the development of the Ego and the personality.

all Egos resemble each other in that each is unique and distinct. Each Ego is an entity, a world in itself, postulating the existence of other Egos without seeking to identify itself with them. The Ego I have in mind is the extra-social and non-objective Ego. The Ego's existence precedes its materialization in this world, and yet it is inseparable from the existence of the Other Self and of other Egos.[2]

The uniqueness and distinctness of every Ego is a condition of personal freedom, and hence Berdyaev insists upon the notion that every Ego is a "world in itself" (a microcosm). The Ego postulates the existence of other Egos because it knows; and thus illuminates its irrational basis (primal will); in knowing *them*. We will see, in Section E, why it seeks to know other Egos and not just things. The Ego's *existence* precedes its materialization in the world; that is, its manifestation as body and soul.[3] "And yet it is inseparable from the existence of the Other Self and of other Egos." "Other Self" refers to God, while "other Egos" refers to other created persons. Berdyaev is trying to show that the Ego is subjective, absolutely free and self-determined; yet, it cannot be an Ego (and a microcosm) in solitude, in isolation from other Egos.

Self-consciousness implies consciousness of others; it is social in the depths of its metaphysical nature. Man's life, insofar as it is the expression of the Ego's, presupposes the existence of other men, of the world, and of God. The Ego's absolute isolation, its refusal to communicate with anything outside it, with the Thou, would be suicidal. The Ego's existence is threatened whenever it denies the potential existence within itself of another Ego, or of the Thou.[4] (my italics)

[1] *Ibid.*, 122.
[2] *Ibid.*, 67.
[3] See *ibid.*, 67.
[4] *Ibid.*, 67.

Not only man's life, the expression of the Ego, but the very existence of the Ego itself, presuppose the existence of other men, of the world, and of God. This is so because its isolation would be suicidal. And, Berdyaev indicates, these are known in another Ego insofar as it is a Thou. "The potential existence within the Ego of another Ego or of the Thou" refers to a knowledge which transcends the division into subject and object. Berdyaev is showing that the Ego and the personality can exist only in a communion with other Egos and with the world.

Berdyaev speaks, in the first citation in this chapter, of a suffering which the realization of personality involves. This suffering is primarily an anguish which arises in the face of the abyss of existence (the *Ungrund*, ultimately) which the person finds in himself.

It is necessary to distinguish anguish (*Angst*) from fear (*Furcht*). Kierkegaard does this, although it is a relative distinction in the terminology of every language. Fear has causes, it is connected with danger and with the every day world of common experience. Anguish, on the other hand, is experienced, not in the face of empirical danger, but in confronting the mystery of being and non-being, when face to face with the transcendent abyss, in the face of the unknown.[1]

While fear is caused, anguish, a truer and deeper experience, is uncaused because it faces not a cause but the condition, the ground, (the *Ungrund*) of existence, the mystery which is beyond being and lies in non-being. Here too, Berdyaev is an Existentialist, using the language of Existentialism.

Nevertheless, in order to understand Berdyaev's position, we must see that this anguish, *Angst*, in the the face of non-being is not the fundamental Existential experience in Berdyaev's philosophy. As James Collins says, in *The Existentialists*:

If the fundamental existential experience is an encounter with utter nothingness, then there is little room for a philosopher who consistently studies such positive attitudes as fidelity and hope and worship.[2]

And Berdyaev consistently studies and propounds such positive attitudes. For him, is anguish a fundamental Existential experience? He asserts a primal will is at the basis of the person and proposes that personality should be achieved in illuminating the will. The radical awareness of freedom of choice produces an anguish. He criticizes the French atheist Existentialists who are captivated, he says, by non-being.

Present-day man, oppressed by fallen and disintegrating being, is being captivated by non-being. Face to face with the very brink of non-being, he wants to

---

[1] *Slavery and Freedom*, 52.
[2] *The Existentialists*, 115.

experience the final ecstasy, whether the ecstasy of heroism for the sake of nothingness, or the ecstasy of creativeness which arises out of his own nothingness. . . . It is in the Godman, in the Son of God and the Son of Man, that the new man takes his beginning, the man of a new and eternal humanity.[1]

Berdyaev is referring here to a new notion of non-being, different from that of his own; and, consequently, he is discussing an Existentialism whose principle is different from that of his own Existentialism. J. H. Randall, in an essay about a contemporary and follower of Berdyaev, Paul Tillich, explains the two notions of non-being which we are here encountering. He says:

The Platonists distinguish between the ὄυκ ὄν which means "nothing at all," and the μη ὄν which meant for them that which does not yet have being but can become being if united with ideas. This Platonic "matter" had a positive power of resisting the evil "nonbeing" – not nothing at all, but something with no positive ontological standing that yet could resist and pervert being. In Boehme's *Ungrund*, Schelling's "first potency," Hegel's "anti-thesis," this dialectical negativity was located in God himself. Existentialism has given to nonbeing a still more positive character and power: Heidegger's "annihilating nothingness" threatens man with nonbeing in the form of death, thus giving his life its "existential" character. For Sartre nonbeing includes the threat of meaninglessness – the destruction of the very structures of being.[2]

Berdyaev's nothingness (*Ungrund*) is that of Boehme, not that of Sartre.[3] This means that he does not view the nothingness, the *Ungrund*,

---

[1] *The Divine and the Human*, 127.

[2] J. H. Randall, Jr. "The Ontology of Paul Tillich," in *The Theology of Paul Tillich*, edited by C. W, Kegley and R. W. Bretall (Macmillan, New York, 1952), 156.

[3] Berdyaev does not associate Heidegger's Existentialism of non-being with Sartre's nihilism. He says, in *Truth and Revelation*, 107–108:
"The idea of non-being, of nothingness, takes a very prominent place in Heidegger's thought, indeed, it might even be supposed that his philosophy is a philosophy of non-being. The last word belongs to death, there is no infinity in man, everything in him is finite. But some reminiscences of the old German mysticism are left in Heidegger. For this reason his non-being may be taken to approximate to the *Ungrund* of Boehme." He says, concerning Sartre's philosophy, *Towards a New Epoch*, 98: "In his great philosophical work (*L'Etre et le Néant*) Sartre's use of the word 'nothingness' remains ambiguous. It can mean either that which precedes being or that which follows it. Consequently the meaning of the term changes. Nothingness in Sartre means the corruption of being, whence, so it seems to him, comes nausea. . . . The word, has, however, another meaning. It is with nothingness that the possibility of creating something new is connected . . . I am afraid that his creative work springs from an already rotten being and not from the freedom of nothingness! . . . There is a difference between the conception of nothingness in Heidegger and that of Sartre. In the former one catches from time to time certain reminiscences of the old type of German mysticism, of the 'undetermined' (*Ungrund*) of Boehme. Nothingness here acquires a deep meaning, but there is nothing like this in Sartre, rather he shows the corruption and falling-away of being while at the same time he wants to save it and to affirm freedom." 103: "The whole Sartrian movement is chilling; it possesses no fire, which alone would make it possible to create the future. The morality of this movement . . . is a cold virtue deprived of every trace of charity."
    We can see, especially in the last quotation, why Berdyaev's nothingness (*meonic Ungrund*) is like that of Boehme and not like that of Sartre. There is a dynamism in the *Ungrund*, ac-

the existence, as merely a nothingness. He does not propose "an ecstasy of heroism for the sake of nothingness," but "the ecstasy of creativeness which *arises* out of (man's) own nothingness." The nothingness is merely a starting-point for Berdyaev, but not the terminus. The terminus is the God-man, "the man of a new and eternal humanity."

Therefore, *Angst* in the face of non-being is not the fundamental Existential experience in Berdyaev's philosophy. His Christian and mystical philosophy of history and his universal history, require a happier and more meaningful Existential doctrine. He asserts the illumination during history of the *Ungrund* and the fallen world in a divine-human creativity, guided by an eschatological metaphysics. We have studied this metaphysics, in Chapter II, in respect to the doctrines of Godmanhood and of freedom and will study it in this chapter with respect to Berdyaev's doctrine of man. The metaphysics of man and Existential doctrine are understood by Berdyaev always in the light of universal history. The philosophy of history and the universal history of Berdyaev posit a creativity of man in a historical progress which is both divine and human. The suffering, the *Angst*, which Berdyaev notes in the formation of personality, is not to be relieved in "the ecstasy of a heroicism for the sake of nothingness." But it is superseded in "the ecstasy of creativeness which arises out of man's own nothingness." And this beginning occurs "in the God-man, in the Son of God and the Son of Man, the man of a new and eternal humanity."

And, since Godmanhood is Logos or divine Truth, Personality is, finally, the child of Truth.

Truth is the meaning of the existent, and meaning is the truth of the existent.

cording to Berdyaev's philosophy, which expresses itself, not only in an intelligent creativity but also in a supernatural charity. Cf. Jacob Boehme, *The Way to Christ* tr. J. J. Stoudt, with a foreward by the Quaker, Rufus M. Jones (Harper, New York, 1947). Stoudt says, in his Introduction, xxvi: "The *Ungrund* is the highest metaphysical principle in Boehme's system. ... Boehme also employs several other descriptions of this idea, notable *Nichts* (nothing) which is reminiscently Neoplatonic in tone." Stoudt then points out that when the unconditioned *Ungrund* becomes conditioned being, the image by which it becomes conditioned and before it has manifested itself in substantial reality is the Great Mystery (the essential Logos of God which has become manifested in the world; namely Christ). The book which follows – *The Way to Christ* – is a devout work where the name of Christ appears on every page, and sometimes on the same page with the word, *Ungrund*. Cf. 177.

Berdyaev defines his notion of *Ungrund* or nothingness as follows: Note that he does not subscribe to a Platonic notion of a μὴ ὄν in the Greek sense: "Is the idiom of the theology and metaphysics capable of explaining *Ungrund*? That is a task which only an apophatic knowledge can undertake. ... *Ungrund* is *nothingness* as distinct from *something* in the category of being; it is not οὐκ·γν, μηδόν. But it is not μὴ ὄν in the Greek sense. Boehme goes beyond the limits of Greek thought, of Greek intellectualism and ontology. Like Eckhart's *Gottheit*, Boehme's *Ungrund* goes deeper than God. We should probably be right in thinking of *Ungrund* as the primal pre-existential freedom." *Spirit and Reality*, 130.

This found its expression in the doctrine of the Logos ... Truth is meaning born in God before all ages, in God the existent one. And this birth is repeated in all who exist, and because of it personality emerges into view.

Personality is not the offspring of a generic process; it is the child of meaning, of truth.[1]

The meaning of the existent is the truth of the existent, and just as meaning (the Logos) is born in God, so it is born in man; and personality appears. The truth which is born in men is, finally, the Logos, the Godman.

Personality, therefore, cannot be the offspring of a generic process; that is to say, it is not the resultant of an interplay of mere essences; it is not, in short, a mere essence or form. For the truth, or meaning which brings about the appearance of personality is ultimately an existent – the Godman. And this is a spiritual problem. The Existentialism is a spiritualism.

C. PERSONALITY IS SPIRIT: AN EXISTENTIALISM OF SPIRIT

Berdyaev's Existentialism of Personalism (which now seems to be the same thing) is a voluntarism in which the primal Will is illuminated by intelligible truth. This recalls Section C in Chapter II where we saw that his philosophy is one of the spirit. Spirit can be understood in the light of a voluntarism which asserts the loving illumination of the Will by the divine Logos.

He defines Personalism in terms of spirit.

Man has to realize personality. Personality is spirit, free spirit and the link between man and God. It is a link of man with God which is outside the false submergence of man in his own closed circle.[2]

Personality is spirit because, so to speak, at the moment in the formation of a personality when the Ego realizes itself as personality, the conditions of spirit are present. These are the conditions, namely, of will and intelligibility.[3] Spirit is the link of man with God because it transcends objectivized knowing through the primacy of the will; and because it transcends a pure subjectivity through the divinity of the human spirit. The way in which the human spirit transcends both objectivization and subjectivization, and thus remains a link of man

---

[1] *The Beginning and the End*, 64–44.

[2] *Slavery and Freedom*, 246.

[3] We will see, in Section D, more clearly why we cannot say that (abstract) intellect is a principle of personality.

with God, will be seen in Chapter IV. Suffice it to say that he distinguishes between the soul and the spirit of man.[1] In refusing to see an identification of the soul and the spirit, Berdyaev considers man especially in his divinity. Insofar as man is ruled by his soul, he is human and not divine; but insofar as the spirit gains the ascendancy, man is human and also divine (like Godmanhood).[2] Such a psychology (but let us use Berdyaev's word: such a *pneumatology*) [3] asserts an alternative to the objectified or isolated knowing of the soul. The spirit is quite distinct from the part of the personality (the soul) which knows objectively or falsely.[4] Spirit is a link of man with God because spirit in itself knows in a perfect manner.[5] Man in this life knows imperfectly, but the progress of history is at the same time a progress of the incarnation of spirit; [6] man is becoming more an incarnate spirit. His knowledge is therefore achieving greater transcendence over the objectivization.

It seems, in Berdyaev's philosophy, that the Ego of a man comes to him through the spirit.

The spiritual principle alone constitutes personality and gives it a permanent center. Personality is created by the logos ... Without the logos, without the spiritual principle, personality disintegrates. The synthesizing spiritual principle embraces both the soul and the body.[7]

The spirit is the principle of both the soul and the body, which is to say, man is an incarnate spirit. When he says that the spiritual principle gives the personality a permanent center, his remark brings to mind the deepest part of spirit and of personality; namely, the Ego, the wilful acting, the will. In addition to the Ego, which is "the constant unity underlying all change," [8] the spiritual principle, the logos, integrates the personality and indeed "creates" it.

Berdyaev calls the spiritual principle the logos because man refers, ultimately, to the perfect prototype: the Godman, the divine Logos. In

---

[1] Berdyaev is clear, in *Freedom and the Spirit*, on the distinction he makes between the spirit and the soul. He says, 27: "The spiritual must not be separated from the 'psychical' and natural; rather, it must illuminate it and spiritualize it."

[2] *Ibid*, 27.

[3] He says, in *The Beginning and the End*, 96: "Does a subject of meaning, value and idea exist? My answer to this question is that it does. It exists as spirit. Spirit moreover is not abstract being ... *Ontology should be replaced by pneumatology*." (my italics).

[4] See Chapter IV, Section B, notes.

[5] Knowledge through spirit, for Berdyaev, is above consciousness. He says, in *Spirit and Reality*, 18: "Consciousness and self-consciousness are related to spirit ... Spirit is the agency of super-consciousness in consciousness."

[6] *Spirit and Reality*, 66–67.

[7] *The Destiny of Man*, 189.

[8] *Solitude and Society*, 67.

Berdyaev's philosophy, consequently, the deepest part of man, the Ego, the primal willing, comes from the spiritual principle; and the spiritual principle, the logos, is based on the Godman. The mystery of how man participates in the *Ungrund*, in irrational Freedom, by means of his spiritual principle, his logos, is not investigated by Berdyaev. He has tried, with his esoteric doctrine, to uncover the mystery of freedom in God and in man, that is, with the Boehmian doctrine of a divine theogony out of the *Ungrund*. But the mystery still remains, both in God and in man, a mystery.

The paradox of freedom and intelligibility becomes more noticeable in Berdyaev's later than in his earlier works. In *Freedom and the Spirit* (1926), for instance, an earlier work in his mature period, the Boehmian voluntarism is uppermost in his mind. Freedom (*Ungrund*), rather than Logos (Christ), is the interest. But the doctrine of Logos or Godman-hood is stressed in the last works.

But God is spirit, and spirit is activity. Spirit is liberty. The nature of spirit is the opposite of passivity and necessity ...[1]

He means, not that spirit is irrational but that the will, the profoundest part of spirit, acts freely in spirit. He takes care to point out in the latest works that spirit is not irrational.

Spirit is not something opposite to the rational or the irrational. The true existentialist philosophy is philosophy of the spirit.[2]

When he says that spirit is not opposed to the rational or irrational, he means that the divine Truth (the Logos) is known by the *integral* human spirit.[3] There are rational and irrational elements. "Spiritual knowing is divine-human, knowledge neither by reason nor by feeling, but by integral Spirit." [4] And when he says that the true Existentialist philosophy is philosophy of the spirit, he means that his Existentialism does not accept the irrational nihilism of Sartre and Simon de Beauvoir, "the idolatry of death," he says.[5] On the contrary, he is concerned with nothing less than the search for truth. The chapter in which he discusses the rejection of nihilistic and irrational Existentialism, has been en-

---

[1] *Freedom and the Spirit*, 2.
[2] *The Realm of Spirit and the Realm of Caesar*, 31.
[3] See Chapter IV, Section G, Part 3.
[4] *The Realm of Spirit and the Realm of Caesar*, 30.
[5] *Ibid.*, 27. Concerning Sartre's nihilism see note above. Concerning Simone de Beauvoir, see *Towards a New Epoch*, 100: "The articles" (in Sartre's Review, *Temps Modernes*) of Simone de Beauvoir, intelligent, and reasonably clear as they are, are superior to those of Sartre, but they also reveal nothing original. If one lays the philosophical language aside in wihch they are clothed, the subjects themselves are ... almost banal."

titled "The Struggle for the Truth." This way of truth, which is the philosophy of the spirit, is Existentialism:

Knowledge of Truth means the transfiguration, the enlightenment of the world and not abstract knowledge ...[1]

That is, his Existentialism seeks the Truth, not an abstract (essentialistic) truth which, he thinks, would be an objectivization. Rationalism would be an unsatisfactory substitute for the irrational nihilism of some Existentialists. But Berdyaev's Existentialism creatively seeks an existent (Truth) which is intelligible. Knowledge of the Truth, which for Berdyaev is one aspect of the ultimate union of man with the existent Truth, means the transfiguration of the world. The macrocosm, the world, is transfigured in the microcosm, man, and brought back to integral unity.[2]

It is clear that Berdyaev has an Existentialism, and it is spiritual rather than irrational; that is, it is something more than rational or irrational. This is the mystery of freedom and intelligibility. Freedom is an absolute principle, but it is not contrasted with knowledge.

As I have already said existential philosophy cannot be ontological. Jaspers [3]

---

[1] *The Realm of Spirit and the Realm of Caesar*, 30.

[2] See Section F of this chapter.

[3] Jaspers, of all the contemporary Existentialists, is most to Berdyaev's liking. He says, in *Dream and Reality*, 103:

"Jaspers seems to be more faithful, and gives a more dramatic relief, to the original Kierkegaardian inspiration (than does Heidegger). His thought contains, moreover, strong Nietzschean elements. ... Jaspers is richer and more sensitive as a thinker than Heidegger; his thought abounds in psychological insights, and he has a deep sympathy for history. I have much more in common with him than with the other contemporary existentialists. An existentialist philosopher should be aware of an identity between his thinking and his personal and the world's destiny."

But Berdyaev inferentially criticizes the subjectivism of Jaspers' Existentialism. He says, in *Truth and Revelation*, 12:

"Kierkegaard regarded as existential only the knowledge which exists in the sphere of subjectivity, not in that of objectivity, in what is individual rather than in the common. In this respect he was a pioneer. It is Jaspers who remains most faithful to (Kierkegaard). ... But Kierkegaard did not take up a position which lies entirely on the other side of the distinction between subject and object. He preserved that distinction and at the same time took the side of the subject."

This criticism of Jaspers' and Kierkegaard's subjectivism, whether Berdyaev realizes it or not, is a criticism of contemporary Existentialism. See *ibid.*, 56, where the supremacy of a Personalism in his Existentialism reveals itself.

Further, the criticism of Jaspers' subjectivism is a criticism of Jaspers' *historicism*. Berdyaev's philosophy is suprahistorical; his solution to subjectivism is suprahistorical. Jaspers' doctrine of "frontier-situations" is a historicism. For Jaspers, "*L'historicité est alors le caractère de tout ce qui est concret* ..." M. Dufrenne and P. Ricoeur, *Karl Jaspers et la Philosophie de l'Existence* (Seuil, Paris, 1947). 181. Dufrenne and Ricoeur observe that (*Ibid.*, 182) Jaspers' philosophy is influenced by the historisicm of Kierkegaard.

A Comparison of Kierkegaard's Historicism with Berdyaev's Suprahistoricism:

Kierkegaard's historicism is apparent in his *Philosophical Fragments* (Princeton Univ.,

speaks truly when he says that the sphere of freedom is *Existenz*, that the Ego actually is freedom of choice, that freedom is an absolute principle. But with him freedom is contrasted with knowledge, and that is true only if it is the objectivization of knowledge which we have in mind.[1]

The ontological, which Existentialism opposes, is an essentialism. Hence, an ontological knowledge with which Jaspers, for example, contrasts freedom.[2] Berdyaev thus indicates he does not contradict Jaspers' Existentialism, but is proposing a free and existent Truth.

Princeton 1946). His historicism is clearly present, and in such a way as to contradict the suprahistoricism of Berdyaev. On p. 50 and following Kierkegaard points out that if we accept the Socratic principle that learning is a process of self-recollection; than the object of faith is the *teaching*, not the Teacher. And Kierkegaard rejects this solution and observes that it is not historical. (St. Augustine, incidentally, does not suffer in this argument because, unlike Berdyaev he asserts the historical teacher as well as the teaching. *De Civitate Dei*, Book 18, Chapter 49).

"But the historical is the past (for the present pressing upon the confines of the future has not yet become historical)."

Then he shows that nature cannot be called historical. It is interesting that Berdyaev, when he considers the possibilities of a philosophy of history, turns to the two unhistorical ones: the cosmic and the supernatural. *Slavery and Freedom*, 262–263. But he leaves out the historical approach. Kierkegaard says:

"... nature is too abstract to have a dialectic with respect to time in the stricter sense. ... On the other hand it is the perfection of the eternal to have no history, the eternal being the only existence that has absolutely no history." *Philosophical Fragments*, 62.

Kierkegaard contradicts the suprahistoricism of Berdyaev on at least two points. He says, *ibid.*, 92:

"It is well known that Christianity is the only historical phenomena which in spite of the historical, nay precisely by means of the historical, has offered itself to the individual as a point of departure for his eternal consciousness ..."

But Berdyaev says that Christianity is a historical phenomenon which, by means of the *suprahistorical* in it, has offered itself as a point of departure. See 129, n 3 and works cited. This is the important difference.

Kierkegaard then says:

"Christianity ... has proposed to base man's eternal happiness on his relations to something historical. No system of philosophy, addressing itself only to thought, no *mythology*, addressing itself solely to the *imagination*, no historical knowledge, addressing itself solely to the *memory* has ever had this idea ..." (my italics).

Berdyaev does assert the historical Christ. Cf. *Truth and Revelation*, Chapter V, but he asserts, far more, the suprahistorical Christ. This philosophy addresses itself, precisely, to concrete thought, imagination and memory; and it is a mythical philosophy (in the sense of symbolism). We will see that the memory is all-important in Berdyaev's Personalism and Existentialism. The concrete Existent, the Godman, is *recollected* and created in the memory; and the recollection is suprahistorical. Berdyaev is interested in the "historical," not in the mere historical as such. See Chapter I, Section B.

Finally, if Kierkegaard encountered Berdyaev's philosophy he would class it with Hegel's universalism. Berdyaev's existent is a concrete universal and, so far as it is an existent, not merely historical. See 114, n 1 below. Hegel, however, intends to be historical. The essence of Hegel's man is defined by the whole historical universe. Berdyaev is suprahistorical; man, according to him, transcends, in his essence, the whole universe.

[1] *Truth and Revelation*, 68.

[2] Berdyaev says, in *Towards a New Epoch*, 96–97:

"*Ontology is a doctrine of essence*. Jaspers is infinitely more right in not admitting an ontological knowledge by means of concepts ... Existential philosophy can only be a knowledge of God, of the world, and of man in the deep subjectivity or human existence ..." (my italics)

That is, he maintains the primacy of freedom, and overcomes irrationalism in the super-rationalism of the divine Logos.

> It is written in the Gospel, "Ye shall know the Truth and the Truth shall make you free." The final and decisive liberation can be reached only by the vital assimilation of truth. In the last resort this is divine freedom, the freedom of the Kingdom of God, freedom which is finally united with grace.[1]

The mystery of freedom and intelligibility is recognized here. "The vital assimilation of truth," he says, "in the last resort is divine freedom ... freedom which is finally united with grace." Berdyaev uses the mysterious terms, *divine* and *grace*. He says, *"finally* united with grace," means that irrational freedom finally is perfectly illuminated after a process. And he refers to this doctrine of truth when he says;

> I have already said many times that spirit ... is freedom, that it is a creative act which is effected in depth, it is what nowadays is called *Existenz*.[2]

We may anticipate Chapter IV in noting how this Existentialism can remain a Personalism and yet posits that the person resorts to a transcendent Truth. The human spirit escapes objectivization and yet goes outside itself. Berdyaev says that the spirit is a creative act, and that is the answer.

D. PERSONALITY: THE CONCRETE AND UNIVERSAL EXISTENT

The philosophy of the concrete existent is typical of Russian philosophers:

> ... it may be said that Russian philosophy, colored as it was by religion, desires to be existential. In it the apprehending and philosophizing self was existential.
>
> ... The fundamental idea of Russian philosophy is the idea of concrete existent, of the underlying real existence which preceeds rational thought.[3]

The most important point Berdyaev makes in this passage is that Russian philosophy has been colored by religion. Berdyaev admits even to a certain quality of Existentialism in the essentialist, Vladimir Solovyev. This is so because Solovyev is a Christian religious philosopher and therefore propounds a philosophy of the Existent, the Godman.[4] And a hundred years' tradition of many Russian thinkers,

---

[1] *Truth and Revelation*, 71.
[2] *Ibid.*, 74.
[3] *The Russian Idea*, 159–160. Cf. *Dream and Reality*, 102.
[4] See Chapter II, Section C.

whose thought has been at once metaphysical and religious, exists.[1]
Russian philosophy has been concrete, existential and religious.

First, the Russian religious outlook is Orthodox and stems from the
mystical way of ancient Orthodoxy. Second, the organicism of Schelling
and his contemporaries, their irrationalism and Schelling's nature-
philosophy, have permeated Russian Philosophic thought. Third,
Russian philosophy has been greatly influenced by Hegel's concrete
universalism. The influence is understandable. Hegel combines a cosmogonical doctrine of Spirit, which is akin to the supernaturalism of
Russian Orthodoxy, with a concrete universalism.[2] The division between the natural and the supernatural is denied, and it is therefore

---

[1] Lossky says, in his *History of Russian Philosophy*, 29:
"The doctrine of metalogical knowledge as the essential complement to logical knowledge
particularly occupies Florensky, Bulgakov and Berdyaev; ... Interest in the metalogical
principles of existence is closely combined in *Russian religious philosophy* with an insistence
upon the concreteness and wholeness of existence." (my italics) See, also, the Table of
Contents, Zenkovsky's *History of Russian Philosophy*.

[2] In the case of Berdyaev, it is misleading to talk of influences concerning many points of
doctrines. The influences are exceedingly numerous and impossible of determination. We
cannot know Berdyaev's mind, and if we could, Berdyaev would probably give an incorrect
answer to himself and to us. But we can point out certain currents of thought, doctrinal
complexes, and observe that Berdyaev participated in them. We cannot even say Berdyaev
was exclusively determined by them.
   Berdyaev's philosophy is a part of that doctrinal complex which asserts the concrete
universalism. But he does not consider himself a Hegelian. "The metaphysical development
of post-Kantian German Idealism as represented by Fichte, Schelling and Hegel, was really
a betrayal of Kant." *Dream and Reality*, 94. He attacks them for their monism, pantheism
and evolutionism.
   On the other hand, Berdyaev recognizes the origin of concrete universalism in German
Idealism. He looks upon German Idealism as a movement which freed philosophy from
intellectualist doctrines. "But concrete living realities have always eluded those metaphysical doctrines." *Freedom and the Spirit*, I.
   The Sophiological doctrine of Solovyev is of great importance to Berdyaev's philosophy –
he defines his doctrine in terms of Sophiology. And Solovyev asserts a concrete universalism.
Cf. Zenkovsky's *History of Russian Philosophy*, 520. Berdyaev's contemporaries, Bulgakov
and Florensky, are both followers of Solovyev. And they assert a concrete universalism.
Cf. Lossky's *History of Russian Philosophy*, 208. But the outlook is already old in Russian
thought. Zenkovsky says, *History of Russian Philosophy*, 529–530:
   "Solovyev did not introduce new themes to the Russian philosophic consciousness; even in
the most original part of his system – his Sophiological doctrine – he merely gives a new *name*
to a complex of problems which had been considered by Russian thinkers many times before
him."
   The Schellingism of Solovyev (and of other Russians) is important. We find, here, the
positing of the organic structure of the world, the world-soul, the notion of totality. Cf.
Zenkovsky's *History of Russian Philosophy*, 119. "Russian Schellingism has not yet wholly
disapperaed; we need only recall Schelling's enormous importance for the world-view of
Vladimir Solovlev, whose influence is still alive in our day". *Ibid.*, 116.
   Berdyaev's philosophy may also be considered a part of a philosophical current which is
called "Romanticism." Zenkovsky attempts to make out an overwhelming case for the
Romanticism of Berdyaev. Zenkovsky fails. All the evidence he gives to prove that Berdyaev
is a Romantic philosopher is true, but he fails to see that Romanticism is only one among the
terms that must be used to describe Berdyaev. Cf. *History of Russian Philosophy*, 760, ff.
The root of Berdyaev's Romanticism, he believes, lies in "his constant readiness to repudiate

propitious for a philosophy centered about the Godman to arise. Western philosophers usually apply the notion of an existent to created things, or to metaphysical entities. But Russian philosophers who follow Solovyev, primarily apply the notion to the Godman.[1] The philosophy refers, also, to created concrete existents.

The religious orientation of Russian philosophy precludes an idealism,[2] or objectivism, in which rational thought (instead of the existent) is known. Religious doctrine is prior to German Idealism in the Russian religious philosophers. Berdyaev himself who began as a Marxist idealist, did not remain an idealist when he became a Christian philosopher.[3]

It is not necessary for our purpose to study the attack Berdyaev makes upon the abstract entity which he and Solovyev associate with the copula in logical predication, and which they believe is an improper hypostasization of the copula. But this distinction, in terms of predication, between abstract being and concrete being shows us well the concrete Existentialism of Berdyaev.

Cat ... is the kernel of the phrase, "the cat exists." [4]

This shows that he wants to avoid the theorizing of existence. He dislikes, in fact, the use of the very word, *existence*, because it stands alone, by itself, and thus becomes an empty abstraction with no concrete content. As he shows some sentences farther, he dislikes the use of the word *existent*, because *existent* is associated with the empty term, *existence*.

Indeed following Solovyev, he establishes his Existentialism from the point of view of logical predication. The doctrine of Hegel (that of concrete universalism) seems to be in the background.

Vladimir Solovyev established an interesting distinction between abstract Being

---

reality – which for him was an intolerable banality.'" *Ibid.*, 780. Berdyaev's Romanticism can be seen in the form his reaction against philosophic essentialism takes.

Like Schelling, he offers, in place of the essentialism, a philosophy of beauty. His organic outlook is Romantic. Likewise his transcendentalism and spiritualism is Romantic. "I have often wondered if I might be called a romantic philosopher. ... But what does romanticism really mean. If it is the opposite of classicism, I must undoubtedly style myself a romantic. ... On the other hand I found myself in opposition to Romanticism..." *Dream and Reality*, 105. In *Dream and Reality*, 106, he shows exactly in what sense he considers himself a Romantic philosopher and in what sense he is not. See also 126, n 1 below concerning the idea of microcosm.

[1] Concerning followers of Solovyev, see preceding note; see also Chapter II, Section C.

[2] The 19th-century Christianity of Holy Russia was a world for which Idealism as such was unreal.

[3] V.V. Zenkovsky, *A History of Russian Philosophy*, 720.

[4] *Slavery and Freedom*, 75.

as the *predicate* and concrete Being as the *subject*. The notion *is*, is an example of abstract Being.[1]

The Russian language completely does away with the copula, so that it presents such phrases as, "he old," "she lovely," "they students." A correct Russian syllogism might be: "All men mortal; Socrates man; Socrates mortal." [2] Clearly in such a language, the copula, *"is"* (which is represented in Russian, when necessary, by the word, *"est"*), represents no reality.

It is the *concrete* cat Berdyaev is interested in, not in the "existence" which is ascribed to it. This is his attitude.

He has then, presented the reader with a distinction between two positions in his Existentialism. We have seen, on the one hand, that existence (as a primal willing) is at the root of the Ego. And Berdyaev uses the term *existence* often. On the other hand, existence, taken in itself in mere logical thought, is an empty concept.

This shows us that Berdyaev denies the opinion which sees existence as something added to something else. What is more, he shows in the context of the passages just cited that he is refuting only doctrines of being in which being is prior to will or freedom.[3] The basis of his Existentialism and Personalism is the concrete existent whose deepest root is the pre-existential will.[4]

Such a philosophy cannot be an extreme realism, where the idea is more real than the thing, nor a nominalism, where the meaning, the logos of the thing is unreal.

... the traditional controversy between the "realists" and the "nominalists." I am, both intellectually and emotionally, opposed to realist conceptualism and do not believe in any general ideas or universals representing not particular and individual images but a supposed essence of things. ... On the other hand, I cannot identify myself with the nominalist position, because it appears to undermine the idea of the human person, and fails to recognize the eternal image of man. I am not concerned to deny any reality to universals or to restrict philosophy to the particular; *rather, I am concerned to find a universal in the particular, to understand the abstract concretely, instead of understanding the concrete abstractly.* ... The revolt against the domination of the "general," therefore, is legitimate and receives its impetus from the Christian conception of God, who is neither Plato's idea of the Good nor Aristotle's concept of the pure act, but the 'God of Abraham, Isaac and Jacob," the God who is made man and with whom

[1] *Solitude and Society*, 41.

[2] Cf. Professor E. Gilson's book, *Being and Some Philosophers* (Pontifical Institute of Mediaeval Studies, Toronto, 1949), 192. The example of a Russian syllogism is Professor Gilson's.

[3] Cf. *Slavery and Freedom*, 75–76.

[4] Berdyaev says, in *Spirit and Reality*, 130: "We should probably be right in thinking of *Ungrund* as the primal pre-existential freedom."

man enters into personal relations. I am convinced that all philosophical foundations demand re-examination in the light of this Christian affirmation of the
pre-eminence of the personal and the singular ...[1] (my italics)

He is opposed to "realist conceptualism" (he has Plato in mind) [2] because to him it is an essentialism which disregards existents. He opposes
nominalism, ultimately, because it denies his philosophy of Godmanhood, where the divine Logos is seen to be knowable by man. Yet, the
universal does exist (in the particular).

He intends "to understand the abstract concretely, instead of understanding the concrete abstractly." We will study this in Chapter IV,
where his noetic is treated. There is no purely intellectual knowing for
Berdyaev, but highest knowledge has an imaginative component. The
existent is properly known by means of an image (or by a perfect
identity between the knower and the known), rather than by an abstract
concept.[3] And the universal is known along with the image. Berdyaev
refers his solution of the problem of universals to the religious doctrine
of the singular and personal Godman. In this philosophy, then, the
Godman is known conceptually and imaginatively by means of an
image. Berdyaev finds the universal, *humanity*, in the singular, the
Godman.[4]

In short, Berdyaev holds that abstract truths (without imaginative
components) are not real truths; but he thinks that truths known both
intellectually and imaginatively are real.[5] Note that this requires every

---

[1] *Dream and Reality*, 289.

[2] *Ibid.*, 289. He criticizes the *general* ideas of Plato. But "I am not concerned to deny any
reality to universals ... rather, I am concerned to find a universal in the particular."

[3] See Chapter IV, Section G.

[4] Cf. *Slavery and Freedom*, 50. When we say that Berdyaev finds the universal, *humanity*,
in the singular, the Godman, we recall Hegel. Russian religious philosophers are interested in
history and reassert the Hegelian doctrine of concrete universals. But Hegel's spiritualism
does injustice to the existent and to the person, and, therefore, to Christianity. Berdyaev has
proffered a doctrine which says: the concrete universal is, finally, the particular Existent,
the Godman, the Second Son of the Holy Trinity. But the concrete world of nature and of
history, in which we move, has suffered in Berdyaev's suprahistorical doctrine.

Hegel's historicism has done better in Solovyev. Historicism for Solovyev is the principle
form and the flowering of existence. "Historiocentrism rather than cosmocentrism, or even
anthropocentricicm, defines Solovyev's approach to all problems ... in the sense that for him
all 'aspects' of being are revealed in history, in the development of mankind." Zenkovsky's
History of Russian Philosophy, 482–483. But then Solovyev falls into a doctrine of "pan-
human organism," where "all human elements form an integral organism."

[5] *Solitude and Society*, 130. "The 'general,' as opposed to the individual, is real only when
it is itself individual and unique. The non-individual 'general' is a logical rather than an
ontological category; and its logical significance is determined by the degree of community
existing between consciousnesses that have no bond of communion; in other words, since the
terms of objective and social are synonymous, its nature is fundamentally sociological."

This notion of abstract universality is Hegelian. Professor Fackenheim of the University
of Toronto, in a personal communication, has made a *bon mot* which is as illuminating for under-

real knowledge to partake of certain conditions of singularity and concreteness.

I want to emphasize in this connection that my whole philosophical approach is radically incompatible with a belief in the possibility of a rational ontology, that is to say, of a science of being in which the process of abstraction is pushed to the point where Being is regarded as devoid of all peculiarities and all concrete characteristic. I can only admit a phenomenology which describes metaphysical reality in symbolic terms. Any rationalization of the divine-human relationship, any attempt at expressing it in terms of a rational philosophy of being, makes nonsense both of that relationship and of that philosophy. It can only be spoken of in symbolic and mythological terms which leave the door open to mystery.[1]

Symbolic and *mythological*, in this context, refer to an imaginative knowledge. Logical reasoning is no proper use of the mind, because logic requires the use of abstract concepts, and he rejects purely conceptual reasoning.[2] A science of a purely intelligible being cannot be accepted in his metaphysics which is neither scientific nor purely intelligible. He admits only a "phenomenology" – that is, a noetic – which describes metaphysical entities with symbols or myths.[3]

He gives special mention to the divine-human relationship; it cannot be expressed by an abstract metaphysics because the metaphysical relationship is between, not two purely abstract minds, or between a mind and a concrete existent, but between two concrete incarnate spirits. And Berdyaev must, with such a definition of man and of the divine Logos, use myths and symbols instead of concepts to describe the metaphysical relationship between them. We will see, in Chapter IV why this symbolism is needed. The divine-human relationship is, on the

standing Berdyaev as it is for knowing Hegel: "For Hegel, there is a sharp contrast between abstract universal (opposed to particularity) and concrete universal (opposed to isolated particularity)." The word, "isolated," is the key. In denying isolation and particularity, he posits the concrete universal. And this belongs to a doctrine of the organic unity of history.

This outlook is Schellingian as well as Hegelian. Schelling said: "Nothing universal exists ... only what is individual exists, and universal being exists ... only if the absolute individual being *is* the former." Quoted in the "Introduction" to *The Ages of the World*, 48. And, for Hegel, there is no such thing as a class of abstract universals. "Class and members go with abstract thinking". *Phenomenology of Mind*, 157. Berdyaev may have got the doctrine of concrete universals from Solovyev. "Yet the realization of Godmanhood implied the universal development of mangodhood. 'Man can assume Divinity only in his absolute totality,' Solovyev insists, 'the mangod is necessarily collective and universal ...'" Zoyboff's "Introduction" to *Lectures on Godmanhood*, 61.

[1] *Dream and Reality*, 209.

[2] See Chapter IV.

[3] The term, *phenomenology*, is used only once by Berdyaev, so far as I can find, and the use has no connection with the Phenomenological School, except to indicate that the knowledge, insofar as it is not the reality known, is only a symbol of it. "In the phenomenology of Husserl the intentional act liberates from the individual and becomes the basis of objectivism." *The Beginning and the End*, 54.

one hand, a metaphysical fact. On the other hand, it is a religious communion.

It is the concrete person, not the epistemological subject or the abstract universal mind, who takes cognizance of and meditates on the object of knowledge, philosophical or otherwise.[1]

The question which was posed in the preceding section, "how can the concrete be illuminated by a spiritual activity?" is now partly answered. The spiritual activity of knowing is itself imaginative and, therefore, in a sense concrete. Thus the philosopher can arrive at the existent by way of his own subjectivity and yet not do away with its concreteness. It is a creative activity because myths and symbols have to be created (invented) in order to illuminate the concrete with the light of metaphysical reality.

Such a metaphysics flows from Berdyaev's philosophy of history. The divine meaning of history, though it is outside historical time, is nevertheless "temporal." And although as the divine Logos it is the reality of which man is only the symbol, it is nevertheless human. Consequently, the divine meaning of history is, in a way, concrete. And when the philosopher of history illuminates the concrete, at the same time he attains the divine Logos.

Man's relation to what is above him is the condition of the personality's existence.

Personality is precisely the divine idea, the divine image and resemblance in man, in contrast with individuality, which is a naturalistic and biological conception. Thus in order to understand himself man must address himself to God, he must fathom the divine idea concerning himself, and direct all his forces to the realization of it.[2]

When he says personality is a divine idea Berdyaev refers to the divine Logos, the Proto-type of human personality. He does not divide the natural and the supernatural; the divine Idea exists in man as the divine image and resemblance. It is a concrete idea.[3]

He contrasts personality with individuality because personality is a concrete universal, and the concrete universal is opposed to isolated particularity. We saw, on p. 107, that "personality is the child of meaning, or truth." And we saw that personality is created by the Logos, the spiritual principle. The true personality is the personality of

---

[1] *Dream and Reality*, 104.
[2] *Freedom and the Spirit*, 213.
[3] See 117 n 2 above.

the divine Logos, and man seeks the divine idea of himself and thus directs all his forces to the realization of personality.

The Suprapersonal world and existence, to which personality strives to rise, is not an abstract universal for which each personality would be a means.

The relation of personality to the universal is certainly not a relation to the species and the common.
. . .

The universal is not the common; it is not abstract, but concrete, i.e. it is plenitude. . . . The individual is by no means a part of the universal. The opposition of universal and singular is incorrect. Personality is certainly not partial, nor particular as opposed to universal. It can be said with more truth that personality is a universal. The very singleness of the individual is permeated not by that which is individual, but by that which is universal. . . . The universal is an essay, an attempt, on the part of the subject, not a reality in the object.[1]

The individual person is not part of the universal; it is not the individual member forming part of a hypostasized species. For the universal itself is concrete and, hence, incapable of being common to many individuals. The opposition, therefore, of the universal and singular is incorrect; and personality is not partial. General predication, in this theory, pertains to objectified knowledge and is a necessary evil for Berdyaev.[2]

The last sentence of the text answers the question, how *does* the individual participate in the universal? The universal is an attempt on the part of the individual; that is, it is a sought-after goal. The subject seeks this goal in his own subjectivity (that is, he does not seek it as an external object). We saw in Chapter I, for example, the doctrine of the the creative knowing of historical cultures, and of the cosmos. The ultimate goal, we have already seen, is the divine Logos, the Godman. The reason it is sought within the subjectivity of the individual is that it is not only transcendent but also immanent. The individual person is an image of the divine Incarnate Spirit and seeks to improve this image in order to realize in himself the true Reality. In short, the concrete universal Proto-type exists, and concrete universal images exist. And this must be understood imaginatively (with concrete conditions) as well as intellectually.[3]

We saw in Chapter I, when the philosopher knows the historical he is,

---

[1] *Slavery and Freedom*, 37–38.
[2] Concerning logical thought and its use, see Chapter IV, Section B.
[3] See Chapter IV, concerning the identification of knowledge of the universal with the universality of the knower.

ultimately, knowing himself and man. This is proper to such a philosophy of history, because temporal history itself is contained within the universality and spiritual "history" of divine Logos, Who is the True Man. Indeed:

... the personality ... can do what no *mere part* can aspire to do – it can realize itself in the process of making its content universal. It is a unity in the midst of plurality, and can thus comprehend the universe.[1]

When the philosopher of history seeks to realize the true Man within him, he does so by realizing himself as a microcosm. And just as the history of the world, with its conditions of concreteness, is contained within the concrete divine Existent, so man progressively brings history within his own subjectivity through the use of concrete historical myths. Berdyaev says:

The hypostatization of man, the endowment of him with the qualities of personality is the real myth about man, and it also requires imagination. In accord with this myth man is not a part, he is not particularized, because he is the image of (God) and is a universe. This is the God-likeness of man ...[2]

The greatest myth of all is the *image* of the divine Personality; namely, man's own personality in which all the other symbols and myths are contained and brought toward the reality he seeks. Everything we know is known by way of myths; [3] the "historical" is known this way, and man progressively improves the myths in the course of history. In this way, the world and man are improved during history, along with man's mythical and symbolic knowledge. The (symbol of) rule of the cosmos in ancient times was replaced by the (symbol of) technical conquest of the world by the spirit.[4]

It is quite clear that the metaphysics we are dealing with is a concrete Existentialism. Man is a concrete existent; the True Man is a concrete existent; and the participation of man in the True Man is concrete and Existential. The image, or symbol, or myth, through which a person creates and knows the reality is itself a concrete existent because it is an

---

[1] *Solitude and Society*, 132.
[2] *Slavery and Freedom*, 50.
[3] See Chapter IV.
[4] *Freedom and the Spirit*, 221, ff. We may see something of this symbolism of the ages of the world in the following:

"Herein lies the religious meaning of technique. It gives man a planetary feeling of the earth, very different from the one he experienced in former ages. He feels differently when his feet touch the depth, holiness and mysticism of the earth than when he sees it as a planet flying into infinite space, amidst innumerable universes, and he himself able to detach himself from it, to fly into the air, into the stratosphere." Berdyaev, *The Bourgeois Mind*, 46–47.

image that is identified with the concrete subjectivity of the person: himself the "immortal and eternal" [1] image of plenary reality.

Personality is not opposed as the particular to the universal; "it can be said *with more truth* that personality is universal." That is, the personality can be called particular or singular,[2] but there is more truth in calling it universal. The universality of the personality is connected with the communion of it with other persons.

E. PERSONALITY
AND EXISTENCE NOT ISOLATED FROM THE THOU AND THE WE

In a concrete Existentialism and Personalism the personality is a subject which is not part of a whole; it is not an object, but a subject, and a whole and which seeks a spiritual union with other Egos. In the coming section, we shall see just what it means after all for the personality to be a whole. At present we will see how it is that this doctrine implies the Thou and the We, the spiritual communion of persons.

... the personality is never a part but always a whole, never a datum of the inner world of existence. ... It is not of this world: when confronted with the personality, I am in the presence of a Thou. It is not an object ... Thus the triumph of the personality will mean the annihiliation of the objective world.[3]

The personality is a whole, a concrete whole; it, therefore, is never an objective datum nor an abstraction. It cannot, then, be of this world (which is objectified). It is, in other words, a subject. Personality is not known as an impersonal It. Berdyaev introduces in his personalism the familiar form of the personal pronoun, the Thou. (We will soon see that one knows his own personality through knowing the Thou, other personalities.) Berdyaev, we will see, speaks too of knowing *me*. This usage shows that, according to Berdyaev, the personality cannot be understood and known except through a personal communion. The use of the word *Thou* also indicates the subjectivity of the other person, as it truly is apart from any encrustation and distortion of objectivity. The personality is not of this (objective) world. The triumph of the personality which is, at the same time, the triumph of its subjectivity, its true reality, therefore means the transfiguration of the objective world. As we will see in the following section, the creation of the true

[2] *Solitude and Society*, 149.
[2] See 95, n 3 above.
[3] *Solitude and Society*, 123.

world, in the microcosm, flows out of the transfiguration of the objective world.

Berdyaev connects the solitude of man and the objectivization of personality. He criticizes the relationships of society:

Solitude, indeed, can be overcome only in communion, only in the knowledge of the spiritual world, and not in the world of social frequentation, of the multitude and its objective relationships. When authentic community is achieved, the personality is strictly itself, and obeys the dictates of its own nature; . . . it unites with the Thou while at the same time preserving its own identity. . . . on the existential plane, on the extra-natural and extra-social plane, the personality insists on being itself; and man seeks to find his own reflection in another human countenance, in the Thou.[1]

The personality, then, cannot become its true self in a state of solitude. And it cannot avoid solitude if its relationships with other persons are ordered according to social formulas. Berdyaev, indeed, condemns abstract logic, itself, in terms of society. Such a logic is bound up with the objective relationships and outlooks found in ordinary societies. He associates all objectified knowledge, and particularly knowledge in the form of abstractions and essences, with ordinary objectified society.[2]

We see, then, what he means when he says: "solitude can only be overcome in communion, only in the knowledge of the spiritual world." The personality, objectified in society, remains in solitude not only because it fails to find other personalities but also because it cannot find itself. So far as it can know itself, it sees itself objectively; and in failing to find its reflection in another human countenance, in the Thou, it lacks a condition of knowing itself.[3]

When by means of authentic community the personality is strictly itself, it is free to "obey the dictates of its own nature." "The personality insists on being itself; and man seeks to find his own reflection in another human countenance, in the Thou." It is a paradox: a man preserves his own identity and yet seeks his reflection in another man's face. Berdyaev refers to the true Man, the true Personality, of Whom we are images. In this respect the personality insists on being itself and yet goes out of itself when it seeks its reflection in another man's countenance. Berdyaev is asserting both immanence and transcendence of the Godman. We may observe, by the way, Berdyaev's reference to the concrete image of personality, the human countenance, the face. He

---

[1] *Ibid.*, 125.
[2] See 117, n 5 above.
[3] See Chapter IV, Section E, which treats communal knowing.

finds the Thou there because the communion is imaginative, as well as intellectual.[1]

But the existence of the We cannot be ignored, and its relationship to the Ego, the Thou, and the It must be considered. . . . the We can be transformed into the It by the operation of socializing or objectifying processes . . .[2]

The We can then be understood in two ways. First it can be viewed in relation to the Thou (and the It); where the relationship is between two Thous, there is a We. Second, the We can be understood as it is in itself, and this is the main intention of the passage. The We exists. The We can be transformed into the It by a socializing or objectifying process (and we have considered the process). It becomes clear then that Berdyaev believes the We is an existent reality. He sees it as one ordinarily sees "society" to be an existent reality; except the We is more existential. It is a spiritual communion.

The personality is not a part of the We (as an ordinary citizen happens to be part of an objectified society). It is subjectively identified with the We.

The personality has a creative function to perform in social and cosmic life. Spiritually, the personality is never isolated, for it postulates the existence of others, of the Thou and the We, without at the same time every being becoming a part or a means.[3]

Thus, the paradox of the personality remaining itself and yet seeking its image in the Thou and the We is solved. It becomes identified with the Thou and the We, and yet within the subjectivity of its own concrete existence. It creates, in its noetic action, an image which approximates closer than before to the true reality of the Thou and the We.

We might at this juncture recall Berdyaev's notion of the historical. The historical is a historical myth or symbol which the philosopher of history creates and, through it, knows the meaning of history. The historical, we saw, ultimately is man. Now, we find, the Thou and the We are taken up into the person's subjectivity in a creative action. And one improves his own concrete existence in this creative act. His existence becomes identified with the Thou and the We. If follows from this, I think, that he clarifies and improves the meaning of history. He has realized further the true man in himself. The true man is a microcosmos in which the world and history are contained.

---

[1] We will see that religious knowledge is imaginative in its religiosity. Cf. Chapter IV, Section G, Part 1.

[2] *Solitude and Society*, 79–80.

[3] *Ibid.*, 131.

... The We is a qualitative [1] content immanent in the Ego, for every Ego is invariably related not only to the Thou but also to multiple mankind.[2]

"Ego" is understood to mean personality.[3] The Ego is noetically and metaphysically related to the We, that is, to multiple mankind, because this is a "social and human metaphysics, that of the We," [4] a "metaphysical sociology." [5] The Thou and the We flow cut of something – the Ego. [6]

Even if we assume that the We, as well as the Thou and the It, are immediate data, it remains none the less true that the Ego is the anterior, primitive entity; I cannot say, "I," without thereby affirming and postulating the Thou and the We. In this light, sociability is a constituent property of the Ego's intimate existence.[7]

The We as well as the Thou and the It are "immediate data." Berdyaev is not asserting idealism; the external reality is really external (as well as internal, in the subjectivity of knowing). Nevertheless the Thou and the We are basically implied in the I (the microcosmos, the image of the True Man). The Ego, therefore, is the anterior, primitive entity. This is why, in this metaphysical sociology, sociability is a constituent property of the Ego's intimate existence. Let us note that Berdyaev does not separate the natural and the supernatural; he distinguishes them.[8] The divine Prototype of man is the Source and Terminus of all men and of all history, and man is the image of Him.

Berdyaev may be classified in a certain philosophical movement which Helmut Kuhn calls "Social Existentialism." In this sense his most eminent companions are Martin Buber and Gabriel Marcel.[9] It

---

[1] When Berdyaev says "the We is a qualitative content immanent in the Ego," he does not mean anything more by "qualitative" than the commonsense idea. That is, he is only pointing out the superquantitative aspect of the union of the We and and the Ego. There is no question of a Scholastic doctrine of quality.

[2] *Solitude and Society*, 80.

[3] *Ego*, here, refers to personality; and Berdyaev uses the word, *Ego*, because he discusses his Personalism for the moment, in terms of that of Martin Buber. He translates Buber's distinction between the *Ichsein*, the *Dusein*, and the *Essein* as a distinction between the Ego, the Thou and the It. Berdyaev claims to go beyond Buber. "(Buber) envisages the relationship between man and God, as expounded in the Bible. His investigations do not extend to the relationship between human consciousnesses, between the Ego and the Thou, between two human beings, or to the diverse relationships. Nor does he consider the problem of social and human metaphysics, that of the We." *Solitude and Society*, 79.

[4] *Ibid.*, 79.

[5] *Ibid.*, 80.

[6] Recall that the person, in his true depths, is the Godman. See the following section.

[7] *Solitude and Society*, 80.

[8] See *Spirit and Reality*, 175.

[9] The notion, "Social Existentialism," is that of Helmut Kuhn. In an article in Virgilius Firm's encyclopaedia, *A History of Philosophical Systems* (Philosophical Library, New York, 1950), 414, entitled "Existentialism," Kuhn describes Social Existentialism. The only devotée of this outlook, however, that he mentions is Gabriel Marcel.

is a personalism in which the role of the social is personalized and stressed in a doctrine of personality.

F. PERSONALITY: THE MICROCOSM

It is because man is a microcosm [1] that his own existence is the "most 'existential'" of all concrete existents.

So-called existentialist philosophy (the novelty of which, by the way, has been greatly exaggerated) regards philosophy as the knowledge of reality through human existence and its concrete manifestations. Now it is a fact that my own existence is the most "existential" of all. In knowing himself man is initiated into mysteries unknown to him through his knowledge of others. I have experienced the world around me and all the historical processes and events of my time as part of myself, as my spiritual biography. At the deepest mystical level everything that has happened to the world happened to me. [2]

The definition of Existential philosophy here given states affirmatively what we have seen stated negatively. We saw before the object rejected, and we see now the subject affirmed. By the "concrete manifestations" of human existence, Berdyaev refers to the creations of man, particu- to historical entities.

"My own existence is the most 'existential' of all existents," because all the historical events and processes have entered into my subjectivity. But my existence is not the most "existential" if we mean merely the coverage knowledge and association give me.

"In knowing himself, man is initiated into mysteries unknown to him through his knowledge of others." Man has experienced history and events as part of *his* spiritual biography. The historical is not the cause of his greater existentiality. Instead, the historical is the effect of his

---

[1] We cannot say what are the historical origins of Berdyaev's doctrine of man the microcosm. Undoubtedly, he has encountered numerous versions of the doctrine. Solovyev's doctrine of "pan-humanity" has probably been one influence. Solovyev writes: "mankind, and not the individual person, is the primary reality; mankind is an entity, which is becoming absolute through universal progress." And he calls the "pan-human organism" a "totally one personality." (Quoted by V.V. Zenkovsky, *A History of Russian Philosophy*, 514). Solovyev's doctrine is the opposite of Berdyaev's Personalism.

Again, we may note the Leibnizian influence which came to him partly through Kozlov (1831–1900), a member of a neo-Leibnizian movement in Russian philosophy. "In (Berdyaev's) early period – clearly under the influence of Kozlov – he was ready to acknowledge a 'hierarchical unity of spiritual monads, bound together into a cosmic whole by the primary Divine Monad ... by means of an *emanation* (!) which is *prior* to the creative multiplicity of being." *Ibid.*, 760. Berdyaev mentions in passing Leibniz' idea of the microcosmic monad in *Dream and Reality*, 89.

[2] *Ibid.*, X–XI.

greater existentiality.[1] We recall from Chapter I that the process of knowing and creating the historical (e.g., the historical culture) is a process of Platonic remembrance. The True Man is, at the core of the personality, the True Microcosm from Whom the world and history flow.[2] This is why Berdyaev concludes saying, "at the deepest mystical level, everything that has happened to the world happened to me." At the deepest mystical level stands the True Man, in whom the eon of temporal history is but an epoch in celestial history.

... the individually personal is the most existential of all things and perhaps the most universal too; it is the most spiritual, and it is that which is most closely linked with meaning. The ego is steeped in its own depths and there it comes into touch with the noumenal spiritual world. This has been better understood by mystics than by philosophers.[3]

Berdyaev says *perhaps* the individually personal is the most universal. He hesitates here because, properly speaking, the individual person is only potentially all things (in their existential and spiritual reality.) [4] Only an extraordinary act of Platonic remembrance would realize the ultimate in universality. He associates the spirituality of the person (since he is a spirit) with meaning and with mysticism. The passage invites the reader, as it were, to conclude that the perfect universality, the one truly proper to the individual person, is to be achieved in the mystical union. The author's conclusion is Berdyaev's, as may be seen in the following cited text.

Further, the connection of Existentialism and philosophy of history may be seen, and Berdyaev is well aware of the connection.[5]

---

[1] Berdyaev, when he discusses his Existentialism in *Truth and Revelation*, 20, considers the temporal priority of the person to the externalization of the world. "The question is asked – by what organ can transcendental man be recognized? It is he himself who recognizes himself in an act which precedes the falling apart into subject and object. The universal spiritual experience of mankind provides the evidence that this is possible."

[2] On 14, *ibid.*, he says: "The spiritual experience of the inner man is not objectified, it is an existence which precedes the formation of the world of objects and things."

[3] *The Beginning and the End*, 45.

[4] "Potentially, (man) includes everything ..." *The Divine and the Human*, 113.

[5] The association of Existentialism and philosophy of history in Berdyaev's mind is to be seen in a passage from *Towards a New Epoch*. Indeed, the connection between Existentialism and philosophy of history in Berdyaev's mind saves the passage from being incoherent. He says, 103:

"Yet a religious form of existentialism remains possible; it is that of Pascal, Kierkegaard, as also that of L. Shestov and Gabriel Marcel. I consider myself a representative of religious and spiritual existentialism. There could not be in Russian thought an existentialism of the type of Heidegger of Sartre. We are children of Dostoyevsky. Russian thought is full of the philosophy of history. The expectation of a Messiah remains alive in us."

He says, in *Dream and Reality*, 103: "An existentialist philosopher should be aware of an identity between his thinking and his personal and the world's destiny. ... what concerns,

The unity of history and of the world is only to be found within the personality, the primary existent:

> Outside personality there is no absolute unity and totality in the world, to which personality would be subordinate; outside personality everything is partial, even the world itself is partial ... Such is the whole objectivized world. ... An existential center, and a suffering destiny are to be found in subjectivity, not in objectivity. ... And everything which is existential in the objectivized ranks of the world, in the nation, in mankind, in the cosmos, etc. belongs to the inward being of personality and is not subordinate to any hierarchical center. The cosmos, mankind, nation, etc., are to be found in human personality as in an individualized universe or microcosm, and their falling away from it, their ejection into external reality among objects, is the result of the fall of man, of his subordination to impersonal reality, exteriorization, and alienation.
> ... The realization of personality, the concentration and actualization of its strength, takes the sun into itself, it inwardly receives the whole cosmos, the whole of history all mankind.... There is no wholeness, no universality of any kind outside personality, it exists only within personality ...[1]

Everything outside the personality, even the inanimate world, is partial because the personality is the principle of total unity. Outside of total unity are parts with respect to wholes; and therefore not unifiable because lacking the subjectivity of the person. This Personalist doctrine is the condition of Berdyaev's universal history, a history and a philosophy which envisages the total unity of terrestrial history and of celestial history within God.

The existential basis exists in every objectified rank of the world: the nation, mankind, the cosmos, etc. Insofar as all these truly exist, they exist in the human personality. Their existentiality belongs to the inward being of personality.

Existents, in their existentiality, are not subordinate to any hierarchical center; that is, to an order modelled, for example, upon the nation or the cosmos. Indeed these orders, in their proper existence, belong within the human personality; they dominate the person only because of the objectivization which occurred in the Fall.

What, then, is the order, if any, to be found in the True World, in the age of the Spirit (Heaven)? Berdyaev terms himself in a sense a "mystical anarchist." [2] But he does not oppose anarchism to order and concrete harmony. He does not assert an anarchy, a chaos or disharmony.[3] After the end of this world, both the cosmos, mankind and nations

---

and absorbs, and haunts me is the destiny of the subject, the microcosmos, in which there stirs and throbs the whole universe, and which bears witness to the meaning of its own and the world's existence."

[1] *Slavery and Freedom*, 41–42.

[2] *Dream and Reality*, 158.

[3] Cf. *The Russian Idea*, 152. This anarchism, Berdyaev says, ' is an ideal of freedom, of

will be integrally preserved in the New Jerusalem, in the Kingdom of God.[1] Berdyaev is impelled by his Personalist philosophy of history to elaborate a theory of the Kingdom of God, a kingdom which is sought after and symbolized in the hierarchical orders of this world. He must do so because: First, he asserts a philosophy of freedom (from objectivization), and a universal history which *progresses* towards the end of history, the Kingdom of God. And this progress can make sense only if the goal transcends the objectivization of worldly orders. Second he asserts a cosmogonical doctrine, according to which the age of the Spirit will be enjoyed in *this* world after it is transfigured and made divine.[2] Consequently, he must figure out how the nations will be preserved in the New Jerusalem and yet without their slavish groupings and organisations.

He rejects worldly hierarchies from his conception of the Heavenly Jerusalem, but not hierarchism. Indeed he proposes a spiritual hierarchism in this life; that is, in the coming New Middle Ages to precede the end of the world.[3] "The 'hierarchism' natural to life will come back ... life cannot prosper without a spiritual aristocracy." [4] "Humanity is moving by way of hierarchical development towards the universal kingdom of freedom ..." [5]

What is this true hierarchy, a hierarchy in the future World? "It is a hierarchy which depends upon gifts, upon the *charismata* [6] of prophets,

harmony and of order which arises from within ..." Let us recall the notion of will (*velya*) or freedom that is held by Berdyaev. We saw, Chapter II, Section C, that his idea of freedom of the will concerns in a large part a freedom *from* objectivization and spiritual slavery. And his notion of mystical anarchism is not a positive ideal but an apophathic theology which denies any slavery of objectified human institutions in the Kingdom of God. "The perfect life, the *Kingdom* of God, can only be conceived in terms of anarchism, which is the apophatic and the only true way of thinking about it, for it avoids any similarity with the Kingdom of the Caesar and severs all connection with the categories of this world." *The Destiny of Man*, 197. (my italics)

[1] See preceding note for ' Kingdom of God."

[2] See Chapter II, Section D, Part 3.

[3] We may note, in passing, the significance of Berdyaev's mystical anarchism in his religious philosophy. Observe that the always denies a division between the natural and the supernatural and asserts the divinity of man. This mystical suprahistoricism joins with an antipathy to the caesaro-papism which has prevailed in the despotic Orthodox realms and empires for a thousand years. Cf. A. J. Toynbee, *A Study of History* (Oxford Univ., Oxford, 1934, 1939), Vol. III, 26–27; Vol. IV, 320–321; 352–363. That is, Berdyaev is the heir of a social order where the Church has been a state-ruled Church for a millenium. He consequently looks forward to a New Middle Ages, preceding the end of the world, where the Christian Church will be without visible hierarchy or definite government. He wishes to bring on a Christianity which is interior (and unhistorical) in place of a Christianity which he thinks is too exterior (and too historical). Cf. *Dream and Reality*, 326; *Solitude and Society*, 91.

[4] *The End of Our Time*, 111.

[5] *Freedom and the Spirit*, 346.

[6] *Charismata* refers to *charism* (derived from the Greek word, meaning *gift*), a special gift, or grace, given in virtue of one's spirituality.

apostles, saints; it is the hierarchy of men of genius in human power to create, the hierarchy of personal nobility of character and beauty of soul. ... What is needed is to set humanity, pure divine humanity, a human idea of hierarchy and a charismatic sense of it against the fearful slaverly of man in objectified society, against the vampire-like tyranny of inhuman and inhumane hierarchical principles and generic ideas." [1]

The cosmos, mankind nation, etc., are to be found in human personality as in an individualized universe or microcosm. [2] And their falling away, their ejection into external objectivity, is the result of the Fall of man. This is the subordination of man to impersonal reality. Berdyaev intends that all of the past history, every aspect of the historical – the City of New York, for instance – belongs to the human personality in its true depths. Every historical entity – even the City of New York – has been present from the time of its founding in the human personality! The Fall of man has involved the fall of the City of New York. Man has forgotten his true self and is painfully creating a history which will enable him to create himself – and the true meaning of history – as he and the historical potentially can be. This is the Existentialism and Personalism of Berdyaev.

Berdyaev seeks the meaning of history rather than history. Yet he asserts man is a microcosm and that in him the cosmos and all of history should and will be preserved. And this seems to put history as history at the basis of his doctrine. But it really does not do so because the microcosm, properly speaking, contains "everything *which is existential in the objectified ranks of the world.*" What is existential in the objectified City of New York is presumable very different from the historical city that we see. According to Berdyaev's apophatic sociology, the existential City of New York is free from objective hierarchy. He is interested in the suprahistorical, in celestial history. The mere historical happens to be objectified. It imperfectly reveals what he seeks: the meaning of history. His is a suprahistorical doctrine. His Personalism or Existentialism is therefore suprahistorical. It is ordered to the mystical realm of celestial history.

Let us note well, however, that Berdyaev's philosophy of history by no means is anti-historical or uninterested in human history. We saw, in Chapter I, [3] that historical traditions are not only spiritual but

---

[1] *The Beginning and the End,* 226–227. See also, *Slavery and Freedom,* 18; *Freedom and Spirit,* XIV.

[2] See 128 above.

[3] Chapter I, Section B, Part 1.

also historical; the philosopher of history is profoundly concerned with history. We saw too that the moral purpose of philosophy of history is to transfigure history.[1] The philosopher of history descends from his speculations and enters into history to transform it. Indeed "Man is an historical being; he seeks to realize himself in history, and his destiny is, therefore, historical. ... By virtue of its objective nature, history is absolutely indifferent to the human personality. ... And yet, for fear of impoverishing and diminishing himself, man cannot refuse to participate in history – his appointed path, his destiny. But he must take care never to become merely historically minded. ... The task of creating culture devolves on man by virtue of his historical existence. Culture is his path and his destiny ..." [2] "Tradition is a supra-personal and *soborny* experience, and the creative spiritual life transmitted from generation to generation, uniting the living and the dead and thereby overcoming death." [3]

Berdyaev's philosophy is suprahistorical; it seeks the religious meaning of history. But this is to seek the transfiguration of the world, the incarnation of spirit in history. According to Berdyaev's Personalist doctrine, man should go outside of himself and enter history in order to bring history within the religious unity of his human and divine personality. He describes [4] the "realization" of the personality in view of the return of the cosmos and of history to their trans-subjectivity. He speaks of "the concentration and actualization of personality's strength." This language shows the essential unity between his Personalism, his cosmogony and his philosophy of history. The personality "inwardly receives ... the whole of history ..." (and makes the past present).

Man has forgotten his true self, and the true meaning of history. He seeks to recover them in a process of creative recollection.[5] The memory is therefore very important in a doctrine of the microcosm.

Memory is undoubtedly man's most profound ontological principle, the one that cements and preserves the unity of his personality.[6]

It may be accident that Berdyaev uses the term, *ontological*, a term

---

[1] Chapter I, Section B, Part 3.
[2] *Solitude and Society*, 150–151.
[3] *Freedom and the Spirit*, 331.
[4] See 128 above.
[5] The platonic doctrine of recollection is found in Schelling's philosophy of history. Berdyaev probably obtains this Schellingian doctrine from Russian philosophers. Cf. Bolman's "Introduction" to his translation of Schelling's *The Ages of the World*, 62.
[6] *Solitude and Society*, 102.

which he does not like. But it seems that he chooses it in place of *existential*. Will is man's most profound existential principle. But insofar as the personality of man is intelligent, memory is the basic principle. "Ontology," Berdyaev says, in *Towards a New Epoch*, "is a doctrine of essences." [1] Hence, the primary ontological principle pertains to knowledge instead of will. Berdyaev understands by "cementing and preserving" a principle of synthesis. Personality is synthetic, rather than analytic.[2] And, since memory is the principle that "cements and preserves," the unity of the personality after all is to be characterized more by its knowledge than by its will. This is so, even though the will is prior. The divine Logos is the terminus.

Yet, the memory is not a repository of static essences, images or associations.

Reminisances belong to museums and archeology, not to real life. Rather, it is a matter of memory, which is creating and transfiguring. ... The beauty of the past is not a beauty of past facts recorded in the text books of history or archeology; it is the beauty of the real, experienced and transfigured past which has entered into the present. ... When I remember the past I perform a creative act, whereby it is transfigured and invested with meaning. I am intent on finding a meaning in the past: but the beauty of the past, of which I am now more conscious than ever before, is not passively reflected in me; I respond to it and re-live it creatively. True life is creation and this is the only life which is worth the having.[3]

That is, the memory of the past is not only a conserving historicism, but it is a spiritual creativity. It is a spiritual memory.[4] It creates and transfigures the past and thus achieves beauty. It is not a beauty composed of past facts. Berdyaev advocates creative recollection of the totality. He does not, therefore, advocate the total recollection of past facts. "The beauty of the past is the beauty of creative acts in the present." [5] Indeed, there is "a need for oblivion, the need to forget many things." [6] Thus the doctrine of the creative memory which preserves what is true in the past is correlative to the notion of the true microcosm which is at the core of the human personality.

Philosophy of creativity is at one and the same time a platonic

---

[1] *Towards a New Epoch*, 96.

[2] Cf. *Solitude and Society*, 41, where Berdyaev points out the synthetic character of the spirit. He says: "Dilthey is much nearer to Existential philosophy when he refuses to resolve the spiritula life into its elements or to analyse it, and studies it, instead, as a whole in its synthetic aspects."

[3] *Dream and Reality*, 284.

[4] *Slavery and Freedom*, 111.

[5] *The Beginning and the End*, 212. See *The Meaning of the Creative Act*, 29: "*Philosophy is creativeness, and not adaptation or obedience.*" (sic)

[6] *Solitude and Society*, 102.

doctrine of recollection. This is so because it is a philosophy of beauty which uses the method of metaphor to recall the reality. Man is an image of the Godman and potentially a microcosm (and microtheos).[1] He strives to create a better image, and this creativity which is effected through philosophy of history, is at the same time a recollection. "Immortality is memory made clear and serene." [2]

Berdyaev made a mistake in thinking that the imaginative knowledge and memory of the past, which is a present memory, preserves the past solely as present. That is, he would have made a mistake if he were not a mystical philosopher. He see the present in the historical image or myth, because he intends the *mystical* symbol of the eternally present Reality.[3] He says in *Slavery and Freedom*:

This spiritual memory ... reminds man of the fact that in the past there lived concrete beings, living personalities, with whom we ought in existential time to have a link no less than with those who are living now. Society is always a society, not only of the living but also of the dead ...[4]

The communion of the Thous and the We thus extends to all the people of history. And thus the microcosm, in recalling everything, recovers and retains a personal communion with history.

This memory is not a "conserving, but a creatively transfiguring memory." [5] It is a resurrecting memory, not a restoration of the past with its mixture of good and evil, but a transfiguration. And it takes the past into the Existential order which is not historical.[6]

He says "true life is creation," [7] and means that it is a creativity in which one invests the past with meaning and thus relives it. The true life of spirit (the best life) and of the personality is a life which finds the meaning in a philosophy of history. Personalist Existentialism thus articulates his philosophy of history in the sense that history is the occasion of finding universal history and bringing it into the subjectivity of the person.

The Existentialism and Personalism are eschatological and complete the messianic doctrine of his meta-history and philosophy of history.

Man ought ... to take all history into his own infinite subjectivity, in which the world is part of man.

---

1 *Slavery and Freedom*, 103.
2 *The Divine and the Human*, 158.
3 See Chapter IV, Section G.
4 *Slavery and Freedom*, 111.
5 *Ibid.*, 111.
6 Cf. *Solitude and Society*, 106–117.
7 *Dream and Reality*, 284.

The resultant and consistent demand of personalism, when thought out to the end, is a demand for the end of the world and of history, not a passive waiting for this end in fear and anguish but an active, creative preparation for it.[1]

Here, he seeks not fear and anguish but a mystical activity. Not that man ought to experience fear and anguish, but "man ought to take all history into his own subjectivity, in which the world is part of man." This is the demand of Personalism when thought out to the conclusion. Personalism moves away from Existentialism (as Berdyaev views Existentialism). He is advocating an eschatological Personalism a mystical, doctrine which looks for the end of the world.

G. SUMMARY

1. The beauty and spirituality of universal history, as well as its human an divine significance, are Existential and Personal. Philosophy of history needs to be articulated by Existential and Personalist doctrines. Berdyaev's creative philosophy of Beauty, which we observed in Chapter II, is an Existential philosophy which knows the world, bringing it into the subjectivity of the knower. He thereby reveals himself to himself, and his knowledge thus becomes the existent microcosm; This Existentialism is a Personalism because beyond *Existenz* is the primordial personal principle, wilful freedom (the Ungrund); and it is illuminated, according to this cosmogonical philosophy, by the divine personal principle, Christ. The philosophy is influenced by German Idealism. Berdyaev asserts a historical scheme of realization of the human Ego which is similar to that of Fichte and which, like Fichte's scheme, assumes a first principle of wilful freedom. The scheme, however, is personalized and etherialized in Berdyaev's philosophy.

There is an anguish, an *Angst* in this Existentialism; and it is experienced in the face of the primal abyss, mystery, or divine nothingness, which is the basis of the personality. But *Angst* is not the fundamental experience for Berdyaev. Rather, "the esctasy of creativeness which arises out of man's own nothingness," is the primary Existential event. "Nothingness" is not absolute non-being; it occurs in the principle, not in the terminus. The Godman, the divine Logos, Christ, is the term. Every personality will finally be illuminated through the full Truth.

---

[1] *Slavery and Freedom*, 267.

2. Existentialism is here a Personalism. Personality, however, is spirit, and spirit is the link of man with God. This is a *pneumatology*; man is an incarnate spirit, a concrete existent. Spirit is the realm of subjectivity and supra-subjectivity, and it enables the person to overcome objectified conditions of knowledge and of existence. That is, it raises fallen man.

This doctrine of spirit denies the division between the natural and the supernatural. Every personality has its logos, its spiritual principle which integrates it. Man is an image of the divine Logos, and the true man is the Godman. Thus Existentialism is here a mystical philosophy of the spirit; it is not opposite to rationalism or irrationalism but transcends both.

This remains a Personalism which asserts the self-identity of every personality, even in change, because the creative memory achieves a remembrance of the divine origin of the person and knows it as a microcosm. The world, every man, and God are my creative act. We create symbols (such as "nation") which approximate closer to the true reality That is why philosophy of history is creative and symbolic; the mere historical is symbolic. The philosopher takes his creations into his own subjectivity. At the same time he approaches their transcendent truth. This is a philosophy according to which the person creatively strives for a platonic recollection of himself as he truly is. All the things he knows become himself by revealing him to himself. Berdyaev's Existentialism, therefore, eminently is subjective, seeking to overcome objectivity. It seeks the meaning of human existence and of the universe as part of the divine Existent.

3. This is a concrete Existentialism or Personalism, and Berdyaev asserts, like Hegel, the reality of *the concrete universal*. He uses this Hegelian doctrine to elaborate a Russian religious philosophy. The supreme concrete Existent, the Godman, is at the center of the philosophy. And this is a cosmogonical outlook. It expresses the doctrine of the total unity of mankind – all men – and the cosmos in God in terms of the concrete universal.

Intellectualism, the metaphysics which asserts the reality of abstract essences, comes under attack. Berdyaev is interested in the concrete existent, and yet he says it is a universal. Its universality is real, not nominal. Such a *concrete* universalism, which attacks the abstraction from the whole requires a noetic which is at once intellectual and imaginative. That is, the truth is known at once intellectually and imaginatively. Concrete universalism accords well with the doctrine of creativity, the notion of mythical and symbolic knowing, and with the mystical Existentialism. Further, it is a concrete Existentialism where man is an actual microcosm. The unity of the person with the world, other persons and with God, approached noetically, is concrete in its conditions. The mystical unity of all things and of history in the Godman is the concrete goal of man, and sought through recollection. True personality is the True Concrete Universal.

4. In a cosmogonical philosophy which says that the world and all men are taken up and divinized in the person's subjectivity, the doctrine of true community and communion is stressed. It is a metaphysics of the Thou and the We. In knowing other persons spiritually and subjectively, man finds his own reflection and approaches closer to his true self. The personality thus becomes subjectively identified with the We. In the last analysis, the Thou and the We are basically implied in the Ego which is the microcosm, the image of the Godman. This is the principle of *Berdyaev's* Social Existentialism. He would transcend subjectivity in the Existential meeting with God, with all persons, and with the interior existence of the world.

5. Since man is a microcosm his existence is the most "Existential" of all concrete existents. At the deepest mystical level everything that has happened to the world happened to me. "I have experienced the world around me and all the historical processes and events of my time as part of myself, as my spiritual biography." This clarifies Berdyaev's philosophy of history. The historical (e.g., historical traditions) is not the cause of greater Existentiality; rather, the historical is the effect of man's greater Existentiality. Further, the unity of history and of the world will be found only within the personality, the primary existent. The realization of personality involves the reception of the cosmos, history, all mankind. Thus, the doctrine of universal history, which is the substance of Berdyaev's philosophy of history, is directly associated with Personalism.

This is a suprahistorical doctrine. All existents so far as they truly exist – the cosmos, mankind, nations, etc. – exist in the human personality. But they are not historical in their true existence. It is the mystical and Existential City of New York, for example, not the objectified and historical City, which belongs to the human personality in its depths.

Berdyaev's philosophy of history is, however, by no means antihistorical or uninterested in human history. Indeed he understands man to be a historical being who should realize himself in history as well as in suprahistory. Man should enter history in order to bring history within the religious unity of his human and divine personality. History as such is not preserved in the human memory; the memory (man's supreme ontological principle) is spiritual and creative. It transfigures the past into the eternal and Existential present. This is not a philosophy of history in the sense of knowing the meaning of history as history itself. It is a universal history, and a Personalism, which seeks a suprahistorical meaning.

CHAPTER IV

EPISTEMOLOGY AND PHILOSOPHY OF HISTORY

A. INTRODUCTION

We saw in the foregoing chapter that there is a historical process in the human personality; at one state it is mainly sub-conscious, at another state, mainly conscious, at another, mainly supra-conscious. A theory of knowledge which parallels the history of the personality will be investigated in the present chapter. Berdyaev's method is not primarily rational and objective and his interest in man is not primarily the consciousness. But since the rational is necessary to any discourse at all and admittedly to his own, his theory of rational knowledge will be studied, as well as his criticism of it.

This study of Berdyaev's theory of knowledge is necessary if we want to know his philosophy of history. There are especially two reasons why we must study his method. First, his philosophy by its nature has a radical unity, so that to understand one part of it one must investigate all the other important parts. Theory of knowledge and knowledge itself, we will find, is one with his mystical philosophy of history in the final position. Second, his theory of knowledge will tell us exactly what his method is. We will learn both the method by which he discovers philosophy of history and the method by which he expounds it, which are the same.

B. THE REJECTION OF THE SUBJECT-OBJECT RELATIONSHIP

Berdyaev's approach to knowledge is both positive and negative: he asserts spiritual knowing and criticizes objective knowing. Objective knowing, we saw, is a result of the fall of man and of the cosmos. And the point-of-view from which Berdyaev refutes the objectification is mystical. Epistemology in this doctrine necessarily is also a metaphysic.

Philosophy is concerned primarily with man's inner life, and it should therefore investigate all problems from the standpoint of human knowledge. The purpose of existence cannot be elucidated either from things or from objects; it is inherent in the knowing subject and in existence itself. Thus purely rational philosophy, as an objective process, cannot apprehend the purpose of existence which is immanent in the depths of Being . . . [1]

Philosophy is concerned with man's inner life because man is a microcosm in his interior depths. It follows that philosophers of history should investigate all problems from the standpoint of human knowledge – man's inner life is intellectual. The purpose of existence cannot be discovered in things alone because they are not the Godman, nor images of Him. Nor can the purpose of existence be elucidated from objects. Objects are the objects of our objectified knowledge, whether they be God, persons or things. Berdyaev will show us that objects do not belong to man's inner life or to existence. Rational philosophy, so far as it is an objective process, cannot apprehend the purpose of existence.

It also follows that, since knowledge is essentially immaterial, its ability to apprehend the material nature of things and objects remains the great enigma. . . . It can only be resolved if we admit the *ontic* nature of knowledge, that it participates in Being, illuminating its obscure depths and integrating the objective world in the spiritual. The faith in the immutability of natural laws, which goes back to Greek geometry, is only a faith in reason as a manifestation of nature's inherent spirituality. This spirituality is oppressed by the objective world; but we apprehend it as our destiny as soon as we become converted to the inner world of existence. Thus the so-called natural laws are actually human destiny. [2]

The enigma presented by the immateriality of knowledge facing the materiality of things is the problem of reconciling knowledge to reality. Berdyaev solves the problem by regarding knowledge as an existential reality. But this requires that knowledge be identified with the interior subjectivity of the person knowing; so much so, that it partakes of his innermost being, his spirituality, and therefore of his existentiality. To clarify the problem of the immateriality of knowledge facing the materiality of things is indeed one of the purposes of this chapter. When we understand this we will understand Berdyaev's noetic.

Knowledge "integrates the objective world in the spiritual." The objective world reflects the objectivization of man, his falsification in the Fall. Knowledge is the way by which man illuminates the world. This illumination reveals the spirituality inherent in the world. We recall that the world is the incarnation of spirit and that man is an

---

[1] *Solitude and Society*, 50.
[2] *Ibid.*, 50–51.

incarnate spirit. Our immaterial knowledge of natural laws is a "manifestation of nature's inherent spirituality." This spirituality is oppressed by the objective world; thus our knowledge of natural laws is rational, a rational manifestation of nature's spirituality. And since, in truth, nature's spirituality is our spirituality, the so-called natural laws of the world are actually part of our inner world, our human destiny.

Berdyaev's notion of objectivization is based largely on his interpretation of the philosophy of Kant. Schopenhauer is influential.[1] Berdyaev says, in *Solitude and Society*:

When in opposing the subject and the object, philosophical theory abstracts them both from Being, it makes the apprehension of Being impossible. ...

Objective processes transform Being into a superstructure of the subject, elaborated for philosophical purposes. ... he loses all contact with Being ...

This is the tragedy of knowledge as expounded by German Idealism ... the manifold superiority of the German post-Kantian philosophers lay in their critical approach to the problem of objectivization and in their recognition of the importance of the knowing subject. ... the advent of Kant and of German Idealism marks a most important stage in the history of human self-conscious-

---

[1] See *The Philosophy of Schopenhauer*, edited by I. Edman (The Modern Library, New York, 1928). This is an Englished edition of Schopenhauer's main work, *The World as Will and Idea*, and there are several notions that Berdyaev shares with Schopenhauer, by whom he has been influenced. The voluntarism is obvious.

The notion of *idea*, especially the very use of the word, *idea*, seems to have been inspired by Schopenhauer. The following text might have been written by Berdyaev:

"The method of our own system is *toto genere* distinct from these two opposite misconceptions (that is, starting a philosophy from the subject or from the object) for we start neither from the object nor from the subject, but from the *idea*, as the first fact of consciousness. Its first essential, fundamental form, is the antithesis of subject and object." Schopenhauer means that there is something prior to subject and object which is not conceptual, yet, on the other hand, is not irrational. And Schopenhauer asserts an *intuitive* knowledge instead of a conceptual knowledge. Cf. *ibid.*, 299.

Indeed what we found in Chapter II, namely, that Berdyaev's philosophy is based on two principles, the irrational will and the (divine) intelligibility, is asserted by Schopenhauer of his own philosophy. "For as the world is in one aspect entirely *idea*, so in another it is entirely *will*." And, like Berdyaev, Schopenhauer resolves these contradictory principles from a historical point of view. The intelligible principle should finally dominate the irrational. "If, however, we wish to give an honorary position, as it were emeritus, to an old expression, which from custom we do not like to discard altogether, we may, metaphorically and figuratively, call the complete self-effacement and denial of the will, the true absence of will, which alone forever stills and silences its struggle, alone gives that contentment which can never again be disturbed, alone redeems the world, and which we shall now soon consider at the close of our whole investigation – the radical cure of the disease of which all other means are only palliations or anodynes. In this sense the Greek Τεòλς and also *finis bonorum* correspond to the thing still better." *Ibid.*, 291–292.

Further, Schopenhauer asserts a concrete knowledge opposed to abstract knowing. He says, 310: "There is a wide gulf between (abstract and intuitive knowing) which can only be crossed by the aid of philosophy, as regards the knowledge of the nature of the world. Intuitively or *in concreto*, every man is really conscious of all philosophical truths, but to bring them to abstract knowledge, to reflection, is the work of philosophy which neither ought nor is able to do more than this." Berdyaev asserts a similar notion of (concrete) intuitive knowledge.

ness. It was a step towards human emancipation, towards freeing man from the constraint and slavery of the objective world. The very fact of a critical awareness of the subject's participation in the objective processes, implied the subject's deliverance from the external tyranny of the objective world. ... Henceforth, Being could only be apprehended subjectively ...[1]

Berdyaev rejects the opposition of subject and object because, in fact, it never gets away from subjectivity. The term, *object,* connotes the dependence of objectivity on subjective states and on human relationships. "My use of the term 'object' will never connote that any form of knowledge is independent of the subject." [2] "Objective processes transform Being into a superstructure of the subject ... he loses all contact with Being." [3] Objectivity is an improper form of subjectivity.

Berdyaev observes two contributions of the German Idealists, especially Kant, Fichte, Schelling and Hegel: a critical approach to objectivization and a recognition of the importance of the subject. He is enthusiastic about the establishment in the German Idealists of "a critical awareness of the subject's participation in the objective processes" and of the "external tyranny of the objective world." Kant, to whom Berdyaev acknowledges indeptedness above all other philosophers,[4] was quite articulate as to the inability of the object to present the reality as it really is. ("We can have no knowledge of any object as thing in itself ..." [5] said Kant.)

Kant rejects the Newtonian philosophy of nature, such as it is understood in his own philosophy, as a knowledge of noumenal reality.[6] And

---

[1] *Solitude and Society,* 35–36.
[2] *Ibid.,* 29–30.
[3] *Ibid.,* 36.
[4] *Dream and Reality,* 93.
[5] *Critique of Pure Reason,* 27.
[6] The objective knowledge which Kant treats in the *Critique of Pure Reason* is an empirical knowledge, a knowledge which was called in the 18th century a philosophy of nature. That is, it is an empirical knowledge which is defined in philosophical terms: i.e., in terms of categories, concepts, sensible intuition, understanding, etc. See *Critique of Pure Reason,* 162. Norman Kemp Smith in his *Commentary on the Critique of Pure Reason* (Humanities Press, New York, 1950), lv–lvi, says: "... the term knowledge has, in the Critical philosophy, a much narrower connotation than in current speech. It is limited to *sense*-experience, and to such inferences therefrom as can be obtained by the only methods that Kant is willing to recognize, namely, the mathematico-physical. Aesthetic, moral and religious experience, and even organic phenomena, are excluded from the field of possible knowledge."

"In holding to this position, Kant is, of course, the child of his time. The absolute sufficiency of the Newtonian physics is a presupposition of all his utterances on this theme. Newton, he believes, has determined in a quite final manner the principles, methods and limits of scientific investigation. For though Kant himself imposes upon science a further limitation, namely, to appearance, he conceives himself, in so doing, not an weakening Newton's natural philosophy, but as securing it against all possible objections."

This is why we can say that Berdyaev is attacking a Newtonian world-outlook in his attack on objectivization. He is attacking an empirical view of reality which is defined in terms of

Berdyaev, in attacking objectivization, is rejecting the claim of such a natural necessitarianism to get at the reality of things. True, as we saw, he is not attacking solely the Kantian "object" but also intellectualist philosophies. His approach, however, is by way of the objective theory.[1]

As for the second contribution of the German Idealists, their recognition of the importance of the knowing subject, Berdyaev again refers to the advent of Kant and his successors. "It was a step towards human emancipation, towards freeing man from the constraint and slavery of the objective world." Kant's categorical imperative, in giving the human soul an intrinsic value, singled it out from all other natural existences and strengthened it to face the cold immensities of the cosmic system.[2] The *Critique of Pure Reason*, in its strict limiting and defining of objective knowledge, cleared the ground for the practical Reason of Kant and secured it in the autonomous control of its own domain.

And thus Berdyaev says above: "The very fact of a critical awareness of the subject's participation in the objective processes, implied the subject's deliverance from the external tyranny of the objective world. Henceforth, Being could only be apprehended subjectively." Berdyaev understands a metaphysical and existential "Being" in the chapter cited from,[3] a true Being instead of the objectified Being mentioned in most of his writings.

He discusses the opposition of subject and object in a later book, *The Beginning and the End*:

philosophical categories and which is necessitarian and outside of the order of human volition. See *Critique of Pure Reason*, 26, as to the use of the categories. Berdyaev uses Kant's terminology. "The subject is created by God, whereas the object is a product of the creature. The subject is noumenon, the object is phenomenon."

[1] Berdyaev's attack upon the object should be understood in the light of the intellectualism. The notion of theoretical object, and the objectivization of philosophy, have predominated in philosophic thought since the end of the middle ages. Cf. J. Maritain, *Les Dégrés du Savoir* (Desclée de Brouwer, Paris, 1946), 247.

[2] Cf. *Commentary on the Critique of Pure Reason*, lvi–lviii. Also, Cf. I. Kant, *The Moral Law, or Kant's Groundwork of the Metaphysic of Morals*, (Hutchinson, London 1948), 121: "How is a Categorial Imperative Possible?"

"A rational being counts himself, *qua* intelligence, as belonging to the intelligible world and solely *qua* efficient cause belonging to the intelligible world does he give to his causality the name of '*will*'. On the other side, however, he is conscious of himself as also a part of the sensible world, where his actions are encountered as mere appearances of this causality." Then Kant goes on to say that a man is not solely of the intelligible world (which pertains to the categorical imperative) nor solely of the sensible world (which refers to natural laws).

[3] Cf. *Solitude and Society*, 30, 31, 35. On 38, Being is described in such a way as to mean existent. This notion of being is unusual in Berdyaev. He constantly attacks the notion of being and the philosophy of being. Here, he accepts the doctrine of being, it seems, because he is discussing Existentialism in terms of the philosophies of being of the German Idealists and the Existentialists.

What are the marks of objectivization, and the rise of object relations in the world? The following signs may be taken as established: (1) The estrangement of the object from the subject; (2) The absorption of the unrepeatably individual and personal in what is common and impersonally universal; (3) The rule of necessity of determination from without, the crushing of freedom and the concealment of it; (4) Adjustment to the grandiose mien of the world and of history, to the average man, and the socialization of man and his opinions, which destroy distinctive character.[1]

Note that all four of the marks of objectivization consider the subject to be prior to the object. The object is estranged from the subject; that is, the object has fallen away from the integral unity in the subject and has thus become object. This refers to the Fall of man and of the world. The object is in the essentialistic order; hence, the objectivization of man is the submission to the rule of the common and impersonally universal. This crushes the freedom of man; that is, it conceals freedom (which is at the basis of man's personality). Finally, he speaks of the socialization of man and his opinions: "adjustment to the grandiose mien of the world and of history ..."

From the viewpoint of epistemology, objective knowing estranges an object from the subject (instead of bringing it into the interiority of the subject); the particular is subsumed in the common and is insufficiently known. The freedom of the knower is crushed, but true knowing requires the exercise of volition; it is volitional. Finally, the socialization of man and his opinions, where he is overcome by the grandeur of the world and human opinions, is due to the rise of objective relations.

Indeed this epistemological and metaphysical problem of objectivization is central to the thought of Berdyaev.

In my opinion the central thought of eschatological philosophy is connected with the interpretation of the Fall as objectivization, and of the end as the final and decisive victory over objectivization.[2]

Thus sin leads not merely to objectivization through cognition – Kant went no further than to assert the objectivization of cognition – but sin actually makes nature a fallen realm of being. And the epistemological problem is therefore two-fold: to overcome objectivization both in the subject and in the world with the aid of true knowing. Epistemology takes account of a temporal sequence and is, therefore, conceived in terms of Berdyaev's philosophy of history. He asserts a religious epistemology, as well as a philosophy, defined in terms of religious doctrine and philosophy of history.

[1] *The Beginning and the End*, 62.
[2] *Ibid.*, 51.

His attack upon objectified knowledge is philosophical; that is, like Kant, he is attempting to take away the pretentions of this knowledge to arrive at metaphysical reality. In the natural sciences objectivization does not destroy the object of knowledge since nature is itself the result of objectivization.[1] This objectivization does not result in the same devastation as do the objectified historical or psychological inquiries about spirit.[2] Concepts especially serve the natural sciences. Indeed they give us our bearing in the dark infinity of the object world which surrounds us.[3] But the concept lowers the reason towards the fallen state of the world and therefore has a limited application.[4] The concept operates in terms of the general and has, Berdyaev believes, no affinity with the particular or the unique.

The concept is fatal to mystical or spiritual experience, and this is why he rejects it from the proper noetic of his philosophy of history. He attacks the use of the concept because his noetic seeks the individual and the unique.[5] We saw that his epistemology is imaginative and that the concrete conditions of individuality and uniqueness are preserved in the highest knowing. Of course he must reject the concept; for in philosophy it is no instrument or means of reaching existential knowing. This is so because it eliminates in itself the very conditions of concreteness that are contained in existential knowing.

The truth is inherent in the existing subject and not in the opposition of the abstracted subject with the object. The objective world has no criterion, or source of truth.

Intellectualist philosophies, whether Greek or Scholastic, tend to make the subject passive by endowing him uniquely with intellectual perceptions. As a result we are in danger of identifying concepts with Being, of regarding the uninterrupted activity of intellection as a purely reflective activity. The human ntellect was originally confronted with chaos; but since its function is to clarify and to illumine, to introduce meaning into a world devoid of any, the very act of apprehending the dark and meaningless world should bring illumination and significance.[6]

The truth exists only in the subject (the knowing person). We saw that the external world is an objective (and rather falsified) world because it has fallen away from the unity of the microcosm, man. The fall of man involved the fall of the world. We saw too that philosophy of history

---

[1] *The Destinity of Man*, 12.
[2] *Ibid.*, 12.
[3] *The Beginning and the End*, 77.
[4] *Ibid.*, 79.
[5] *Ibid.*, 120.
[6] *Solitude and Society*, 33.

describes the process through which man takes up the world and history into his truth and his subjectivity. Truth, in fact, is primarily the divine Truth, the divine Logos – a concrete truth of whom man is the image.[1] Primary Truth is not a comparison (as of the subject to the external object), but a concrete existent, True Man.

Berdyaev criticizes "intellectualist philosophies" for asserting that the knower is passive. And he does because they identify concepts with Being.

He has two reasons for attacking "intellectualist philosophies." One reason is given above: the conceptualism of them and hence their unreality. The other reason is based on the cosmology of Berdyaev. The world at the time of the Fall of man became enslaved to essences and to laws because it fell from its integrality with the Godman, the divine Meaning.[2] An "intellectualist" philosophy would accept the objects of a "world devoid of any meaning" and assert them as the meaning.

This twofold attack on objective philosophy should be noted. (1) The philosophy is false because it does not know primary reality, but objects and essences. It never gets beyond the superficial objectivity or a superficial knowing.[3] (2) The philosophy is false because it provides no way of introducing meaning into a meaningless world; which is to say, it prevents the spiritualization, the taking up of the world in the microcosm. The second reason, Berdyaev's interest in cosmogony and philosophy of history, is more important. An Existential noetic serves his own cosmogony.

Knowing is an act, though not a purely reflective activity. It is, we have seen and will see, a creation.

Rational knowing (which depends upon concepts) is objective, not only because of its nature, but also because it is the accepted means of communication in (fallen) societies. Berdyaev says in his work, *Solitude and Society*, a book of which we have seen so much in the preceding chapter:

---

[1] See Section G, Parts 3 and 4 of this Chapter.
[2] Cf. *The Beginning and the End*, 87.
[3] But Berdyaev does not deny the (limited) validity of objective knowledge. It is based on nature, and nature does reveal, though imperfectly, the truth from which it springs. "The word, *nature*, can be interpreted in two ways: there is a preconscious existential nature and there is a post-conscious and objectified nature. The first admits of spiritual communion, the latter only of scientific or technical relations." *Spirit and Reality*, 175.
We will see later on how Berdyaev asserts the limited validity of objective knowledge. Suffice it to say, here, that objectified nature is a (useful) symbol of existential nature, and objective knowledge is a (useful) symbol of a truer knowledge.

(Existential philosophy's) aim is to study the unifying principle which integrated philosophy and the community of men, and also to demonstrate the social character of logical communication. For this reason, my principal endeavor in this book has been to establish the relationship between knowledge as an instrument of objectified society and knowledge as a means of achieving existential communion.[1]

When he speaks of a "unifying principle which integrates philosophy and the community of men," he refers to the spiritual principle: spirit integrates society and philosophy. Logical communication – that is, rational, conceptual and objectified communication – is contrasted with the spiritual principle. Objective knowing never gets beyond the superficial and isolated subjectivity of the knower. Existential knowing does. And objective knowing, that of concepts and rationalization, organizes and systematizes the chaotic world in our thought. It is a preparation – and a necessary one for the knowing which creates and transforms. Logical knowing (and logic itself) is social.[2] Logical, rational, conceptual knowing is a social communication on a low level, on the objectified level. It is not entirely other than spiritual.[3]

Berdyaev practises what he teaches: he says of his method of philosophy:

... my manner of thinking ... is intuitive and aphoristic rather than discursive and systematic. I am unable to expound anything by way of ratiocination, and I do not believe in the need to do so. ... what carries conviction ... is not discursive argument but the original insight.[4]

Philosophy is preoccupied with the original insight. That is why Berdyaev's books seem endlessly repetitious, though each book has a different aim and teaching; for the original insight is constantly brought into the exposition. The ratiocinative way is allowed to influence the exposition only to a certain degree. The books and chapters are planned and divided logically, but what stands out in the writing is the original insight. Philosophy is the constant revelation and unfolding of the original insight, not the ratiocinative deduction.

The opposition to the objective and rational method is seen in the metaphysics we considered in the foregoing chapter. It is a metaphysics of all men and the Godman. It is a metaphysics of the Thou and the We

---

[1] *Solitude and Society*, 57.
[2] *The Beginning and the End*, 74.
[3] *Ibid.*, 125. Cf. *The Realm of Spirit and the Realm of Caesar*, 16. Berdyaev never denies the validity of rational knowledge. And he pays his respects to it. Cf. *The Beginning and the End*, 87: "Knowledge and science have their own worlds, religion has its own world, so have art and politics. This does not in the slightest degree mean that the world of science is a world of phantasy and is devoid of reality. It is of immense importance to man as he takes his way through life ... This is particularly so in the case of historical science ..."
[4] *Dream and Reality*, 81.

(not a metaphysics of a general Mankind), and the knowledge is intuitive, subjective and mystical. And hence Berdyaev associates the logical and ratiocinative way of knowing with an objective socialization.

There are two aspects of knowledge: one comprehends the relationship between the knowing subject and Being; the other includes the relationships between the knowing subject and other Egos, the multiple world of men and society.[1]

He thus conceives his epistemology in terms of mankind through all of history as well as in terms of the Godman. And he refuses to accept the sociological image, the logical and conceptual knowledge as proper to philosophy.

Yet, he does not entirely reject the rational type of knowing. Indeed, we need only glance at his books, which after all are rational, in order to see the wealth of concepts and ideas which he uses. He continues:

... Because knowledge is invariable concerned with the *general*, the abstract and the universal, it tends to overlook the individual, the singular and the personal ... in terms of Existential philosophy, knowledge is primarily concerned with the Ego and the Thou ...[2]

This passage is valuable for the link it shows existing between the rational and the intuitive in Berdyaev's theory of knowledge. First, he admits that "knowledge is invariably concerned with the general." Second, he says: "the general, the abstract and the universal." But the universal, we have seen, belongs not only to rational knowledge but also to intuitive knowledge. The existent is a concrete universal. Consequently, the general and the abstract, which are here associated with the universal, play some part in the attainment of philosophic intuition. Proper philosophical knowledge is primarily, not exclusively, concerned with the Ego and the Thou. That is, philosophical knowledge is primarily but not exclusively intuitive. Philosophy of history is rational and conceptual because "knowledge is invariably concerned with the general, the abstract and the universal." But it is primarily intuitive.[3]

[1] *Solitude and Society*, 87.

[2] *Ibid.*, 87.

[3] Berdyaev's psychology and his pneumatology are helpful in a consideration of his theory of knowledge. Though "man's being is an aggregate in which spirit, soul and body are unified" (*Freedom and the Spirit*, 261), yet, if man knows only with his soul he knows only objectively. Berdyaev says he interprets, here, St. Paul's words on the soul of man in his own way. The psychological goal is the gradual conversion of soul into spirit. *Ibid.*, 8. He stresses the distinction between the soul and the spirit. "The confusion of spirit and soul ... was one of the causes alike of a false naturalism and a false 'spiritualism' in philosophy." *Ibid.*, 9. Yet, he asserts the unity of man. "In the history of spiritual consciousness, the error has often been perpetuated of identifying spirit and soul, the spiritual and the psychic. ... *Spirit is the*

C. KNOWLEDGE NOT ANTI-RATIONAL, BUT SUPER-RATIONAL

Berdyaev's positive affirmation of the rational occurs only in his last writings, those published since 1941. He seems to have felt the need to admit and assert its validity. It has value as seen from the perspective of philosophy of history. That is, it is one of the steps in the historical ascent of man's knowing from the irrational beginnings of the world to the future transfiguration of the world.

Knowledge within the objectified world does admittedly reveal truths. There is a reflected light in it which helps us to take our bearings in the darkness of this world, but it does not reveal primary and original Truth. ...[1]

The truths that objectified knowledge reveals are not primary truths. (Thus, Being, we saw, is not primary in Berdyaev's philosophy). When he says there is a reflected light in our knowledge of the objectified world which helps us take our bearings, this must be understood in the light of his symbolism and imagism. Every human knowledge is symbolical, objective knowledge more so than existential knowledge.[2] The logical concept then is a symbol, diminished though it is, of the true reality. "For in its depths, even the most positive, exactly scientific, knowledge of the natural world holds within itself a reflection of the Logos." [3] Indeed we just saw that Berdyaev asserts that philosophical thought must be conceptual (his own thought, of course, included). The

highest quality of the soul ..." (my italics) Spirit and Reality, 39. Again, he says: "The soul is the kernel of the human creature and the function of spirit should be to endow the soul with the highest quality and purpose." Ibid., 40.

However, "Spirit is the masculine active principle whereas the soul is the feminine passive principle. Spirit comes from the Logos, while the soul is cosmic. Spirit performs an act in relation to the soul; it informs it with purpose and truth, it liberates it from the power of cosmic forces." Ibid., 40. Berdyaev's mystical noetic is connected with spirit, in contradistinction from soul. Cf. Ibid., 240. The soul is the faculty of knowing the fallen cosmos as such. It is a "passive principle," which is to say its knowledge is (passively) conceptual.

And so Berdyaev has written: "It is only the soul which can regard itself as opposed to the known object and can interrogate the criterion of its own knowledge. But no object can be set in opposition to the spirit, and in the spiritual world the question of a criterion does not arise. Only an object which appears to us as something alien and impenetrable can raise a question as to the criterion of our knowledge of it. ... The criterion of truth is the spirit itself ..." Freedom and the Spirit, 25.

For Berdyaev, then, the soul knows in a relation of subject and object; that is it knows, by itself, only objectively. The soul sets up a criterion outside itself. In Berdyaev's doctrine, we saw, an exterior criterion is a falsified criterion; it is a universal, an essence, by itself an objectivization. The soul is the principle of knowing an essentialistic and objectified thing, according to Berdyaev. When he says the soul "can interrogate the criterion of its own knowledge," he is referring to rational process, logical reasoning; and this is the proper to the soul but not to the spirit.

[1] The Beginning and the End, 49.
[2] See Section G of this chapter.
[3] The Realm of Spirit and the Realm of Caesar, 16.

concrete universal, as the term *universal* shows, is a foundation of conceptual knowledge. It amounts to this: Berdyaev's philosophy cannot be anti-rational because the anti-rational would be irrational and consequently would be completely unavailable to knowledge.

Equally false is the naturalist ... type of mysticism, which would remove the conflict between subject and object, not from above, but from below. This type of mysticism is not super-rational, but irrational; not super-conscious, but unconscious. It would plunge us into the abyss.[1]

Berdyaev's mystical philosophy of history, which is at the same time symbolic and imaginative, cannot assert itself ratiocinatively. It seems to be opposed to the rational because its type of knowing – mystical – is the type that Berdyaev recommends to the *philosopher* (as distinguished from the scientist). But his philosophy is not anti-rational. To deny reason and consciousness would be to assert the irrational and the unconscious. But Berdyaev seeks the super-rational and the super-conscious. His philosophy of history cannot be irrational because, finally, the divine Logos, the Godman, is the Truth he seeks.

This attitude toward rational cognition and objectivized thought is also to be seen in terms of the human consciousness.[2] Just as the rational imposes order on the irrational, so consciousness brings light into the darkness of unconsciousness.

Human nature is rooted in fathomless, pre-existential meonic freedom, and in his struggle for personality, for God's idea in him, man had to fashion consciousness with its limitations, to bring light into darkness, and to subject subconscious instincts and strivings to the censorship of consciousness.[3]

The very limitations of consciousness (which are rational and logical limitations) serve the progress of man by imposing themselves on the limitless freedom. It is an intelligible principle, God's idea of man, whose realization is sought. The intelligibility which plain consciousness finds is a step ahead of the primitive sub-conscious.[4] Consciousness in itself is the objectified mind that was heretofore discussed. It is the knowledge of reality so far as it is objectified. The reader will recognize an attitude which originates in the German Idealists: the notion of the progress of consciousness out of unconsciousness and to supra-consciousness.[5] Indeed:

[1] *Ibid.*, 180.
[2] Concerning rational cognition, see Section B of this chapter.
[3] *The Destiny of Man*, 69.
[4] *Freedom and the Spirit*, 101–102.
[5] Cf. Schelling, *The Ages of the World;* Hegel, *The Phenomenology of Mind; The Destiny of Man*, 38–39.

Hegel speaks of the "unhappy consciousness" which implies division and for which God is transcendent; but this is true of consciousness as such. Unhappy consciousness can only be overcome through super-consciousness.

There are three stages in the development of the spirit: the original paradisaical wholeness, pre-conscious wholeness which has not had the experience of thought and of freedom; division, reflection, valuation, freedom of choice, and, finally, super-consciousness wholeness and completeness. . . . [1]

This is a historical treatment of consciousness. Consciousness is seen to be the second part of a grand historical dialectic of the progress of man toward supra-consciousness. Consciousness, for Berdyaev as well as Hegel,[2] is "unhappy" because it suffers division, endures ratiocinative reflection and subordinates itself to valuation. Berdyaev, therefore, is committing himself to a great deal when he rejects the rational and logical as unworthy of autonomous functioning. He is doing nothing less than attacking the autonomy of consciousness itself.

He is asserting a mystical doctrine; for, in asserting a universal history, he has committed himself to a mysticism of history. It is not irrational (which is meaningless), it is not rational (which is conceptual and general), but it is supra-rational (which is both concrete and universal). We will find that it refers, somehow, to the unique as well as to the universal.

Though Berdyaev attacks the autonomy of consciousness along with that of reason, he does not reject consciousness, just as he does not reject reason.

To overcome the unhappiness of consciousness through the supra-conscious is not a rejection of consciousness. The positive acts of consciousness enter into the supra-conscious . . . [3]

Consciousness, which belongs to man, participates in the unity of man (for man, we saw, is a unified incarnate spirit). There is also a unity of knowledge; that is, the truth of rational knowledge is preserved in mystical knowledge. "The positive acts of consciousness enter into the supra-conscious . . ."

We may stress (Berdyaev has never been kindly enough disposed

---

[1] *The Destiny of Man*, 39. See *The Meaning of the Creative Act*, 34: "Discursive thought is a formal, automatic apparatus, brought into action by forces which lie outside it. In the final analysis, discursive thought is only an instrument of intuition." Berdyaev adds, in a Bergsonian vein, "Discursive thought is an apparatus beautifully adapted to operations on the given world which is forced upon us . . ."

[2] Berdyaev doubtless accepts Hegel's notion of the unhappy consciousness. "Hegel, too, (that is as well as I) connected the unhappy consciousness with relation to the object, with dichotomy and disruption." *The Divine and the Human*, 198.

[3] *The Beginning and the End*, 81.

towards Reason to point it out) that his attack on rational philosophy has now lost some of its sting. For he must, at one and the same time, attack philosophical consciousness itself. Of course his rejection of the method of logical process is also a rejection of unmystical thought. But we just noticed that he allows concepts and ratiocination to be used in philosophy of history. And he uses them constantly. The ratiocination is reduced to a minimum and the concepts are taken up into symbols. He tells us how he writes:

I have already spoken of the unsystematic nature of my thinking. . . . When I begin to write I am sometimes carried away to the point of dizziness. My thought flows so fast that I hardly have time to write it down . . . I write in response to an inner voice which commands me to transmit my mental experience.[1]

Thus, his practice follows his theory. It is not scientific. He points out a little further, however: for all that, the written sentence is ratiocinative and objective to a degree.

It is now time to examine his mystical theory of knowledge. To understand it will require the remainder of the chapter. In the following section we will investigate some of the attributes and the necessary conditions of true knowledge.[2]

---

[1] *Dream and Reality*, 219–220.

[2] Just as we found Berdyaev's doctrine of the soul to shed light on his theory of objectivized knowledge, likewise we can find a doctrine of a changing human nature. It elucidates his synthesis of the irrational, the rational and the supra-rational. The soul, human nature, is not unchanging, but it changes during history.

He says, in *Truth and Revelation*, 17: "Transcendental man is not what is called unchangeable human nature, for it is not nature at all. It is creative action and freedom. Neither spirit nor freedom is nature. The nature of man changes, it evolves, but behind it is hidden the transcendental man, spiritual man . . ."

Berdyaev distinguishes the nature of man from his transcendental (and eternal) principle. He wants to show that man is changing in history (in nature) and yet is eternal (as transcendental).

He says again, in *Truth and Revelation*, 56: "the soul and mind of present day man is now entirely different from his soul and mind in earlier Christian ages. A ray of divine humanity has lighted upon man inwardly." The nature of man, for Berdyaev, is the soul of man, and it changes because of the changes of history. However, "man changes, he progresses and regresses; his consciousness expands and deepens, but it also contracts and is thrown on to the surface." *The Divine and the Human*, 126. Berdyaev means that the progress of man in history is a chequered career, a progress with its gains and losses.

He understands soul from the point of view of mind. He purposely ignores the soul so far as it is the principle of corporeal functions. That is, he views the soul only in its function as consciousness. The development of consciousness is identified, in his theory, with a development of the human soul in history. This is the sense in which he means the soul changes during history. Its change, then, is a change of mind, of consciousness, and is directed towards a goal. That goal is spiritual. "Spirit is truth, the purpose of the soul. . . . Spirit is axiological . . . truth, beauty, purpose . . . The soul is invariably, fragmentary and partial; spirit alone is whole and universal." *Spirit and Reality*, 39.

However, the significant part of Berdyaev's doctrine of the soul at the present time is precisely the change itself, not the progress (for there are regresses). And the change is significant because it allows man to turn to something new, to a new knowledge. Old

D. KNOWLEDGE AN IDENTITY

True knowledge seems to be an identity and also a vision, for Berdyaev, a sight, a seeing.

It is not an adequation of subject with object.

... truth is not the relationship or the identity of the comprehending, judging subject with objective reality, with objective being, but rather is entrance into divine life which is beyond both subject and object.[1]

Truth is not the type of identity achieved between knower and known object. Berdyaev does not allow that apprehension of the object, or even the judgment of its truth, attains true and spiritual knowledge. (This is not a natural way, nor the way of Grace, but a spiritual way).[2] Truth, he says, is the entrance into the divine life. "The apprehending mind has never discovered truth by the assistance of the logical apparatus by which he endeavors to convince others." [3] Berdyaev admits that the knowledge which is for the sake of communications is a real knowledge. But "knowledge above all ... places (the knower) face to face with ... truth." [4]

Knowledge is a vision because the truth is a light.

The knowledge of truth ... Truth is the light of the Logos, lighted within being itself, if we use the traditional terminology, or in the depths of existence, or of life itself. This one complete Truth is divided into a multitude of truths. A sphere of knowledge lighted by one path of light (such as a given science) may deny the source of light, the Logos-Sun. But it could never be lighted save for this one source of light.[5]

He is talking about a divine or spiritual illumination. True knowledge is the sight of the divine Logos-Sun.[6] The knowledge achieved in the

knowledges and outlooks, and hence old states of human nature, are experiments tried and discarded. Thus, change, whether it is progress or regress of the human soul, is the condition of new and better states. It is the condition of the spiritualization of the soul.

He says, in *Spirit and Reality*, 119: "Mysticism is essentially a spiritual as distinct from a psychic state and implies a spiritual penetration of the soul." Hence, Berdyaev's noetic, in asserting a supra-rational which is not irrational, is parallel to a psychology which asserts that the soul (and its objective consciousness) can be spiritualized by the spirit (with its mystical knowledge).

[1] *The Realm of Spirit and the Realm of Caesar*, 16.
[2] *The Beginning and the End*, 39.
[3] Cf. *Truth and Revelation*, 141.
[4] *The Beginning and the End*, 39.
[5] *The Realm of Spirit and the Realm of Caesar*, 19.
[6] The Russian word for *truth* favors the definition of Berdyaev, for whom truth is religious. The word, *pravda*, means not only *truth* but also *justice*. Thus, the Russian notion of truth is not as theoretical as the English, but is practical. Zenkovsky in his *History of Russian Philosophy*, 364, quotes a "well known" passage from the works of the philosopher, Mikhailovski: "Whenever the word '*pravda*' comes into my mind I cannot help admiring its

logical and rational sphere, in the adequation of subject and object, is true in so far as it dimly sees some ray if the Logos-Sun. The truth of judgment and of adequation is a "diminished Truth." [1]

We can understand better now how it is that Berdyaev's philosophy of history approaches the truth of the "historical," whether through a concept-symbol such as the "nation," or a more inclusive symbol.[2] In knowing and creating these symbols, the philosopher of history is glimpsing dimly a ray of the Logos-Truth. He is not seeking a rational knowledge in which he forms a concept adequated to an external object. But he is seeking and creating a vision which will reveal the meaning of history. That is why, according to Berdyaev, the philosopher of history insists upon the symbolism of his concepts, and why he calls them symbols or myths instead of concepts. He is not engaged in a rational process where the reason comes to rest in the truth of adequation of subject and object; for example, in the understanding of the *concept, "nation."* Instead he he creates the *symbol, "nation,"* in a knowledge directed toward a mysticism of history.[3] He is discontent with any vision save the religious one, that of the Logos-Sun. The universal history of the philosopher is based on that revealed in Holy Scriptures, and historical symbols serve it. The ultimate meaning of universal history is Christ, the Godman. He and the universal history to which He gives meaning provide the mystical light in which the philosopher creates and discovers historical symbols.

The true knowledge, or the symbolic approach to it, is not only a vision but is also a complete or partial identity of the knower and the known. I say it is an identity rather than an adequation because:

... The Truth is within me, in the depth of me, in the depth of the knowing subject, since I have my roots in the noumenal spiritual world. But it is within me in a drowsy state and awakening of it within me is an awakening to truth.[4]

This has been seen in the preceding chapter, in Berdyaev's metaphysics of Man. The Truth is within man because he is an image of the Godman;

---

striking inner beauty. It appears that no such word exists in any European language. Only in Russian, it seems, are 'truth' and 'justice' designated by the same word, fusing, as it were, into one great whole."

This notion of truth, however, is not exactly Berdyaev's. He seeks a Truth which he thinks is beyond good and evil, beyond justice. See *The Destiny of Man,* Chapter II. Nevertheless the notion of truth described above is practical and religious and Berdyaev's notion is likewise.

[1] *Truth and Revelation,* 45.

[2] For Berdyaev all historical traditions are symbols, useful for philosophy of history. Cf. *The Meaning of History,* 12. Concerning cultural epochs, Cf. *Ibid.,* 18.

[3] *The Beginning and the End,* 47. Concerning symbolic knowledge, see Section G, Part 2 below.

[4] *The Beginning and the End,* 47.

and he knows the Godman in his own most existential depths.[1] We recall Berdyaev's doctrine of remembrance.[2] The greatest truth that man recalls is the Godman. Man is a Godman by virtue of his divine origin, not through nature or by Grace.[3]

Berdyaev states the notion of the identity between knower and known in *Dream and Reality*. He makes some concession to the validity of objective knowledge, but at the same time he shows the difference between objective and philosophical knowledge.

I regard as "object" not the subject-matter of knowledge but that which makes a certain relationship within the existential sphere, whereby man takes up a cognitive attitude *toward* something, whereas his attitude ought to *be* that something. In true knowledge man transcends the object or rather possesses the object creatively and, indeed, creates it himself. ... Inasmuch as science and scientific method evince critically the grounds on which any given piece of knowledge is based, I am all for it ...[4]

This concession to objective and scientific knowledge is definite but note that the difference between the true knowledge of philosophy and the less true knowledge of science is stated more clearly than ever. In objective knowledge, man takes up a cognitive attitude towards the known reality (the "subject-matter"); that is, he notes the general in the reality without knowing *it* in its concrete universality. But the true, proper and philosophical attitude is to *be* that reality, to be identical with it. One becomes that reality because he creates it – the symbol expressive of the plenary truth in Christ.

Scientific and objective knowledge is good because it evinces critically the grounds of true (symbolic or mystical) knowledge. I may clarify Berdyaev's statement with my own example. Historical sciences, which are objective and scientific,[5] evince critically the grounds upon which part of philosophy of history may be based. Thus the chapter in *The End of Our Time* entitled, "The End of the Renaissance," is based partly on the findings of historical science. However, Berdyaev's own ("true") knowledge of this era of history is not an objective attitude toward the disclosures of historical science. It is a creative knowledge, illuminated by the mystical doctrine of Godmanhood; it utilizes the grounds provided by science and scientific method; and it knows a reality, Godmanhood and universal history, through the symbols it creates.

[1] See Chapter III, Section F.
[2] Chapter I, Section B, Part 2.
[3] See *Truth and Revelation*, 141.
[4] *Dream and Reality*, 287.
[5] *The End of Our Time*, 148.

The identity of the knower and the known is established. But we have
yet to find out what this true knowledge is. It is not an identity according to concepts because knowledge does not truly know conceptually, but symbolically or mystically.

... throughout the whole history of philosophical thinking men turned to self-
knowledge as the way of knowing reality. But was this knowledge of "self" a
knowledge of the concrete, unique and unrepeatable human self or was it merely
knowledge *about* man, man in general, or the species called man? [1]

As Berdyaev implies and as we already know, the true knowledge of
reality and of one's self is a knowledge of the "concrete, unrepeatable
human self." A conceptual identity would be an objectified knowledge.

True knowledge is therefore at once a self-knowledge and a knowledge
of a reality which is not the self. It is an identity of knower and known;
it is a creation of the knower; and it is a knowledge of a concrete
existent. In order to find Berdyaev's explanation of this theory, let us
investigate two preliminary aspects of knowledge in the following
sections: namely, the communal character and the volitional aspect
of knowledge.

E. TRUE KNOWING IS COMMUNAL IN CHARACTER

Berdyaev calls objective knowing sociological because it is the generalized mode of communication between civilized men. Communion of
persons in society, however, plays an outstanding role in true knowing,
according to Berdyaev. We can see that Berdyaev in particularly en-
couraged to stress the relationship of the knower and society (other
persons) in his theory of knowledge. For we have seen that the knower
does not discover the truth in nature as nature but in himself. Berdyaev
must find a way of obtaining true knowledge other than merely by
means of objective nature or even by means of self-analysis. That means
is the communalty of men.

The ego, man, can be a source of truth when he is steeped in his own depth, he
can be in the truth, whereas the object, on the other hand, cannot be in it. Hence
we shall see that the knowledge of truth is dependent upon the social relations
which obtain among men. [2]

We may note in passing that man can exist in the truth when he is
steeped in his own depths. Truth here refers to the mystical Godman

---

[1] *Dream and Reality*, 303.
[2] *The Beginning and the End*, 54.

as reflected in him. The identity of the knower and known is therefore not a perfect identity of one with the other, since created man is not the Godman but eternally distinct.

Berdyaev in some way connects the (true) knowledge of man with the social relations that obtain between him and other men.

> We should distinguish above all between two types of knowledge: there is ... rational and objective knowledge ... and secondly, there is the knowledge immanent in Being and in existence ... this knowledge is synonymous with *community* and participation. ... Knowledge can thus be considered from two different standpoints; from that of society, of communication between men by means of the objective and the general; and from that of community, of existential communion and of penetration into the heart of the individual.
>
> This is the very core of my thought.[1]

True knowledge is "immanent in Being and in existence": This is so because man knows the truth when "he is steeped in his own depth," and because existence and being pertain primarily to the human self.[2] This knowledge, immanent in existence," is synonymous with community and participation." This community is an existential communion with the heart of the individual.

The implication is that true knowledge is immanent in man in his true self; and this true knowledge is therefore attained in knowing the true man, both as it is in one's self and as it is in the selves of other men. That is, the communion of the Ego with the Thou and the We is a very important condition of existential knowledge. When he speaks of a penetration into the *heart* of the individual he is using a technical philosophical word; to commune with the heart of another is to know that person in the intelligible and volitional depths of his spirit.[3] It is a spiritual knowledge.

All our paths converge upon one metropolis when we investigate the philosophy of history of Berdyaev: True Man. Just as we found, in Chapter I, that the "historical" is in the last analysis man, so we find now that true and existential knowledge is knowledge of man. So significant is this that Berdyaev tells us it is of the very core of his thought; "this existential knowledge is synonymous with *community*." The theory also agrees with his Hegelian concrete universalism; for, in asserting the community of knowing he is denying the isolation and particularity of the concrete man as cut off from the universality of manhood.[4] We

---

[1] *Solitude and Society*, 48–49.
[2] Cf. Chapter III above.
[3] See Section F of this Chapter.
[4] See Chapter III, note 108.

saw indeed in the preceding chapter that the realization of one's personality involves the reception of the whole cosmos, the totality of history and all mankind.[1] But we find here that true knowledge is of man primarily because it is through man (and ultimately the Godman, the True Man) that history and everything else is truly known.

We are beginning to complete the outline of the doctrine of knowledge of Berdyaev. We are commencing to see a notion of man where the philosopher of history spiritually identifies himself with every man and, thereby, with the meaning of history and with the true cosmos. For man is a concrete universal, known in his universality and in his concreteness. The stress on communion as the mode of true knowing is strengthened by the doctrine that all nature has emanated from man and is potentially returned to man. Inasmuch as history and the historical are implicated in the concrete conditions of the cosmos, and since the cosmos emanates from man and is potentially returned to man, the stress on communion as the mode of true knowing again is justified.

Berdyaev tells us in his autobiography that he asserted this communal doctrine of knowing in his earliest book (1901), when he was a Marxist (idealist):

The character of knowledge is not only a matter of logic, but also of society, for the subject, in the act of knowing is not the ... German ... universal Mind, but concrete man endowed with certain mental and emotional qualities and placed within certain social relations with other men.[2]

This doctrine, he says, always remained. He adds that he expounded it in *Solitude and Society* and might have entitled the latter book "The Sociology of Knowledge." [3]

Thus we see that this doctrine of communal knowing *is* at the core of Berdyaev's epistemology. We saw in Chapter III that man "seeks to find his own reflection in another human countenance, in the Thou." [4] We found that "the We is a qualitative content immanent in the Ego," [5] because it is a question of "a social and human metaphysics, that of the We." [6] And we saw that sociability is a constituent property of the Ego's intimate existence.[7] And in this metaphysical and epistemological sociability man emerges from his own subjectivity and passes over

[1] See Chapter III, Section F.
[2] *Dream and Reality*, 124.
[3] *Ibid.*, 124.
[4] *Solitude and Society*, 125.
[5] *Ibid.*, 80.
[6] *Ibid.*, 79.
[7] *Ibid.*, 80–81.

into the trans-subjective.[1] Indeed Berdyaev attaches this sociology of knowing to a religious outlook which he found in the Slavophile philosophers of the 19th century. It is what "might be called a corporate Church gnosiology ... a method of apprehension which is opposed to the Cartesian *cogito ergo sum*. It is not *I* think, but *we* think, that is to say, the corporate experience of love thinks ..." [2]

However, Berdyaev defends the subjectivity of the individual person against the domination of rational and logical forms of social communication. There is not, I want to point out, any question but that Berdyaev affirms the value and dignity of the individual person so far as he is distinct from other persons.

Intuition is the foundation of communion, the faculty of being able to identify oneself with all things ... In the case of communion, the community becomes a part of the personality ... In the case of society ... the personality is merely a part of the community.[3]

The intuition of the individual person is the condition of his communion with others. And the communion of persons itself is of service to the single person: "the community becomes part of the personality."

Yet, true knowledge is a corporate experience, and an experience in which love operates. This Russian *We think* is a religious doctrine and, as Berdyaev says:

There is to be noted a very original gnosiology which might be called a corporate Church gnosiology. Love is recognized as the principle or apprehension; it guarantees the apprehension of truth; love is a source and guarantee of religious truth. Corporate experience of love, *Sobornost'* is the criterion of apprehension. ... The will is united to reason, not cut off from it.[4]

In such a Russian outlook, since true knowledge is communal and religious, it will therefore be an affective, a loving knowledge. This is a criteriology based on the experience of *Sobornost'*, altogetherness. Apprehension is judged in the light of communal knowing. And this Russian idea of knowledge is profoundly Berdyaev's own.[5]

Thus in this theory of knowledge we are witnessing the way in which the human personality realizes itself as a microcosm. Noetic is beginning to join Berdyaev's metaphysics now that we are at the mystical and religious level. Berdyaev himself discusses his epistemology and his

---

[1] *Slavery and Freedom*, 29.
[2] *The Russian Idea*, 161.
[3] *Solitude and Society*, 136.
[4] *The Russian Idea*, 161.
[5] Cf. *Solitude and Society*, 136; *The Beginning and the End*, 37, 70, 77.

religious metaphysics practically in the same breath at times. Knowledge is concerned with social communion, and society is existentially part of the individual's personality.[1]

Knowledge of communion and *Sobornost'* depends upon love more than upon intelligibility (See action following). It is not like the physical and mathematical knowledges which are universally binding upon men of different beliefs and outlooks. It depends, not upon intellectual community, but spiritual community.

> ... the universally binding character of cognition is to be found in its highest degree in mathematics and the physical sciences. ... On the other hand, knowledge in the historical and social sciences and in sciences of the spirit and of values, that is to say, in philosophy, has a lower degree of universally binding character just because it pre-supposes a greater spiritual community in which people share. Least of all universally binding are truths of a religious character, because they pre-suppose the maxium of spiritual community.[2]

According to this passage, Berdyaev's communal theory of knowing is correlative to his mysticism, a mysticism where the will leads the intellect and, consequently, where intelligibility does not trammel or destroy the freedom of the will. Berdyaev says the historical and social sciences and the sciences of the spirit are less universally binding than the lower sciences. This is obviously so according to his philosophy.

> The significance of communion as a goal of human life is essentially religious. ... This participation must take place in the very heart of the Ego's union with the Thou. The interpenetration of the Ego and the Thou is consummated in God.[5]

Berdyaev develops his theory of the commonalty of knowing with the guidance of the Christian doctrine of communion of saints. And the main guide is the doctrine of mystical communion of man and God. It is a guide because Berdyaev describes the partially communal knowledges of history, of social sciences and spiritual sciences as degrees of the true communal knowledge. We may note that his metaphysical doctrines of *Sobornost'* and microcosm and his cosmogonical approach have predisposed him to develop a sociology of knowing. His first principles have caused him to distinguish carefully the objectivized knowledge, common to the ordinary dwellers of societies, from the trans-subjective knowledge mutually enjoyed in a communion of saints. He wants to make denizens into citizens.

---

[1] Cf. *Solitude and Society*, 136 amd 137.

[2] *Slavery and Freedom*, 115.

[3] *Solitude and Scciety*, 141.

General-validity, which is always external and related to objectivity, is replaced by a sense of community, spiritual kinship, and reciprocal penetration of feeling.[1]

This statement sums up in a way how a communal knowledge happens to be superior to the knowledge limited by the objective mode of communication in a society. The important words are: *General-validity* and *feeling*. Berdyaev asserts a communal knowledge which is affective and loving. The meaning of history, we recall, is at the same time a metaphysical Existent, the Godman, Christ. The knowledge of history reaches its apogée in Him; at the same time, the knowledge becomes a metaphysical and mystical union of persons. True knowledge in philosophy of history is therefore loving. What is the role of love in Berdyaev's epistemology?

F. TRUE KNOWING IS LOVING AND CREATIVE IN CHARACTER

"Freedom," Berdyaev said, in *Freedom and the Spirit*," ... raises us up towards the idea of the divine."[2] We saw when we considered Berdyaev's voluntarism in Chapter II that his philosophy of history is a philosophy of beauty. It is, therefore, a philosophy which is loving, one where the reason places itself under the guidance of love. Berdyaev is most profoundly convinced of the affectivity of metaphysical thought and not only concerning a religious metaphysic (such as his own) but every metaphysic.[3]

The process of intellection discovers the meaning, the cosmos, underlying the meaningless and chaotic universe. ... It is essentially creative and promotes organization by helping the human mind to master chaos and the obscurities of existence; in a word, to master the world both theoretically and practically by the exercise of the human faculty of creation ...[4]

To begin with, Berdyaev does not deny intellection in his doctrine of loving knowledge. Intellection discovers the meaning of history (and of the cosmos) because and only because the human mind masters the world *both* theoretically and practically. So far as it masters the world theoretically it knows conceptually and abstractly; so far as it masters the world practically it knows affectively and lovingly. And this occurs because the knower creates that which he knows in his own subjectivity. He creates a symbol or true myth which approximates closer to the true

---

[1] *The Beginning and the End*, 77.
[2] *Freedom and the Spirit*, 124.
[3] Cf. *Solitude and Society*, 20.
[4] *Ibid.*, 52.

reality contained in the Godman.[1] And this creativity – by virtue of the very nature of creativity – is more volitional than rational. In creatively mastering the world, the philosopher of history proceeds by way of a loving knowledge.

When Berdyaev says that knowledge is properly active rather than passive, he is speaking from the point of view of his creative noetic.

Knowledge is essentially active because man is active. When philosophical theory is based on the opposition of intellect and Being, the affirmation that philosophy only reflects being passively ... is no longer tenable. Intellection is the outcome of free human activity; it is not merely reflection, but also creative transfiguration ... (Man's) creative freedom should extend to all spheres and it should pursue its creative work in the sphere of knowledge itself.[2]

I cite this passage at this time; the assertion of activity of knowing against the notion of passivity of knowing is a religious statement and not merely an ontological statement. Proper knowing is not an act of the intellect but an act of the man, a human act, guided by his *love*. This rejects any purely intellectual epistemology and asserts a voluntaristic noetic in its place. In the text above Berdyaev is preoccupied with the controversy between objectivism and existentialism; he only touches upon the religious aspect of his noetic. The loving knowledge here considered is that of the creator for his work, that of the philosopher of history for the symbols and true myths which he creates. "Knowledge," he says, "is essentially active, because man is active."

This is a greatly loving knowledge, even if the immediate object of the will is only the symbol, for the symbol participates in the Beauty of that which it symbolizes. The creation of the philosopher of history, here, is a metaphor of history. And the metaphor of history, we saw in Chapter I, becomes identified in the knower with a mystical knowledge of the highest Reality.[3] The affective knowledge of the philosopher of history when he creates the meaning of history is guided by a loving and mystical knowledge of religious truths. The lower affective knowledge is transformed by the mystical knowledge, while at the same time it merges in its more spiritual heights with religious and mystical doctrine. Thus the lesser love of the creative thinker is taken up into the greater love of his religious and mystical communion. There is no separation of experiences here.

In Berdyaev's doctrine philosophical intuition is loving:

---

[1] See following section.
[2] *Solitude and Society*, 33.
[3] Cf. 42, n. 1 above.

Philosophical intuition cannot be deduced from anything else; it is primary, and secretes in itself the light which will illuminate every act of knowledge. ... Philosophical knowledge depends upon the range of experience, and it also supposes an essentially tragic experience of all the contradictions of human existence *Philosophy is therefore based upon the maximum experience of human existence*. This experience integrates man's intellectual affective and volitional life.[1]

Intuition is intellectual, but it cannot be intellectual only. It is also emotional and volitional. As Berdyaev said in a last work, "it is the activity, the intense effort of the spirit as a whole. ... The dispassionately intellectual is a figment of the imagination ... primary intuition itself is above all emotional." [2]

The above quoted passage is the assertion of Berdyaev the philosopher of history and Existentialist. He speaks of a *"maximum experience of human existence."* Philosophical intuition is based upon this experience, a tragic and Existential experience. The primary intuition of the philosopher of history is the intuition of the Godman. And the philosophical intuition when it is less strictly understood, is attained in the light of meta-historical principles, at the very time that it bases itself upon the maximum experience of existence.

Berdyaev connects his idea of philosophical intuition with the doctrine of the activity of knowing. "Intuition is not only the perception of something; it is also a creative penetration into meaning; and more than that, the very existence of meaning presupposes a creative condition of spirit." [3] He understands the creativity of knowing from the point of view of the unifying action of intuition. The synthesis of creativity is at the same time the strong unity of intuition. We need only think for a moment of his philosophy of history. The philosopher, when he creates his historical symbols, achieves the unity of his synthesis in a spiritual intuition. Berdyaev opposes the concrete and synthetic unity of creative intuition to the division and abstraction he finds in objective knowledge.[4]

When Berdyaev speaks of the "contradictions of human existence," he is expressing one of the tenets of his philosophy: He believes that contradictions and antinomies belong to the very order of the world and God.[5]

---

[1] *Solitude and Society*, 13.

[2] *The Beginning and the End*, 68.

[3] *Ibid.*, 38.

[4] *Dream and Reality*, 286; "Objectivity ... is the product of disruption, disunion, estrangement and enmity. Knowledge, which is an activity of the subject, depends on the victory over disunion and estrangement, on the extent and intensity of spiritual communion."

[5] Cf. *The Beginning and the End*, 18, where Berdyaev discusses Boehme's Heraclitean metaphysics of opposites.

The paradox and contradiction that he finds follow from his peculiar peculiar notion of knowledge. In particular, the cause of his outlook is his notion of the concept. All that we have seen of his attack on intellectualist philosophies show that the concept for him is purely univocal in meaning. There is an example of the univocity of his idea of concept in his theory of good and evil. He calls his philosophy a "philosophy of beyond good and evil." [1] He must do this in order to hang onto his philosophical (and religious) insights, because the concepts of good and evil, he thinks, are univocal concepts. "Good" (legality),[2] for him, means only one thing; furthermore, since it is a concept, it is non-existential. He must not, therefore, predicate (human) good of God. Hence God is beyond good.

> Herein lies the fundamental paradox of ethics: the moral good has a bad origin and its bad origin pursues it like a curse. This paradox is brought to light by Christianity, which shows that the good understood as a law is powerless. For Christian consciousness law is paradoxical ... Law comes from sin ...[3]

He is simply asserting the Christian doctrine that natural good is powerless to bring man to Salvation unless it is perfected by Grace. And there is a paradox that good is not good enough. But Berdyaev will not see any sense in this notion of good which is not paradoxical. He will never state that human natural good is analogous to the Divine Good, but he denies that the Divine can be good.

Thus Berdyaev, believing in the univocity of concepts, proceeds from his *thoughts* about the world to the assertion that the world actually *is* paradoxical and antinomical to its depths. James F. Anderson, in his metaphysical work, *The Bond of Being,* has shown how this notion of the concept not only leads to a paradoxical metaphysics but requires a symbolism in place of any other kind of noetic. "Symbolism moves in the order of univocal concepts." [4]

Berdyaev asserts the notion of univocal concept, and this univocity has served his mystical philosophy of history by setting up a dialectical necessity requiring him to assert an affective and loving noetic of symbolization.[5]

---

[1] *The Destiny of Man,* 17, ff.

[2] Concerning the legality of "good," see *The Destiny of Man,* 84, ff.

[3] *The Destiny of Man,* 84–85.

[4] James F. Anderson, *The Bond of Being* (Herder, St. Louis, 1949), 226. See, too, section entitled, "The Neo-Platonist Symbolism of Nicholas Berdyaev," 198–203. He says, 200: "Evidently Berdyaev has seen that univocal ideas, like the idea of *being,* considered univocally as a logical concept, simply do not work in theology."

He says, again, 201: "In place of (the science of theology), Berdyaev would substitute a 'mysticism' whose terms are 'symbols'."

[5] Symbolization is necessary if (1) the ultimate reality is to be known and if (2) the ultimate reality is non-conceptual; because concepts are univocal.

A person seeking to know by way of symbol or metaphor is obviously not content to remain in the metaphor but looks beyond it to what it symbolizes. Furthermore, through his knowing, which is affective and loving, he seeks an individual person. The reality which Berdyaev's metaphor symbolizes is ultimately a divine Person. Knowledge properly speaking is a religious knowledge, a "movement of the spirit, a direction of the will, a sensitivity, a search for meaning, a being shaken, elated, disillusioned and imbued with hope." [1] The divine person, an existent, which *this* knowledge seeks, must be concrete (as we saw in Chapter III).

(Intuition is a passionate break-through of the will towards the light towards truth as a whole. Then the universal is revealed in the concrete and the individual without crushing it and turning it into a means. Truth is not common and abstract, truth is concrete, it is individually personal. Indeed, it is the incarnate Logos [2].

The knower properly knows the Truth as a totality, a whole. He knows not only its intelligibility but also its concreteness. Knowing is not an adequation by way of abstract concepts; truth is individual and personal.

The passage brings to our attention the most difficult problem that has been encountered in this chapter: how the philosopher knows the concrete existent in an identity which is not merely conceptual? We turn, then, to the last and by far the most important section of this chapter to answer this question. [3]

---

[1] *Dream and Reality*, 89.

[2] *The Beginning and the End*, 124.

[3] Berdyaev's theory of the heart is helpful in understanding his idea of living knowledge. The notion of the heart in philosophy has a long tradition in Russian thought. See Lossky's *History of Russian Philosophy*, 385. Berdyaev says: "In Eastern Christianity there is a special comprehension of the heart as the kernel of the human creature and his spiritual life. In the light of this concept the heart appears not as man's emotional-psychic nature but as a spiritual-psychic whole, comprising also a transfigured mind. Man's longing for truth and purpose, for spirituality, is an essential part of his nature; it is not deducible from the psychic and vitalistic process but emanates directly from the Divine spirit inherent in man." *Spirit and Reality*, 41. Berdyaev has synthesized the doctrine of the heart with his philosophy of spirit. The notion of heart indicates especially the aspect of spirit which is affective and loving, even though the heart is the organ of wisdom as well as the "organ of moral conscience." *Solitude and Society*, 128. The Spirit may be considered apart from the heart: "We may in truth say that ours is the age of technique and of the spirit, not of the heart." N. Berdyaev, "Man and the Machine," *Hibbert Journal, A Quarterly Review of Religion, Theology and Philosophy*, XXXIII (1934–1935), 83. That is, a spirit without a heart, so to speak, is one in whom knowledge is not loving.

In brief, the notion of the heart refers to the kernel of the human person, the incarnate spirit, in the sense that the heart combines loving and knowing and the former rules the latter. "We must not seek the criteria of truth in reason or the intellect, but rather in the integral spirit. The heart and the conscience remain the supreme agents of value as well as of knowledge." *Solitude and Society*, 12.

G. IMAGE, SYMBOL AND MYSTICAL EXPERIENCE:
CONCRETE AND CREATIVE KNOWING

(1) *Image*

But although philosophy may start by discrediting the myth, it ands by acknowledging it as the sum of philosophical knowledge. Plato demonstrated this
fact when he passed on from *concept* to *myth* as the means of attaining true
knowledge.[1]

Myth, we will see, is synonymous with *symbol* in Berdyaev's philosophy.
The passage quoted above gives us our bearing as we set out to investigate the symbolic epistemology of Berdyaev. The myth or symbol
is the sum of philosophical knowledge, and he refers to Plato's use of the
philosophical myth. The philosophical myth, as we can plainly see in
Plato's dialogues, is imaginative because it describes concrete
circumstances in space and time.[2]

The creative act always calls up the image of something different; it images
something higher, better and more beautiful than this – than the "given." ...

Productive imagination is a metaphysical force which wages war against the
objective and determinate world ... The creative imagination builds up realities.
The forms which are constructed by the creators of works of art lead a real existence and they are active in the world. Imagination is a way out from an unendurable reality.[3]

In creative activity... images arise which are not determined by the empirical
world, or if they are determined by it, it is through the medium of creative
transformation. ... There occur, it is true, radiant, luminous visions ... It is not
only the subconscious which is operating in creative activity but the supra-
conscious also; there is a movement upward.[4]

He says "the creative act always calls up the image of something
different"; for, in his theory, the primary creative act is that of the
knowing person, and the imagination has a noble function. It is involved
in creative (and true) knowing; it has an important and essential role.
In fact, he believes the imagination is at work in the highest, the mysti-

---

[1] *Ibid.*, 6.
[2] Cf. *Symposium*, 203.
[3] *The Beginning and the End*, 174–175.
[4] *Ibid.*, 179–180. Berdyaev refers to Boehme's doctrine of imagination (175). Indeed,
Boehme's notion of the imagination is similar to Berdyaev's. Boehme says in the *Epistles:*
"*Through Imagination and an earnest serious desire*, we become again Impregnated of the
Deity." *Epistles of Jacob Bemen* (London, 1649), 69, No. 10. And in No. 13: "But the New
man which in an earnest serious will and purpose, ariseth through imagination (or the ef-
fectual operation of true Faith) abideth stedfast in the rest of Christ ..."

cal knowing. But, unlike Boehme and Schelling,[1] he does not place imagination in God's knowing.[2]

The myth of a divine imagination is not present in his theory. Imagination is a way out of an unendurable reality. And though the imagination is determined by empirical sources, it creates new images and thus transforms the old. The images from the subconscious are transformed in the supra-conscious.

Further, "the forms which are constructed by the creators of works of art lead a real existence and they are active in the world." Berdyaev, as we saw in Chapter I, is philosophically very aware of the *reality* of the forms men create and retain in the memory.[3] Their existence – indeed their concrete existence – is real. Their existence comes from the existence of the existent men who know them. The imagination, then, is the creator of these forms and hence of existent realities.

We saw in Chapter III that Berdyaev rejects both nominalism and realism in favor of a concrete existentialism. This metaphysical doctrine requires the theory of a thought which works with images.

The antithesis of nominalism is integral intuition, the intuition of wholeness, thinking in terms of images, in which the intellectual is combined with the emotional.[4]

Berdyaev here connects the concrete wholeness of the metaphysical reality with knowledge's image. "The intuition of wholeness" – "thinking in terms of images." The identity of the knower with the concrete existent, of the philosopher of history with the meaning of history, occurs through mental images. And the intellectual is combined with the emotional in thinking in terms of images because the images are created. The knower creates new images in transfiguring old images which mirror the external world.

---

[1] Boehme refers as follows to God's imagination in the *Epistles*, 93, No. 79: "The four elements likewise have such a ground (birth or original) from the imagination of the Eternal One ..." And Schelling says, in *Of Human Freedom*", 35: But there is born in God Himself an inward, imaginative response, corresponding to this longing, which is the first stirring of divine Being in its still dark depths. Through this response, God sees himself in his own image since his imagination can have no other object than himself."

[2] The myth of a divine Imagination is not in Berdyaev's theory. Indeed, in a last book, *Truth and Revelation*,75, he distinguishes between "imagination" and "knowledge." "The act of appraisal which must always be made by man if he is to rise above a given situation which is doing violence to him is associated with the *imagination*. But the appraisal is linked also with *knowledge*, though not with objectified knowledge nor with rationalized knowledge." (my italics).

[3] Philosophy, too, is an art,"... a special art, differing in principle from poetry, music, or painting – it is the art of knowing. Philosophy is an art because it is creation. ... (it) creates existential ideas rather than images." *The Meaning of the Creative Act*, 29.

[4] *The Beginning and the End*, 120–121.

(2) *Symbol and Myth*

The philosophical myth or symbol comes into its own in such a philosophy.

> History is not an objective empirical datum; it is a myth. Myth is no fiction, but a reality; ... Myth is the story preserved in popular memory of a past event and transcends the limits of the external world revealing an ideal world, a subject-object world of facts.[1]

Berdyaev's use of the word, *history*, refers, not to the historical science, history, but to something higher. He is referring to the historical, the meaning of history insofar as it is preserved in popular memory.[2] His terminology is less exact than it is in later books. When Berdyaev says myth is no fiction but a reality, he means that myth partakes of the concrete existentiality of the man who knows it. He is referring, ultimately, to the "microcosm (which) seems to contain in itself all the historical epochs of the past which have not been entirely covered over by the subsequent strata of time and of more recent historical life." [3]

Myth is here understood in the sense of historical symbol, not in the restricted sense in which we usually say *myth*. "All great historical epochs, even those of modern history ... give rise to myths." [4] Plato is soon mentioned.[5]

The word, *symbolize*, is used: "The tradition of a people is valuable in so far as it symbolizes the historical destiny of that people." [6] The word, *myth*, is used in order to convey to the reader the sense of popular and widespread knowledge of a certain historical tradition or symbol. The word, *symbolize* (or *symbol*), is used to indicate the epistemological and metaphysical significance of the myth. *Myth* is synonymous with *symbol*.[7]

---

[1] *The Meaning of History*, 21.

[2] In this use of the word, history, he intends to propose that historical science itself, as it is commonly understood, should change. Historical science, Berdyaev suggests, should adopt Berdyaev's philosophy of history to its needs. Cf. *The Meaning of History*, 22–23. To give the reader an idea of what he is suggesting, I refer to a contemporary achievement in historical writing. A. J. Toynbee's *A Study of History* is an example which gives an idea of the sort of history Berdyaev wants historians to write. Not that Toynbee is a Berdyaevian. Toynbee seeks to write history always in the light of the meaning of history as he understands it. Unlike Berdyaev, he is not interested in cosmogony or cosmology but devotes his stupendous genius to the moral significations of history.

Concerning the relationship between the notion of history and the notion of the "historical," see Chapter I, Section B.

[3] *The Meaning of History*, 23.

[4] *Ibid.*, 21.

[5] *Ibid.*, 22.

[6] *Ibid.*, 24.

[7] Berdyaev, in his mystical and supra-rational doctrine, cannot consider the Holy Trinity by way of concepts, but only in a mystical way. In this, he uses myth and symbol synonymously: "With regard to the mystery of the Trinity, *myth* and *symbol* alone can be used, and conceptual thinking is out of the question." (my italics)

The myth or symbol is the noblest way of knowing.[1]

But although philosophy may start by discrediting the myth, it ends by acknowledging it as the sum of philosophical knowledge. Plato demonstrated this when he passed on from *concept* to *myth* as the means of attaining true knowledge.[2]

The myth is the sum of philosophical knowledge because, being supraconceptual, it is able to transfigure a large amount of conceptual knowledge. Berdyaev gives Plato's philosophy as an example, and we may note an example in Plato. Thus, Plato, with the myth of the cave attempts to attain a true doctrine of the relationship between the lower and the higher worlds.[3]

Note, however, that in propounding a philosophy of myth Berdyaev is not suggesting revelation to be fiction, or even myth or symbol. Myth and symbol refer to knowledge in Berdyaev's philosophy; revelation is not a knowledge. "There is no essential affinity between revelation and knowledge, since the former contains no cognitive element," even though revelation is known and is a philosophical experience.[4] This doctrine of revelation combines the spirituality of Berdyaev's philosophy of history and the existentiality of his metaphysics. It is a peculiarly modern Russian outlook, as we saw in the preceding chapter.[5] Western philosophers usually apply the notion of an *existent* to created things or to metaphysical entities, but Berdyaev primarily applies the notion to the Godman. Revelation is both eminently religious and eminently metaphysical, it is existential and more than knowledge – beyond symbol and myth.

When Berdyaev says, in *The Meaning of History*, that history is a myth, and the myth is no fiction but a reality, we must qualify the bare statement. The myth or symbol is an imperfect reality, just as the external world of nature (itself a symbol of a truer reality) is an imperfect reality. And, as we saw, historical traditions and myths which indeed give meaning to history merely "symbolize the historical destinies of peoples."[6] True enough, "this symbolism is of primary importance for the elaboration of a philosophy of history and for the

---

[1] See preceding note.

[2] *Solitude and Society*, 6.

[3] *The Republic*, VII, 514A, ff.

[4] *Solitude and Society*, 5. Berdyaev goes on to say of revelation and knowledge that "Revelation may therefore prove to be of capital importance to knowledge, for it constitutes a distinct philosophical experience, a transcendent event which philosophy can transform into an immanent datum." Concerning the peculiar use of *philosophical*, see Chapter I, Section C, Part 2.

[5] See Chapter III, 113–114 above.

[6] *The Meaning of History*, 24. Cf. Chapter I, Section B, Part 1.

apprehension of its inner significance." [1] But the symbol or myth is a secondary reality. It, along with historical traditions, is the condition of the knowing the "historical." [2]

It is essential to grasp the inner meaning of the myth and symbol in a spiritual manner in order to free oneself from that naively realist influence which they may possess ...[3]

Hence, though historical traditions and myths give a meaning to history, this meaning in turn has an inner meaning. The meaning of history for Berdyaev is like a large onion. Beneath the topmost layer of onion is another layer, beneath that is another layer, and so on down to the kernel of the onion. And just as a given area of an inner layer refers to a larger extent of the cover the closer to the center it is obtained; so in Berdyaev's philosophy of history, the layers of meaning of history become truer as they become more comprehensive and closer to the kernel, the Godman. And just as the outer layer of the onion is a true reality and existential participant in the totality of the onion, though rather dry; so the merest symbols found in history are true realities, participating in the existence of the Godman, in whom the knower participates and in whose image the knower exists. This idea of an onion is useful for understanding Berdyaev. However, the merest symbols in history are less real than the cover of the onion is part of the onion.

The symbol, we saw (p. 168), is not revelation; it is, therefore, not the "historical," truest reality. And in objectification there are only symbols, no primal realities.[4] However:

The corporeal world is capable of issuing out of objectivity and entering into subjectivity. ... It can be said that the whole material world, the whole natural world, is a symbol of the spiritual world. ...[5]

The symbol tends toward primal reality, toward the events which take place in the spiritual world, toward meta-history. "The events take place in the spiritual world but the image of them is formed in the world of nature and history. ... the symbolic embodiment." [6] Berdyaev will want to distinguish sharply between symbol and true knowledge in his epistemology.

---

[1] *The Meaning of History*, 24.
[2] See Chapter I, Section B, Part 1.
[2] *Freedom and the Spirit*, 71.
[4] *Spirit and Reality*, 52.
[5] *The Beginning and the End*, 65.
[6] *Truth and Revelation*, 144.

In the spiritual life there is a struggle between symbolism and realism. The interpretation of symbols as ultimate realities is not only a misunderstanding of symbolism, but also an evil system of servitude. It is a form of naive realism. In contradistinction true realism is concerned with the knowledge of symbolism, with an awareness of the distinction between symbolism and realism. It is the task of the symbolist theory of knowledge to prepare the way for realism. We must distinguish between *symbolized* and *realized* forms of spirit and spirituality. ... We cannot dispense with symbolism in language and thought, but we can do without it in the primary consciousness.[1]

Berdyaev is presenting a "symbolist theory of knowledge" which insists upon a distinction between symbolic knowledge and real knowledge. We have to think symbolically and yet realize at the same time that our thinking is merely symbolic. Naive realism, for Berdyaev, is the acceptance of the superficial knowledge of the objectified and symbolical world as primary knowledge.

Realism, true knowledge, on the other hand, is the name Berdyaev gives to the strange and non-conceptual knowledge which is first. He indicates in the context quoted from above that the "realism" is a mysticism; this is the "primary consciousness."

But note something rather interesting: Berdyaev passes, in this quotation, from speaking of knowledge to speaking of metaphysical reality. "It is the task of the symbolist theory of knowledge to prepare the way for realism. We must distinguish between *symbolized* and *realized* forms of spirit and spirituality." He is not saying that symbolical knowledge is to be replaced by something that is not knowledge; instead, he means that symbolical knowledge is to be followed by something that is more than knowledge. He is asserting, in his philosophy of history, that the goal to be immediately and directly worked for is the mystical union.

This mystical doctrine throws more light on the problem we have encountered: the problem of how, in knowledge, the knower can be identified with the concrete known concretely. Knowledge passes into something which is not merely knowledge (objectified knowledge), nor a union in which knowledge and the knower can be distinguished (symbolic knowledge participating in the existentality of the person), but a mystical union in which knowledge and knower cannot be distinguished. Hence the knower, in this final phase, becomes identified with the known, with the Godman, a concrete Existent. And this is a concrete identity according to Berdyaev's intention because it is a real identity. We will presently see how the identity is concrete, not only on

---

[1] *Spirit and Reality*, 170–171.
[2] Concerning "*historical*," see Chapter I, Section B.

the side of the concrete Existent, the Godman, but also on the side of man. Man in his own concreteness is identified with the known.

We also see the indication that the problem of the concrete identity of knower and known, of the identity of the philosopher of history and the concrete "historical," is solved in the mystical order of knowing. For, in that order, knowledge becomes the metaphysical (and concrete) reality, that is, the man and the Godman. There, the microcosm realizes itself and achieves the concrete identity with all of remembered history and with the world. This *remembered history* (in the existentiality of of remembrance) is the "historical," and the *world* is the existential reality of the visible and fallen world.

Indeed, both the mystical aspect of knowledge and the historical (not to say "historical") aspect are so important that Berdyaev considers them each to be a principle of knowledge.

Knowledge is based upon the action of three principles: the human, the divine and the natural. It is the outcome of the reciprocal action of human culture, Divine Grace, and natural necessity. The philosopher's tragedy has its origin in the attempt to restrict his pursuit of knowledge by the invocation of Divine Grace or by an appeal to the universal character of natural necessity. If God and nature are the objects of philosophical investigation, then its antagonism to both dogmatic religion and science is inevitable. But its true sphere is the investigation of human existence, human destiny and human purpose. Man is the real subject of the philosopher's knowledge ...[1]

The first assertion, "knowledge is based upon the action of three principles, the human, the divine and the natural," has been implicit in the presentation of Berdyaev's epistemology and metaphysics. The natural itself is real, though a symbol. The natural is, consequently, a principle of knowledge; and Berdyaev refers to the "universal character of natural necessity." The human and the divine are the other two principles of knowledges.

The second sentence deserves close attention: "(knowledge) is the outcome of the reciprocal action of human culture, Divine Grace and natural necessity." Note that Berdyaev associates "action of human culture" with the human principle of knowledge. This is very interesting because Berdyaev implies that what is particularly *human* (with a small 'h') in our knowledge is not the inner dynamism of the knower but the action of human culture. The inner dynamism of the knower refers to the *Godman* of which every man is an image; every man is human and divine. And every man is divine in so far as he is truly

---

[1] *Solitude and Society*, 14–15.

human.[1] To sum it up, the human aspect of knowledge (as distinguished from the divine and the natural aspects) is based upon the action of human culture. That is, our knowledge of man, insofar as he is not the Godman, comes from the action of human culture.

Knowledge of human culture [2] is the condition of knowing the "historical." Philosophy of history is the term of the knowledge of human culture. Philosophy of history, in fact, is intimately related to all three sources of knowledge because (1) it is a mystical philosophy, (2) it is attained through knowing human culture, and (3) it is a doctrine which makes use of reason. These three principles are unified in philosophy of history.

I said that, according to Berdyaev, the identity of the knower and the known is an identity, concrete both on the side of the known and on the side of the knower. The known must be understood by the knower under the concrete conditions in which the knower exists. The mystery of such a knowing, we saw, is partially illuminated when we realize that the knowing (when it is true) is mystical.

The mystery is illuminated a little more by the foregoing passage. The quotation ends, saying: "Man is the real subject of the philosopher's knowledge." And Berdyaev means both man and the Godman, created and uncreated man. It is according to this notion we must understand Berdyaev's doctrine that knowledge passes beyond itself to the metaphysical and religious existent. This mystical union which is more than knowledge is approached by way of the knowledge of man; and it should be so approached because it is a union with the True Man. The approach takes the path of philosophy of history because philosophy of history knows the intelligibility of human culture – its meaning – the source of the human aspect of knowledge. The question remains, how is it possible to know concretely?

(3) The Whole Man Knows

The answer is that it is the whole man who knows, not the reason of man or his mind so far as it is merely intellectual.[3] Not only the consciousness is involved in it, but "wholeness is peculiar to the sub-conscious or to the superconscious." [4]

---

[1] Concerning the divinity of man, see *Truth and Revelation*, 141.
[2] Cf. Chapter I.
[3] *Truth and Revelation*, 20.
[4] *Spirit and Reality*, 103.

Spiritual life is a whole in which separate mental elements are synthesized. There may be more truth and wholeness in the unconscious than in consciousness which introduces division and separation. But this may only be the case when the unconscious is hallowed, purified from resentment and ennobled by lofty religious symbolism. . . . The unconscious, with its instincts, emotions and affective states, must be ennobled and sublimated.[1]

Berdyaev is then saying that the corporeal states of man, instincts and emotions, understood in the term, *unconscious*, enter into the makeup of true knowledge. He means that man truly knows instinctively as well as mentally and that these knowledges are ennobled and sublimated in the *via metaphorica* enroute to the true knowledge of mysticism. This union of instinctive knowledge with what is higher is understood when he speaks, in *The Beginning and the End*, of "Integral Intuition, the intuition of wholeness, thinking in terms of images, in which the intellectual is combined with the emotional." [2]

The imaginative knowledge, the loving knowledge, the symbolic knowledge must be understood not only with regard to the human will and the imagination. It is based also on the corporeal states, the bodily emotions and instincts. "Consciousness is not whole but divided. Wholeness is peculiar to the subconscious or to the superconscious."[3] The ideal of integral knowledge. i.e., of knowledge as an organic all-embracing unity is being asserted. And it can be attained only if the subrational aspect of the world (sense qualities), its rational aspect, and the supra-rational are all given together in experience which combines sensuous, intellectual and mystical intuition. This is the sense in which Berdyaev believes that the whole truth is revealed only to the whole man.

Man, we saw, is an incarnate spirit. It is only by combining all his spiritual powers – subrational experience, rational thought, esthetic perception, moral experience and religious contemplation – that man begins to apprehend the world's true being and see the super-rational truths about God.[4] Berdyaev's doctrine of incarnate spirit underlies

---

[1] *The Destiny of Man*, 230.

[2] *The Beginning and the End*, 120–121.

[3] *Spirit and Reality*, 103.

[4] Lossky, in his *History of Russian Philosophy*, describes this doctrine of integral knowledge very well and is worth quoting. He not only presents the doctrine, but he also shows that this is a peculiarly *Russian* doctrine, well-established in Russian thought. He says, 404: "The ideal of *integral* knowledge – i.e., of knowledge as an organic all-embracing unity, proclaimed by Kireyevsky and Khomiakov – appealed to many other Russian thinkers; but it can only be attained if the subrational aspect of the world (sense qualities), its rational (or ideal) aspect, and the superrational principles are all given together in experience which combines sensuous, intellectual and mystical intuition. The whole truth is only revealed to the whole man, said Kireyevsky and Khomiakov. It is only through combining all his spiritual powers – sense experience, rational thought, aesthetic perception, moral experience and religious contem-

this noetic. "It is the whole man who receives and interprets revelation, not abstract, partial and merely *psychological* man." [1] (my italics) It is not the *psyche*, the soul, which gives true knowledge, but the spirit; and the spirit is incarnate, includes the whole man; and hence there are irrational elements in knowing.[2]

This theory of knowledge raises new problems when we turn our attention from the knowledge of revelation and the knowledge of external things to the historical knowledge of the past. The philosopher of history is particularly concerned with the remembrance of past entities, events and cultures. This remembrance, we saw, is a concrete knowledge. But it is not concrete in the fullest sense of the word; culture is not perceived through the external senses. It is, however, a concrete knowledge upon the condition that the imagination, the fancy, participates in knowing. This is so in the sense that the past is known as past, even though it is a present knowledge. Although this creative memory is "a victory over the empire of time," [3] and escapes from historical time, it preserves the past.

Let us affirm once more that the past has never existed in the past. The ontologically real experience of the past is based upon memory and remembrance. which alone ontologically resists the ravages of time. Memory alone can apprehend the inner mystery of the past; it is the temporal agent of eternity. ... History, like everything else, has two aspects; on the one hand, it is an objective process in so far as it investigates the past as an object and is, consequently, relegated like nature to the objective world; on the other hand, it is a spiritual event, in the inner sphere of existence. As a spiritual event, history can only be apprehended by means of the ontological memory and active communion with the past.[4]

Memory, according to this passage, both spiritually preserves the past and also "apprehends the inner mystery of the past," since it is creative as well as retentive.

Berdyaev here affirms the spirituality of the concrete identity of knower and known. The philosopher of history identifies himself with the historical in its concrete reality and this identification is "a spiritual event in the inner sphere of existence." It is spiritualized (either in popular consciousness or in the representation of popular consciousness by others, or in the mind of others). This is certainly no sensory identi-

---

plation – that man begins to apprehend the world's true being and grasp the superrational truth's about God. It is precisely such integral experience that underlies the creative work of many Russian thinkers ... Berdyaev ..."

[1] *Truth and Revelation*, 19.
[2] *The Realm of Spirit and the Realm of Caesar*, 103.
[3] *Solitude and Society*, 106.
[4] *Ibid.*, 106–107.

fication with the past. This historical knowledge is that of a "past" which did not historically exist but which is created in the historical memory. It seems to be Berdyaev's intention that this concrete knowledge has spiritualized the corporeal aspect of historical knowledge.[1]

[1] Indeed the corporeal body is spirit in its inner essence as it is, also, in Schelling. Cf. *The Ages of the World*, 171. And, therefore, the spiritualizing of the corporeal state is the spirit ualizing of what is already spiritual. In Berdyaev's concrete spiritualizing, where he asserts that the whole world is redeemed in man, he does not mean that the corporeal conditions, as we sense them are immortal. "The form of the body pertains to man's personality and will inherit eternal life. But the matter ('flesh and blood') do not inherit eternal life. . . . The body is not to be equated with matter. . . . body is spirit. The splendour and the beauty of the body for me is contained in its form rather than in its material substance, which is a source of necessity." *Dream and Reality*, 175–176.
    As we saw in the preceding chapter, the world of reality, the true world, will differ from the world that we sense. The true world will be contained, in its imaginative reality, in man the microcosm.

Berdyaev's theory of incarnation of spirit is helpful in understanding his doctrine of concrete knowledge and mystical experience – the goal of knowledge.

We have seen that man is an incarnate spirit and that historical entities, such as nations and cultures, are incarnations of spirit. Cf. *Spirit and Reality*, 66. Indeed, "Man is an incarnate spirit and his vocation is creative incarnation." *Ibid.*, 56. And, "Spirit is incarnated both really and existentially in the human personality, in its creatively intuitive attitude to life, in a fraternal communion with other men." *Ibid.*, 57. Berdyaev means that the objectivization of the human spirit, seen in poor social orders or bad human customs or outlooks, is overcome by this diffusion of spirit. This is incarnation of spirit, carried on by man. "In reality, incarnation implies descent of the Divine Spirit and its union with real human and world destiny, . . . But spirit does incarnate itself in the real ascent of the subject, of the personality towards God, and in the real descent of Divine love and charity towards the subject, in the intuitive communion of the knowing with the known, in the real creation of the hitherto non-existent, in original judgment." *Ibid.*, 65.

The above-quoted description of the incarnation of spirit is very similar to the definition of true and concrete knowing we have studied. Incarnation of spirit is the same as true concrete knowing because concrete knowing is at once spiritual and incarnated; it is incarnated because it preserves the concreteness of the known. Incarnation, let us note, is not moving toward the solid and tactile qualities of bodies, according to Berdyaev. It refers, rather, to spirit, so far as it partakes of the concrete (integral, total) condition either in the true world or in the fallen world. The world moves towards spirit. True incarnation, I think, is not more concrete than is the imagination and memory, according to Berdyaev. Man, by definition is (1) an incarnate spirit and (2) eternal. He therefore does not fall into a material body, but is eternally incarnate. Incarnation is eternal. According to Berdyaev, for spirit to be truly and fully incarnate means, I think, for the spirit to be, so to speak, with a form. The human form, I think, is the true human reality so far as it is concrete, in the last analysis of Berdyaev's writings. Cf. *Slavery and Freedom*: "But the body belongs to the image of man." (31) "The spirit also includes the body in itself." (32).

Spirit is incarnated in the flesh; "flesh is the incarnation and symbol of spirit." *Freedom and the Spirit*, 18. But this does not mean that man, when his spirit is fully incarnated, is fleshly. It means, rather, that flesh is incarnated spirit; and when a spirit is fully incarnated, his flesh will be spiritualized Berdyaev shows in *Freedom and the Spirit*, 18, that: (1) flesh is part of the absolute unity of man; (2) yet, flesh is a symbol of spirit and is associated with historical life; (3) "but the exterior reality of history is only the image of spiritual life under the conditions of time and divisibility. Everything without is but the symbol of that which is within." *Ibid.*, 18. Hence, flesh is not all opposed to spirit (for it owes its reality to spirit); but the historical conditions of flesh, Berduaev means, are to be transformed and spiritualized in a further incarnation of spirit. ". . . flesh and blood do not inherit eternal life." *Dream and Reality*, 175.

As we saw in the preceding chapter the world of reality, the true world, will differ from the world that we sense. Berdyaev tends to be unhistorical with respect to the history of man. He tends to be unhistorical also with respect to the empirical history of bodies. It is the spiritual truth of the corporeal world and historical world which interests Berdyaev. This is a concrete truth with the concrete conditions of the imaginative *sight* or *vision*, but not a solid.[1]

Thus the mystery of the concrete identity of knower and known is further cleared up. It is simply a total identity. True knowledge is an identity, but the concrete truth is not solid or tactile. Just as true knowledge is unhistorical, so the concrete truth itself is unhistorical, whether it refers to human history or to the empirical history of corporeal bodies. In brief, the vision of truth, the identity of the knower and the concrete existent, is no more concrete than the human imagination itself. Berdyaev's "concrete" is not very concrete. He seems to intend that the "concrete" is total and includes (spiritualizes) the concrete conditions of its historical existence.

(4) Mysticism

According to this theory of knowledge, Berdyaev's metaphor of history (which approaches the meaning of history by way of symbol and myth), easily affiliates with a mysticism of history (which sees the Meaning of history). The highest knowledge becomes one with the concrete existing Logos. The concrete conditions of true knowledge, contained in the imagination and the memory, remain in the mystical vision according to Berdyaev's philosophy. Mystical experience, the mystical knowledge of the philosopher of history, begins in the symbolic realm of knowing. Mysticism begins in knowing the meaning of history by the merest symbols. It begins very early, according to this mystical philosophy, because the symbolic knowledge already overcomes the separation of the divine and the human.

In mystical experience there is no longer any insurmountable dualism between the supernatural and the natural, the divine and the created, for in it the natural becomes supernatural and the creature is deified.[2]

The soul of man, with its logical and objective knowledge is contained in the spiritual unity of the human personality, *Slavery and Freedom*, 30–31. As soul is thus related to the spirit, so the consciousness, which pertains to logical knowledge, is related to supra-consciousness. *Spirit and Reality*, 18. Only objectified spirit submits to the limitations of consciousness, says Berdyaev. *Ibid.*, 55. Thus, the mystical action of supra-consciousness pertains to the human spirit, qua spirit.

[1] See preceding note.
[2] *Freedom and the Spirit*, 243.

We have noted frequently that Berdyaev stresses the unity of the natural in the supernatural, and attacks the dualism of the natural and the supernatural. His description of mysticism above defines his philosophy as mystical. And, as we have amply seen in previous pages, Christ is He in Whom the mystical union occurs.

Berdyaev distinguishes kinds of mystical experience:

We may distinguish three types of mysticism, in the past: the mysticism of individual souls' approach to God. This is the most churchly form. Second, gnostic mysticism which must not be confused with the gnostic heretics of the first Christian centuries: this is a mysticism involving not only the individual soul, but cosmic and divine life, as well. Third, we have prophetic and messianic mysticism; this is a super-historical and eschatological, the beginning of the end. And each of these three types of mysticism has its limits.[1]

This general classification serves Berdyaev as a definition of mysticism with respect to its intention and goal. Besides a mysticism of the individual person, there is also a communal mysticism, one of *Sobornost'*, and *Sobornost'* both with other persons, with the cosmos and with history. By implication of the text above, the communal type of mysticism is also an "historical" one, achieved in communion with the "historical." The third type of mysticism, he says, is super-historical and eschatological. This is a mysticism whose intention is to bring about the end of the world, the transfiguration of creation. The divine meaning of history, the return of creation to its unity with Christ the Godman, is the goal.

Berdyaev continues:

The world is moving through darkness towards a new spirituality and a new mysticism. ... The prophetic-messianic element will be strong in the new mysticism ...[2]

This doctrine of mysticism simply does not make sense unless Berdyaev's metaphor of history and mysticism of history (and therefore his philosophy of history) are understood also. The temporal element (which, we found, exists even in the divine life and processes), as it is "historically" known in every level of human experience, is understood along with the divine principles. The very classification of mysticism which Berdyaev presents here, a classification which adequately describes the mysticism of his own doctrine, assumes for a condition the concrete noetic we have been studying.

At the same time, the classification of mysticism that he describes

---

[1] *The Realm of Spirit and the Realm of Caesar*, 181.
[2] *Ibid.*, 181–182.

indicates that his own philosophy has the noetic and the metaphysics which is proper for the third type, the New Mysticism. This messianic mysticism (as well as the cosmogonical and communal mysticism) is an essential part, and the noblest, of Berdyaev's epistemology. Thus we see that his theory of knowledge not only serves his philosophy but becomes, finally, identical with his philosophy of history. The return of the world to its Truth occurs through the loving knowledge of man.

H. SUMMARY

1. In rejecting the subject-object relationship in philosophical knowing, Berdyaev is continuing in a tradition of philosophy which begins with German Idealism. Kant has destroyed the philosophy of the abstract object for Berdyaev. Yet Berdyaev is still faced with the problem of the immateriality of knowledge facing the materiality of things. The spirituality of man faces the materiality of fallen nature.

He rejects the opposition of the subject and object because it never gets away from subjectivity; the object is an expression of the subject. But he seeks reality in his knowledge, not to be found through objectivist, intellectualist philosophies. Objectivization submits knowledge and the freedom of man to the common and impersonal and to the grandiose mien of the world and of history. What is more, according to Berdyaev's philosophy of history, objective knowledge is an adjustment to the objectivized world instead of a transfiguration of the world and history in the existential subjectivity of the knower. The (objective) concept, though it is necessary and useful, impedes a mysticism of history. Mysticism is concrete while the concept is abstract. Mystical truth is primarily the divine Truth, the concrete Existent Christ. Philosophy is primarily an intuitive approach to universal history and to the divine Logos, rather than ratiocinative. Philosophy is rational but primarily intuitive.

2. Berdyaev's philosophy of history cannot be anti-rational. The rational method and the concept are necessary instruments of thinking and communication. However, like all things, conceptual knowledge is symbolic of a higher knowledge or reality and gives place to a symbolic, imaginative and metaphorical method which leads to the suprarational, the mystical. The concept is truer if used as a symbol. The symbol – the metaphor of history – brings the knower to the reality, to the mystical

meaning of history. This noetic may be understood also in terms of the
progress of consciousness to supra-consciousness. Autonomous consciousness, by itself the realm of objective and conceptual knowledge,
gives no true philosophical knowledge. Berdyaev is opposed to unmystical philosophy.

3.   True knowledge is an identity of knower and known. Truth is not
a relation or adequation but the divine life. True knowledge is a vision,
a sight, where the knower is face to face with Truth. It is a vision which
sees Truth even in the imperfect symbols imbedded in historical life.
This vision is an identity of knower and known because the Truth (the
Godman) is at the existential kernel of the knowing subject. The true
philosophical attitude is to be the reality.

4.   True knowing is communal in character. This is so because man
cannot discover the truth in nature; and to find it in himself he must
see the reflection of his true self in other persons in a spiritual communion. The knowing of truth is being steeped in one's own depths, and
this is synonymous with community of existential communion. This
notion of community fulfills the concrete universalism of Berdyaev;
for the mystical theory asserts the multiple unity of the cosmos, history
and mankind in the universality of Christ the Godman. It is proper to
this cosmogonical doctrine of history to stress communion in knowing
because the philosopher of history identifies himself with every man
and, thereby, with the cosmos, history and the meaning of history. We
recall the metaphysical doctrine of the *We* in the foregoing chapter.
True knowledge is corporate: *"We think."* This doctrine of communal
knowledge is religious; indeed, Berdyaev's theory of knowledge joins
his metaphysics at the mystical level.

5.   Such a knowledge must be loving in character. In fact, the primacy
of freedom and volition in his metaphysics requires a volitional noetic.
The philosopher of history creates his historical symbols. Creativity
proceeds by way of a loving knowledge. For this reason, knowledge is
properly active rather than passive. And this active knowledge passes
from the metaphor of history to the most loving knowledge, mysticism
of history. Berdyaev's notion of the (purely intellectual) concept is
univocal, and this concept is therefore inadequate to carry the freight
of any metaphysical doctrine. To remain true to his metaphysics, he
must turn to symbolism and assert a loving knowledge. Love carries the

philosopher beyond the symbols that he knows to the plenary Reality that he seeks in mystical union.

6. To understand how the knower can know a concrete existent in its concreteness, according to a knowledge which is not only a vision but an identity, we had to consider the use of image, symbol and mystical doctrine in philosophy of history. For Berdyaev, the symbol or true myth is the sum of philosophical knowledge, the means of attaining the ultimate Truth. The myth is imaginative, and the intellectual imagination creates the symbols.

The knower, according to Berdyaev's philosophy of intuitive knowledge, intuits images and through them, reality. This is possible because the symbol is an image of reality, contains some reduced ray of the Sun-Logos. Such are, for example, the historical myths of the philosopher of history. Revelation, however, is not a symbol or myth; it is the reality rather than the knowledge.

The historical symbols and myths are themselves a meaning of history, but this meaning in turn has an inner meaning, and the ultimate meaning is the divine Logos. Berdyaev therefore, seeks not the symbol but the reality. But his philosophy of history is symbolical in method. Symbolic knowledge is to be superceded by something which is more than knowledge.

In Berdyaev's doctrine of man the microcosm, the historical culture is one of the primary principles of knowledge (along with the rational and the mystical). Historical culture is a source of knowledge about both man and the cosmos: particularly, about man insofar as he is distinct from the divine Prototype of man. Philosophy of history is the spiritual philosophy which sees through historical cultures to the "historical," the meaning of history. The three principles of knowledge are unified in philosophy of history.

The problem of knowing concretely is solved by the doctrine that the whole man knows in true knowledge. The sub-conscious and the supraconscious, as well as the conscious, operate; in addition the corporeal states, the emotions and instincts, as well as the will, act in true knowing. The imaginative, symbolic and loving knowledge, asserted in Berdyaev's philosophy of history, is partly based on corporeal states. Yet, it is a spiritual knowledge because man is an incarnate spirit. The spirit includes the whole man; the spirit knows when the whole man knows.

True knowledge, however, is not concrete to the extent that it includes knowledge of the exterior senses. The philosopher of history, by a creative act of remembrance, attains an in imaginative and symbolic knowledge of culture. It is not a sense knowledge; yet it is a concrete knowledge, and the concrete conditions of imaginative knowing become part of the knowledge. Berdyaev, however, tends to be unhistorical with respect to the history of corporeal bodies as well as with respect to the history of man. It is the spiritual truth of the corporeal and historical world which interests him. The vision of truth is no more concrete than the imagination itself; and its attainment is the spiritualization of the concrete conditions of sense and imagination.

This noetic is suited to the *via metaphorica* enroute to mysticism of history. The highest knowledge in mysticism becomes something more than knowledge. The person becomes one with Christ the concrete existing Logos. The meaning of history, which involves the person, the cosmos and Universal History, is perfectly attained in mystical union. Here the theory of knowledge becomes identical with the philosophy of history.

CONCLUSION

Now that I have made a close analysis of Berdyaev's text, I shall draw the threads of my findings together. Philosophy for him has revealed itself as a typically Eastern Christian doctrine. That is, philosophy has shown itself to be concerned with both purely philosophical matters (such as Existential metaphysics) and also with theological subjects (such as the doctrine of Incarnation, its key doctrine in Berdyaev's estimation).

In his philosophy of history he has had to distinguish between the historical and "historical." The "historical" – with quotation marks – is the spiritual reality which philosophy of history studies. It is the spiritual meaning of history, beyond history and yet known and attained through historical traditions. The "historical" is indeed the ultimate Reality in Berdyaev's Christian doctrine, Christ the Godman. He is the True Man, the perfect Proto-type, and every man is an image of Him. The "historical" is identical with the true spiritual being of man. Thus philosophy of history studies true man, redeemed man, the existential reality at the core of every man, in studying the "historical."

If history is a symbol of the "historical" towards which it moves, the "historical" itself has a historical quality. That is why Berdyaev posits a divine, a celestial "history" within the Godhead. Though God is timeless, yet He suffers a "historical" progress and illumination. To account for the "historical" unity of divine and terrestrial histories, Berdyaev posits an *Ungrund*, a divine Will, a primordial and irrational basis of God. Celestial and terrestrial history contain the divine and human spiritual illumination of the *Ungrund*, through Christ and through man. Berdyaev asserts a voluntarism in which the dark Will and radical Freedom is illuminated so that it becomes perfect freedom in Christ, in God and in Man. Through the revelation of Christ the fallen world – fallen by virtue of man's radical freedom – can be taken up into the unity within true man from which it fell.

For man is indeed a microcosm attempting to bring back the world – the macrocosm – and mankind into unity within Christ. Philosophy of history enables us to find the meaning of the world and thereby shows us the goal of history. We see universal history according to this view, both in the light of Christian doctrine and in the light of historical traditions and cultures.

This Russian philosophy is mystical. Only mystical knowledge is true knowledge; conceptual knowledge is just a symbol of the truth. Historical traditions and cultures are grasped as metaphors or symbols rather than as concepts. A given historical entity – a nation or an era – is a symbol of the true "historical," of the age of the Spirit, when man and the world will be again reunited with God. The metaphorical knowledge of philosophy of history is the path to the final mystical attainment of the age of the Spirit.

The metaphorical path is a concrete knowledge, one that takes concrete reality (in its spiritual truth) as a whole, with all particular conditions. Because it is concrete (and imaginative), the knowledge can function as a metaphor; because concrete, the knowledge becomes mystically the existential reality itself. Thus history is being mystically taken up, through man and his creative knowledge, into integral unity with man and with True Man, Christ. It is in his explicit mystical doctrine that the voluntarism, the doctrine of Incarnation, the cosmogony, cosmology and spiritualism are all united in service of Berdyaev's Christian philosophy of history.

The voluntarism of Berdyaev is seen at work in the very philosophy of history, as well as in the metaphysics of *Ungrund* on which the philosophy stands. And his philosophy is one of beauty: we actually create metaphorical and beautiful symbols in a mystical way in philosophy of history. It entails a practical and loving knowledge guided by love of beauty. At the same time, symbols bring the cosmos and history – in their true reality – within the true unity of man. And thus occurs the cosmogonical return of man and the world to their truth. The enslavement of man by nature and the cosmos, or by technics, is superseded by spiritualization. The incarnation of spirit, which occurs through man, the human spirit, will finally be consummated at the end of history in the age of the Spirit. Then, all history, all cultures and nations and cities, will exist spiritually and mystically in their true reality.

Such a philosophy of history – at once universal and concrete, meaningful and "historical" – requires a metaphysics which is Existential. Berdyaev, following the lead of his philosophy of history, turns with fellow Existentialists from intellectualist doctrines to a philosophy of the concrete existent. The existent, even the divine Source of man and the world, is "historical" in some way. At the same time, a cosmogony and cosmology, wherein the roles of man and the Godman command an outstanding place, will be personalist in nature. Berdyaev, therefore, uses a personalist Existentialism in his philosophy of history. The Existential emphasis upon the subjectivity and personality of the knower properly serves his mystical doctrine of the microcosm. Thus his philosophy of history is essentially a personalist Existentialism; for he sees man – and indeed history – as an image of Christ, and this is to view man and history Existentially.

In this philosophy are expressed the mysticism of Eastern Orthodoxy, the messianism of the Slavic races and the *Sobornost'* – the commonalty, the doctrine of the We – of Russia. The earthly futurism of Western philosophers of history is spiritualized into a doctrine of the age of the Spirit, vitalized by Christian eschatology. The ancient doctrines of the brotherhood of man and communion of the Saints are invigorated. Berdyaev both examines the conditions of true social communion and investigates the means of true communion between man and Nature. These doctrines – the eschatology and the *Sobornost'* between men and between man and nature – express in different ways the unity of his philosophy. Indeed the outstanding place of cosmogony in the doctrine and the mysticism of it guarantee its doctrinal unity. Everything in Berdyaev's doctrine pertains to philosophy of history because everything pertains to the return of man and the world to God. And every assertion, every notion of his philosophy relates to his mysticism of history, to his mystical doctrine of Christ, the true Man and true Microcosm in Whom the cosmos, all history and every man belongs.

BIBLIOGRAPHY OF SOURCES

I. PRIMARY SOURCES: BERDYAEV

The Beginning and the End (Bles, London, 1952).
Opyt eschatologiceskoj metafiziki. Tvorcestyo i objektivacija (Y.M.C.A.-Press, Paris, 1947).
The Bourgeois Mind and Other Essays (Sheed and Ward, London, 1934).
Christian Existentialism. A Berdyaev Anthology. Selected and translated by D. A. Lowrie (Allen & Unwin, London, 1965).
The Destiny of Man (Bles, London, 1948).
O naznacenii celoveka. Opyt paradoksal'noj etiki (Y.M.C.A.-Press, Paris, 1931).
The Divine and the Human. (Bles, London, 1949).
Dialectique existentielle du divin et de l'humain (Paris, 1947).
Ekzistencial'naja dialektika bozestvennago i celoveceskago (Y.M.C.A.-Press, Paris, 1952).
Dream and Reality (Bles, London, 1950).
Samopoznanie. *Opyt filosofskoj avtobiografii* (Y.M.C.A.-Press, Paris, 1949).
The End of Our Time (Sheed and Ward, London, 1935).
Novoe srednevekov'e. Razmyslenii o sud'be Rossii i Evropy (Obelisk, Berlin, 1924).
Freedom and the Spirit (Bles, London, 1935).
Filosofija svobodnogo ducha. Problematika i apologija christianstva (Y.M.C.A.-Press, Paris, 1927).
"Man and the Machine," *Hibbert Journal, A. Quarterly Review of Religion, Theology and Philosophy,* XXXIII (1934–1935).
The Meaning of the Creative Act (Harper, New York, 1955).
Smysl tvorcestva. Opyt opravdeanija celoveka (Moscow, 1916; partially revised for a German edition, Berlin, 1927).
The Meaning of History (Bles, London, 1949).
Smysl istorii. Opyt filosofi celoveceskoj sud'by (Berlin, 1923).
The Origin of Russian Communism (Bles, London, 1948).
Les sources et le sense du communisme russe (Paris, 1938).
The Realm of Spirit and the Realm of Ceasar. (Gollancz, London, 1952).
Carstvo Ducha i carstvo Kesarja (Y.M.C.A.-Press, Paris, 1951).
The Russian Idea (Bles, London, 1947).
Russkaja ideja. Osnovve problemy russkoj mysli XIX veka i nacala XX veka (Y.M.C.A.-Press, Paris, 1946).
Slavery and Freedom (Bles, London, 1943).
O rabstve i svobode celoveka. Opyt personalisticeskoj filosofii (Y.M.C.A.-Press, Paris, 1939).
Solitude and Society (Bles, London, 1947).

Ja i mir objektov. Opyt filosofii odinocestva i obscenija (Y.M.C.A.-Press, Paris, 1934).
Spirit and Reality (Bles, London, 1946).
Duch i real'nost'. Osnovy bogocel-oveceskoj duchovnosti (Y.M.C.A.-Press, Paris, 1937).
Towards a New Epoch (Bles, London, 1949).
Au seuil de la nouvelle Epoque. (Neuchatel-Paris, 1947).
Truth and Revelation (Bles, London, 1953).
Pravda i otkrovenie (Paris, c. 1950).

Bibliographical Note: I have encountered one book in which scores of articles of Berdyaev have been listed, numerous translations of his books noted and an extensive list of works about Berdyaev has been prepared: M. A. Vallon, *An Apostle of Freedom: Life and Teachings of Nicolas Berdyaev* (Philosophical Library, New York, 1960).

II. OTHER PRIMARY WORKS REFERRED TO

Anderson, James F., *The Bond of Being* (Herder, St. Louis, 1949).
St. Augustine, *De Civitate Dei.*
Boehme, Jacob, *The Epistels of Jacob Bemen* (London, 1649).
— The Way to Christ, translated by J. J. Stoudt Harper, New York, 1947.
Fichte, J. G., ,,The Science of Knowledge" (Introduction), in *Modern Classical Philosophers*, edited by B. Rand (Houghton Mifflin, Boston 1908(.
— "The Vocation of Man," translated by W. Smith, in *Modern Classical Philosophers*, edited by B. Rand (Houghton Mifflin, Boston, 1908).
Gilson, Etienne, *Being and Some Philosophers* (Pontifical Institute of Mediaeval Studies, Toronto, 1949).
Hegel, G. W. F., *The Logic of Hegel*, translated from *The Encyclopaedia of the Philosophical Sciences* by W. Wallace (Oxford Univ. Press, Oxford, 1959).
— *The Phenomenology of Mind* (Allen & Unwin, London, 1949).
— *The Philosophy of History* (The Colonial Press, New York, 1900).
John Scotus Erigena, "De Divisione Naturae," in J. Migne, *Patrologia Latina* Paris, 1853).
Kant, Immanuel, *Immanuel Kant's Critique of Pure Reason*, translated by N. K. Smith (MacMillan, London, 1950).
— *The Moral Law, or Kant's Groundwork of the Metaphysic of Morals*, translated by H. J. Paton (Hutchinson, London, 1948).
Kierkegaard, S., *Philosophical Fragments* (Princeton Univ. Press, Princeton, 1946).
Leibniz, F. W., ,,The Monadology," in *Leibniz, Discourse on Metaphysics, etc.*, translated by G. R. Montgomery (Opencourt, La Salle, Illinois, 1945).
Maritain, Jacques, *Les Degrés du Savoir* (Desclée de Brouwer, Paris, 1946).
Merejkowski, D., *The Menace of the Mob* (Nicholas L. Brown, New York, 1921).
— *Peter and Alexis* (Modern Library, New York, 1931).
Plato, *The Republic.*
— *The Symposium.*
Schelling, F. W. J., *The Ages of the World*, translated by F. Bolman, Jr. (Columbia Univ. Press, New York, 1942).
— *Of Human Freedom*, translated by J. Gutmann (Opencourt, Chicago, 1936).
— *Sämmtliche Werke* (Stuttgart and Augsburg, 1856 seq.), II, Vol. 3 and 4.

Schopenhauer, A., *The World as Will and Idea*, in *The Philosophy of Schopen-hauer*, edited by I. Edman (Modern Library, New York, 1928).

Solovyev, V., *Lectures on Godmanhood* (Dobson, London, 1948).

Spengler, O., *The Decline of the West* (Knopf, New York, 1939).

St. Thomas Aquinas, *Summa Theologiae* (Marietti, Rome, 1949).

Toynbee, A. J., *A Study of History* (Oxford Univ. Press, Oxford, 1934–1953).

III. SELECTED SECONDARY SOURCES

Arnold, E. V., *Roman Stoicism*. Being Lectures on the History of the Stoic Phi-losophy with Special References to Its Development Within the Roman Empire (Cambridge Univ. Press, Cambridge, 1911; reissued 1958 by the Humanities Press, New York).

Baldensperger, F., *Mélanges d'Histoire Littéraire Générale et Comparée offerts à Fernand Baldensperger* (Librairie Ancienne Honoré Champion, Paris, 1930), Vol. II. *Edgar Quinet et Auguste Cieszkowski*.

Bett, H., *Joachim of Flora* (Methuen, London, 1931).

Bolman, F., Jr., "Introduction," in F. W. J. Schelling, *The Ages of the World* (Columbia Univ. Press, New York, 1942).

Borowitz, (Rabbi) E. B., *A Layman's Introduction to Religious Existentialism* (Dell, New York, 1966).

Calian, C. S., *The Significance of Eschatology in the Thoughts of Nicolas Berdyaev* (Brill, Leiden, 1965).

Clarke, O. F., *Introduction to Berdyaev* (Bles, London, 1950).

Collins, James, *The Existentialists, A Critical Study* (Regnery, Chicago, 1952).

Dufrenne, M., and P. Ricoeur, *Karl Jaspers et la Philosophie de l'Existence* (Seuil, Paris, 1947).

Fackenheim, E., "Schelling's Philosophy of Religion," in *University of Toronto Quarterly* (October, 1952).

Gilson, Etienne, *Les Métamorphoses de la Cité de Dieu* (Nauwelaerts, Louvain, 1952).

Hartshorne, C. A., *The Divine Relativity; A Social Conception of God*. The Terry Lectures, 1947 (Yale Univ. Press, New Haven, 1948).

Kuhn, H., *Encounter with Nothingness, an Essay on Existentialism* (Regnery, Hinsdale, Illinois, 1949).

— "Existentialism," in *A History of Philosophical Systems*, edited by V. Ferm (Philosophical Library, New York, 1950).

Lossky, N. O., *A History of Russian Philosophy* (International Universities Press, New York, 1951).

Löwith, K., *Meaning in History* (Univ. of Chicago Press, Chicago, 1949).

Lowrie, D. A., *Rebellious Prophet. A Life of Nicolai Berdyaev* (Harper, New York, 1960).

Munzer, E., "Nicolas Berdyaev," in *University of Toronto Quzrterly*, Vol. XIV (1944–1945).

Nygren, A., *Agape and Eros* (S.P.C.K., London, 1953).

Pfleger, K., *Wrestlers with Christ* (Sheed and Ward, London, 1957).

Porret, E., *Berdiaeff Prophète des Temps Nouveaux* (Delachaux & Niestle, Paris, 1951).

Randall, J. H., Jr., "The Ontology of Paul Tillich," in *The Theology of Paul Tillich*, edited by C. Kegely and R. Bretall (MacMillan, New York, 1952).

Shryock, J. K., *The Origin and Development of the State Cult of Confucius* (Paragon Book Reprint Corp., New York, 1966).

Smith, N. K., *Commentary on the Critique of Pure Reason* (Humanities Press, New York, 1950).

Spinka, M., *Nicolas Berdyaev: Captive of Freedom* (The Westminster Press, Philadelphia, 1950).

Werkmeister, W. H., "Scientism and the Problem of Man," in *Philosophy and Culture. East and West*, edited by C. A. Moore (Univ. of Hawaii Press, Honolulu, 1962).

Whitehead, A. N., *Process and Reality. An Essay in Cosmology* (MacMillan, New York, 1927; Harper Torchbook, 1960).

Zenkovsky, V. V., *A History of Russian Philosophy* (Routledge and Kegan Paul, London, 1953).

Zimmer, H., *Philosophies of India*, edited by J. Campbell (Pantheon, New York, 1953).

Zoyboff, P. P., "Introduction," in V. Solovyev, *Lectures on Godmanhood* (Dobson, London, 1948).

INDEX

(Also see Table of Contents.)